Build, Upgrade & Repair Your PC Network on a Shoestring Budget

Wayne N. Kawamoto

Build, Upgrade & Repair Your PC Network on a Shoestring Budget

Limits of Liability and Disclaimer of Warranty

The author and publisher of this book have used their best efforts in preparing the book and the programs contained in it. These efforts include the development, research, and testing of the theories and programs to determine their effectiveness. The author and publisher make no warranty of any kind, expressed or implied, with regard to these programs or the documentation contained in this book.

The author and publisher shall not be liable in the event of incidental or consequential damages in connection with, or arising out of, the furnishing, performance, or use of the programs, associated instructions, and/or claims of productivity gains.

Trademarks

Trademarked names appear throughout this book. Rather than list the names and entities that own the trademarks or insert a trademark symbol with each mention of the trademarked name, the publisher states that it is using the names for editorial purposes only and to the benefit of the trademark owner, with no intention of infringing upon that trademark.

The Coriolis Group, LLC
14455 N. Hayden Road, Suite 220
Scottsdale, Arizona 85260

602/483-0192
FAX 602/483-0193
http://www.coriolis.com

Library of Congress Cataloging-in-Publication Data
Kawamoto, Wayne N.
Build, upgrade, and repair your PC network on a shoestring budget/Wayne Kawamoto.
p. cm.
Includes index.
ISBN 1-57610-411-7
1. Computer networks--Equipment and supplies. 2. Network computers--Repairing. 3. Microcomputers--Upgrading. 4. Computer networks--Computer programs. I. Title.
TK5105.5.K42 1999
004.6--dc21 99-10036
CIP

Printed in the United States of America
10 9 8 7 6 5 4 3 2 1

Publisher
Keith Weiskamp

Acquisitions Editor
Stephanie Wall

Marketing Specialist
Diane Enger

Project Editor
Meredith Brittain

Technical Reviewer
Robert Hummel

Production Coordinator
Wendy Littley

Cover Design
Jody Winkler

Layout Design
April Nielsen

CD-ROM Developer
Robert Clarfield

About The Author

Wayne Kawamoto is a longtime freelance writer who has published hundreds of articles, columns, and reviews in a variety of national publications, including *PC Computing*, *Computer Shopper*, *Home Office Computing*, *Small Business Computing & Communications*, and *Computer Currents*. In addition to writing about computers, Wayne writes about small business topics, movies, and family entertainment and issues. Wayne also performs magic and is a member of the Academy of Magical Arts, which is centered at Hollywood's Magic Castle.

When he's not writing, Wayne enjoys spending time with his wife and three children. Wayne lives in La Verne, California.

Acknowledgments

I could never take on the daunting task of writing a book on my own. I have lots of people to thank for everything that they have done to make this book a reality:

- To the pros at Coriolis who reviewed drafts, provided technical suggestions and advice, laid out the pages, and caught my mistakes. In particular, thanks to Robert Clarfield for his work in making the CD-ROM possible, and his advice and expertise in creating the videos. Thanks to Robert Hummel, who did a great job of double-checking everything. I also want to thank Wendy Littley and April Nielsen for making the inside of this book look great, and Diane Enger and Jody Winkler for perfecting the cover copy and design. A special thanks to Meredith Brittain for her patience when I was behind schedule (I did catch up!), and for tracking the myriad details that go into a project such as this.
- To Stephanie Wall, Acquisitions Editor, for giving me the opportunity to write this book.
- To Martha Kaufman Amitay, my agent, who got me into the book-writing business, and who made this book possible.

More thanks:

- To Mark Kurtz, friend and network guru, who provided advice over lunches of cheap (but quality) burritos, let me borrow equipment, and always has the answer to any networking question that I can think up.
- To Serge Handschin, for lending advice and equipment. You're still the teriyaki chicken connoisseur.
- To Janet Kawamoto, my wife, and the best writer in the family, who tolerated my crazy hours, let me convert the living room into a makeshift photo and video studio for weeks, and barely said a word about the network cable that was running throughout the house.

- To my kids, thanks for being quiet when I was trying to film the video sequences, and for lending helping hands during the photo shoots. Now, get back in there and clean your rooms and finish your homework.

Contents At A Glance

Table Of Contents

Part 2
Building Your Network

Part 3
Using Your Network

Part 4
Upgrading Your Network

Part 5
Appendixes

Introduction

What is *Build, Upgrade & Repair Your PC Network on a Shoestring Budget* all about? I've written this book to provide solid advice and all the information you need to build a network of your own. This book will show you the hardware that you'll need, illustrate the steps necessary to build a network and improve its performance, and explain how to save money in the process. Throughout, I've done my best to provide this material in a form that's easy to understand, without compromising the information and steps. If you're a small business or home user with systems that you wish to link together, this book will walk you through the entire process.

Who Can Use This Book

Most books on building networks are geared toward people who already know a lot about computers and networking. Such books discuss in endless and laborious detail the workings and principles of each and every component, bogging down in all the minute and techy options. However, this book takes the simple and easy route for beginner and intermediate computer users, never assuming that you're a technical whiz. And although this book features in-depth discussions, the emphasis is on what the network components and software features do, and how you can use them. Also, you'll find lots of information on what to look for when buying network and computer components.

First, this book explains what you'll need to build a network, and then it shows you, step by step, how to set up your network and get it running. With the right information and instruction, you can do it—trust me. Later chapters explain how to improve the performance of your network and upgrade the individual computers. Here you'll find step-by-step instructions on performing the upgrades yourself. I'm also proud of the multimedia videos that come on the enclosed CD-ROM that demonstrate the steps. In addition, this book contains valuable troubleshooting advice that will help you through almost any computer catastrophe.

And if you get cold feet and decide to have someone else build your network or make computer upgrades for you, you'll find that this book provides an excellent introduction to networking. Armed with this knowledge, you'll be able to talk with technicians at your local computer repair store and not be intimidated by them and their technical jargon.

If you're new to building a network and upgrading computers, you'll find this book useful. With just a little work, you'll soon have those computers connected and talking with each other.

What's Inside

This book is divided into five parts:

- *Part 1: Introduction to Networking*—This part talks about networking basics and explains the concepts and necessary hardware.
- *Part 2: Building Your Network*—This part shows you how to put together your network.
- *Part 3: Using Your Network*—This part shows you how to configure and use your network.
- *Part 4: Upgrading Your Network*—This part talks about ways to improve your network's performance by changing settings and upgrading components.
- *Part 5: Appendixes*—This part includes lists of vendors for parts and hardware.

Here's a chapter-by-chapter rundown:

Part 1: Introduction To Networking

In this part, you'll learn network basics: network concepts, necessary hardware, and what a network can do for you.

Chapter 1: An Introduction To Networks

Before you can build a network, you have to understand what tasks it can perform. This chapter talks about what a network can do, including sharing files and printers between computers, letting several people work on network programs, and allowing you to play multiuser games.

Chapter 2: Network Basics

This chapter discusses basic network concepts and explains topics such as peer-to-peer, servers, clients, and network operating systems.

Part 2: Building Your Network

Here's where I discuss the nuts and bolts of actually building a network.

Chapter 3: Planning For Your Network

To build the network that works best for you, you should have a plan. This ensures that there will be fewer surprises along the way, and you're far less likely to spend money on hardware or software that you don't need. This chapter discusses topics such as planning for adequate disk space, using systems as print and file servers, and planning for the number of stations on your network.

Chapter 4: What You'll Need To Build A Network

This chapter discusses the hardware that you'll need to build your network, which includes network interface cards, cables, and hubs.

Chapter 5: Bargain Basement: Shopping For The Best Network Values

Where can you get the best prices on network components? Refer to this chapter for the pros and cons of buying at your neighborhood mom and pop computer store, from the general warehouse or discount saving stores, at computer superstores, through mail order, and at computer swap meets. With the advice found here, you can save some cash. I'll also present strategies to protect yourself when making purchases so you don't get burned.

Chapter 6: The Tools

To build your network and work on your computers, you must have the right tools. This chapter discusses the various items that make up a computer tool kit, including screwdrivers, pliers, and more. I also talk about how to organize your work area.

Chapter 7: Installing And Configuring Network Cards

This chapter shows you how to install and configure network interface cards and troubleshoot any problems that you may encounter along the way.

Chapter 8: Making Network Connections With Cables

Once you install your network interface cards, this chapter shows you how to make the necessary cable connections to link your computers together.

Chapter 9: Other Network Connections

New technologies let you make network connections through wiring that already exists in your home or office, or with no wiring at all. In this chapter, we'll discuss some of these new technologies that may change the way you build a network.

Part 3: Using Your Network

After you've installed the necessary network hardware, this part helps you configure and use your network.

Chapter 10: Basic Network Concepts

This chapter explains the concepts you'll need to understand when building your network and shows you how to share files between networked systems. Say goodbye to floppies.

Chapter 11: Sharing Printers

Beyond sharing files, this chapter shows you how to configure your network so you can share printers among several computers. Some of the concepts in this chapter include print redirection, print queues, and tips for networking printers.

Chapter 12: Email

Once you install a network, you may want to use it to support an email system that lets you send messages from one computer to another, either across the office or home network, or through the Internet. This chapter explains what's involved in bringing email into your network, and what you'll need.

Chapter 13: Network Security

If you don't want to share all of the information on a computer with everyone else, you'll want to use the security features built into Windows 95 and Windows 98. This chapter discusses how you can control access on your network and protect key folders and files from prying eyes. Also, concepts such as user accounts, passwords, and rights are defined.

Chapter 14: Backups, Viruses, And Drive Maintenance

In this chapter, I'll discuss how you can keep your data safe, as well as things you can do to keep your network drives in top shape. Topics in this chapter include performing backups, protecting against viruses, and checking your drives for problems.

Chapter 15: Adding And Configuring Peripherals

Beyond sharing files and printers across a network, you can share other devices and peripherals as well. In this chapter, I talk about sharing CD-ROM drives, voice mail, and fax capabilities across a network.

Chapter 16: Connecting To The Internet

Because the Internet is so important, this chapter discusses ways that let you connect your network to the Internet. This way, everyone on your network can access the resources of the Internet. Also, you can post a page to advertise your business or simply make a point.

Chapter 17: Dial-Up Networking

Because you can't be in two places at the same time, this chapter discusses things you need to know to access your network and use it as if you were in the office. This way, you can use your network when you're away from your computer—for example, in hotel rooms and other offices. I'll explain the different solutions, as well as provide instructions on using Windows 95/98 Dial-Up Networking.

Chapter 18: Troubleshooting The Network

I hope that you never have to refer to this chapter, but if you do, you'll find strategies for figuring out what's wrong with your network. Here you'll find troubleshooting tips for fixing problems with workstations, servers, network hardware, and other issues.

Part 4: Upgrading Your Network

Once you have your network in place, you may discover that you would like it to perform better. If this is the case, this part shows you ways to improve your network's performance.

Chapter 19: Improving Your Network

Although many of the chapters in this part talk about ways to improve your network's performance by either upgrading components in a system or purchasing new systems, this chapter discusses options that aren't as much work. Topics in this chapter include looking for bottlenecks and fine-tuning your network.

Chapter 20: Ways To Upgrade Your Server And Workstations

To improve the performance of your networked computers, you can upgrade the components within them. This chapter discusses how changing the memory, hard drives, and CPU/motherboard can improve system performance.

Chapter 21: Upgrading Your System's Memory

You'll learn how adding memory to your system can significantly improve a PC's performance, the different types of memory available, the types that you should consider for an upgrade, and issues to think about when adding memory. I explain how to install memory, from pushing the tiny levers on a memory slot to seating a new board in its place. You can follow the step-by-step instructions and photographs to add RAM quickly, and if you run into problems, there's troubleshooting advice to help you solve almost any problem.

Chapter 22: Adding Hard Drives

If you keep running out of space to store data and applications, turn to this chapter for explanations of the terms that define a hard drive's performance, and what to look for when buying one. This chapter also discusses how to install and configure a hard drive and get it running, as well as ways to solve potential problems.

Chapter 23: Swapping The CPU And/Or Motherboard

In this chapter, I talk about the different types of motherboards that you might encounter and aspects that you should consider when you decide to upgrade a PC's CPU and motherboard. You'll find detailed instructions on how to replace a motherboard, including removing the various components, connectors, and the motherboard itself, and then securing a new motherboard into the case, reconnecting the cables, reinstalling the components, and then testing the system. There are also plenty of precautions and tips, and a troubleshooting guide to consult if anything goes wrong.

Chapter 24: Buying New Workstations And Servers

In previous chapters, I discussed hardware upgrades that you can perform on systems to increase their speed and improve network performance. However, there may be times when the best solution is to purchase a new workstation or server for your network. If this is the case, you can follow the suggestions in this chapter to help you purchase new systems to improve network performance.

Chapter 25: Buying And Installing A CD-ROM Drive

In this chapter, I cover what you need to consider when purchasing a CD-ROM drive, including raw speed, how fast a drive transfers data, and the different types of drives that you can buy. The chapter shows you how to install and configure CD-ROM drives, and it also provides suggestions to get you through any problems you may encounter.

Chapter 26: Installing A Modem

To go online, send and receive faxes from a PC, answer the phone and record messages, and control other PCs across telephone lines, modems are necessary. This chapter discusses modems and tells you what to look for when shopping for one. Once you have a modem, you can follow the instructions in this chapter for installing a modem in a system.

Chapter 27: Mobile Networking

If you want to connect a notebook computer that's running Windows 95 or Windows 98 to your network, this chapter shows you how to do so. You'll also find troubleshooting steps in the chapter that should fix almost any problem that you may encounter.

Part 5: Appendixes

Appendix A: Upgrade And Network-Related Vendors

A comprehensive list of vendors that you can turn to for parts and hardware. The vendors are listed alphabetically.

Appendix B: Vendors By Category

Use this appendix to locate vendors for a part that you need to buy.

Glossary

A detailed listing of computer terms and their definitions.

I hope you find this book useful and that it helps you create and maintain a productive network. Enough of this introductory stuff. Let's get on with it so you can get on with your computing!

Wayne N. Kawamoto
wkawamoto@compuserve.com

Part 1

Introduction To Networking

1

An Introduction To Networks

You may have used a computer for years and reaped its many benefits. Whether you use it to process your words in letters, memos, and reports, work with spreadsheets and databases, or even play games, your computer is a personal workhorse. But at some point, whether you're a home or business user, you may find that you have more than one PC in the house or office. That's when you need to know about a concept called *networking* that lets your computers work together and share their capabilities.

If you're not sure what a network is, but you've heard that it might help your home or small business, this is the book for you. I'll explain everything you need to know about networks, help you figure out the type of network that you should build, describe the necessary hardware and software that you'll need to purchase and install, and offer step-by-step instructions and illustrations that show you every step of the installation and configuration process. Although a computer network isn't a magic answer—no application of smoke and mirrors will instantly make your computers brew coffee or end world hunger—networking is a viable way of making several PCs work together in ways that they can't on their own.

Definition, Please

A *network* is a system that consists of two or more computers that are connected together, either with cables or a wireless system, so that they can share resources (printers, drives, modems, etc.) and information, usually in the form of files.

Networks come in all types, from simple to complex. You may have heard that installing a network is a time-consuming and complicated job that requires years of training and a Ph.D. to perform, and that you'll need to call in a network expert or consultant if you are considering a network installation.

A network expert is definitely needed when businesses install complicated networking hardware and software. On the other hand, if all you want to do is install a simple network in your home or business, you don't need to call a professional. With this book, you can handily do it yourself. It's fairly easy to build a network, and the price is quite reasonable, too.

Besides providing all the information you'll need to build your own network, this book has a definite money angle (because we all know that everything always comes down to money), as the "Shoestring Budget" part of the title implies. Therefore, I'll discuss hardware tradeoffs that you can make so you don't spend extra money on pricey hardware that does more than you need; I'll also show you where you can find the best bargains when you're shopping for your network hardware, peripherals, and software.

What Will A Network Do For Me?

In this section, I'll discuss the many benefits that a network offers.

Sharing Information, Files, And Resources

If you have more than one computer in your home or office, you have, no doubt, copied files from one computer to another. To do so, you probably relied on *sneakernet* (using floppy disks to move files from one PC to another).

Definition, Please

Sneakernet is a humorous term that describes the low-tech method of transferring files from one computer to another by copying them to floppy disks, walking (in your sneakers) to another machine, and then copying the files from the floppy to the hard drive.

If you have your computers linked together in a network, you can transfer files through special cables that connect the computers. It's actually a bit more complicated then this, but I'll explain this aspect in detail throughout the book. Another name for a network—at least, the kind that we'll talk about in this book—is a *local area network* (LAN).

Definition, Please

LAN stands for local area network, meaning a network in a home or office.

I have always found that using floppy disks to move files from one PC to another is a tedious job. I often have to move image files from one PC (the one that's attached to the scanner) to other computers in my house. Many times, these graphic files are too big to copy onto floppies. "Spanning" files onto several disks with a compression utility or connecting and carrying around a portable Zip drive (a special drive that uses a 100MB disk) is too much trouble. I also have had to move files from one computer to another so I can use the printer that's attached to my second system.

With a network, I simply copy the files from one computer to another in the same way that I copy files to a floppy disk or between system hard drives. By doing so, I don't have to copy single files onto disks, carry them around, and load them onto other PCs; I also never run into problems with large files.

A network also lets you share disk drives, such as a CD-ROM or floppy drive. This means that if another computer on the network has a CD-ROM drive, but yours doesn't, you can read a CD on that computer's drive with your own computer. The CD-ROM drive on another machine appears as a drive on your own computer; you can access it using Windows Explorer or any other Windows application.

The network was a real lifesaver when my three-year-old destroyed the CD-ROM drive on my wife's computer. Using the network, we could still install programs and copy CD-ROM-based clip art to her system from the drive on my PC. (We also did some reprogramming of the three-year-old, who soon understood that one does not play with CD-ROM drives). The network came in handy again when the floppy drive on my computer went out. Until I found the time to replace my floppy drive, I inserted floppies into my wife's computer and copied the files to my own machine. In addition to sharing drives, you can also share modems and high-speed Internet connections. This way, anyone on the network can send email or faxes, or access the Internet, without having a modem and telephone line hookup at their own machine.

Another network benefit is *email;* this allows you to send messages electronically from your computer to other computer users who have email addresses. Email has several benefits:

- The message travels fast, usually within a matter of minutes.
- The recipient can read it at any convenient time.
- You can save all incoming and outgoing email messages, creating a permanent record on your computer.

Definition, Please

Email is an electronic letter that you send from one computer to another.

While this is definitely a big-business solution, the concept of an *intranet* has steadily gained in popularity. While the word "intranet" looks as if someone misspelled "Internet," it's really a private, company version of the Web that runs inside a business. In use, an intranet looks just like the Web.

The company's employees use common Web browsers such as Internet Explorer or Netscape Communicator as a convenient way to view business documents, work with company databases, and check schedules and calendars. To get around the intranet, employees click on *links*, just as they do with Web pages. Another advantage is that all workers—whether

Definition, Please

An *intranet* is a specialized network that looks and works like a company version of the Web. To use an intranet, workers use the same browsers that they would use to surf the Web in order to look at company documents, work on databases, and refer to other business information.

they are running Macs, PCs, or Unix workstations—can refer to the same data on an intranet. Intranets are popular in large corporations and businesses, but can offer benefits to small companies as well. However, setting up an intranet is a complicated process best left to professionals. If your company needs an intranet, call your computer consultant for help.

Sharing Printers

Because I have several computers in my house, it's not practical for me to buy a printer for every computer. In the old days, I used to carry a printer around from computer to computer (it was lighter and easier to disconnect and carry than a PC) and connect it in order to print from different machines. The alternative was to copy the necessary file onto a disk (if it would fit), carry the disk to the machine with the printer, fire up the desktop publisher on that computer, open the file from the disk, and then print it.

With my in-house network, I use the Print command in whatever application I'm using and then tell the network to use the inkjet printer that's connected to my wife's system. The document flies through the network cables and emerges from my wife's printer on the other side of our home office.

Keep in mind that you can use a device called a *switch box* that accepts cables from every computer and then lets you select a printer connected to another system. The down side of these devices is that only one computer can use the printer at a time. And when you want to use the printer, you have to walk over to the device and turn the knob so the printer connects with your computer. If you happen to change the switch while someone else is printing, you can ruin that print job and garble the output, an occurrence that will not contribute to serenity in the home or office. A manual switch box is only practical for very small offices with few users whose computers are placed close together.

Definition, Please

A *switch box* is a simple device that accepts the printer cables from two or more PCs and provides a connection to a single printer. When you want to print from a particular PC, you set the switch box to accept information from that PC so the device can route it to the printer.

A more expensive alternative—an automatic switch box—can determine which computers are trying to print; it separates—or *queues*—the jobs so they don't get in each other's way. In many ways, using an automatic switch box is similar to printing across a network, although a network has far more capabilities.

Sharing Applications

With a network, you can share software applications. You can buy a network version of a program and install it in a central location where everyone can use it, instead of buying a copy for every machine and having to install it on each one. Many office applications, such as databases and word processors, come in networked versions specifically for this purpose.

Networked programs are particularly useful when several people need to use a program and access the same data at the same time. For example, if a company has a networked accounting program, the sales department can use the program to enter invoices at the same time payroll is entering time sheets and printing the paychecks. An example of such a program is shown in Figure 1.1.

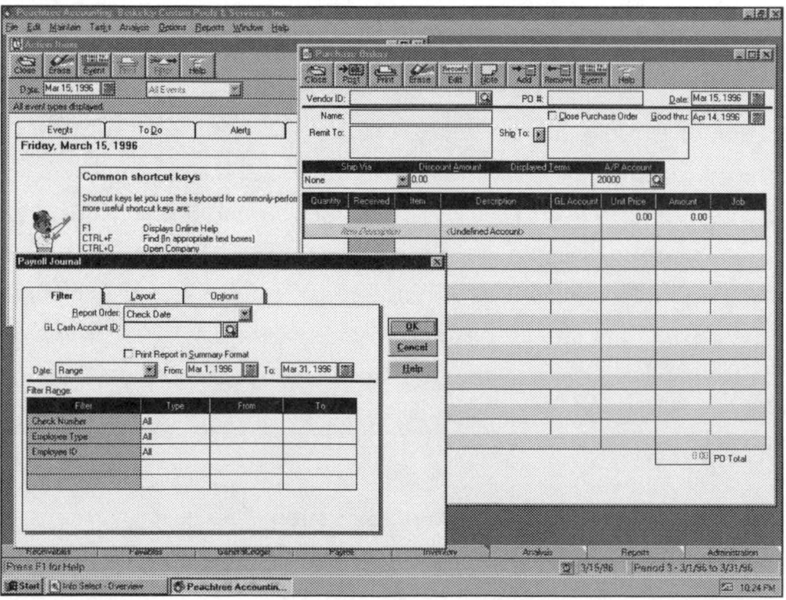

Figure 1.1 Applications such as Peachtree Complete let several users access an application and the same data at once.

Contact managers and personal information managers have offered networking capabilities for years. These programs offer sophisticated telephone address books and schedulers that help you organize your contacts and time. If the computers are networked, workers can use these programs to share calendars and contact files, schedule appointments for others, announce meetings, and manage resources, such as conference rooms and projectors. Workers have their own schedules on their own computers, but across the network, others can view these schedules to check availability, deadlines, and other information.

If you have a small business and several employees who need to use the same applications and data, a network can solve this problem.

Games Networks Play

When I installed a network in my home office, I thought that local area networks were staid business tools that let companies share PCs, files, hard drives, and printers. This is why I installed it, and for the most part, I've enjoyed being able to quickly transfer files among computers and print from any system. Recently, however, this productivity booster has turned into a definite productivity buster in one regard: the network is being used more for playing games with family and friends than for home office purposes.

Although I've played multiuser games across the Internet, I find that when all the players are crammed into my tiny 10-foot by10-foot office, it makes for a more raucous and fun game. It's not unusual to find four people in my office playing Quake, as shown in Figure 1.2. And the constant banter that goes back and forth as we decide how to share health and ammo or taunt fellow players is almost as entertaining as the game itself. This network has rekindled my interest in games that I had tired of long ago; it is a cool multimedia toy.

Some network games give each player an individual view of the action, so that he or she can move about and interact with other players within the game. Flight and car simulations are good examples of network games, and so are first-person fighting games such as Quake, a clear favorite in my house. In Quake, you move your character through the game's mazes and cooperate (or not) with other players, sharing health and ammo in

Figure 1.2 Quake lets several players battle it out over a network and gives each player an individual view of the game.

order to conquer the enemy. You can also fight each other in exciting head-to-head matches.

You can also have a blast playing strategy games—such as Blizzard's WarCraft II and Westwood Studio's Command & Conquer: Red Alert—across a network. These programs show each player an individual view of the game area and a map. Players can choose to battle it out in realtime combat or work as teams by forming alliances. It's like a cool board game, but with explosions and sound effects. Not only is it fun to play against your friends, but you'll find that human players usually make for more responsive and clever competition than the computer's artificial intelligence.

Installing a network just to play games may be a bit frivolous, but the hardware for connecting several computers together doesn't cost much more than a couple hundred dollars, and for serious gamers, it can be worth it.

Networks: The Dark Side

I've listed the many advantages of building a network, but it also has some disadvantages, particularly for those of you who like being independent and take to heart the "personal" in personal computer (PC). When you install a network, you do lose some of your computing freedom.

You may find that others are storing files on your system and gobbling up your hard drive space. You can start with a drive that has lots of space, but if four or five people save their day-to-day work on your drive, your free space will go down to nothing in no time.

If your system is connected to the printer, you'll find that you may want to print a document but can't. Someone else is printing 400 mail-merged letters, and you'll have to wait until the print job is over. Also, if it's your system that connects to the printer, you'll automatically be in charge of seeing that the printer is full of paper and that the toner cartridge is full. When several people use your printer to print their daily email and other documents, the paper really flies—you may begin to feel like you're refilling the paper at the same rate as one of those guys who shoveled the coal on an old steam train or on the Titanic.

Another down side is that you may see a decrease in the performance of your computer—it may run a lot more slowly if others are using its resources. The amount that your system slows down depends on the applications and devices that others are using. The disadvantages don't offset the advantages of installing a network, but they definitely exist. In Part 4 of this book, I'll discuss ways of increasing network performance in order to correct some of these problems.

Networking Time

If you're tired of carrying and swapping floppies, and if you need to share applications, data, and printers so more people can use them, it's probably time to think seriously about a network. The following list of questions summarizes the issues you need to consider to determine whether your home or office can benefit from a network:

- Do you want to share files without copying them onto floppy disks?
- Do you want to share printers?
- Do you want to install an email system so everyone can communicate more easily?

- Do you have applications and data that you want several people to be able to work with at the same time?
- Do you want to play network games?

If you're answering "yes" to many of these questions, it's time to start your networking odyssey.

Can I Really Do It Myself?

At this point, you're probably saying to yourself, "Well, this all sounds fine on paper, but can I really build my own network?" If you're having second thoughts, read on for some advice and encouragement. I asked myself these very same questions when I installed my first network years ago.

Can I really install the network myself?
Yes, absolutely. Some tricks and some knowledge are involved, but I'll explain everything you need to know. Just by buying this book, you've taken the first step toward building your network. You can do it.

Doesn't building a network mean that I have to open the computer case and install components?
Yes, you will have to get your hands dirty (so to speak), but I'll walk you through each step and discuss the tools that you will need. As you'll see, adding hardware components isn't difficult.

But how do I know which parts to buy for my network?
In upcoming chapters, you'll find explanations and charts that tell what hardware components your system will need, based on your network requirements. I'll talk about each of the components in detail so you can gain an understanding of what they do and what to look for when you go shopping. I'll suggest where to shop for the lowest prices. Finally, I'll walk you through the installation process.

What if I mess something else up when I change a component?
Unfortunately, this is a possibility, and it's natural to be nervous. (You should have seen me the first time I opened a computer case.) I'll do my best to help you and provide warnings and precautions along the way. Some computers are very sensitive and seem to go crazy at the slightest

provocation, but you can usually undo any mistakes that you make. Also, if something should go wrong, consult Chapter 18, which should get you out of almost any mess.

Moving On

By purchasing this book, you've already taken the first major step in building your own network and saving money in the process. You've learned the advantages of networking and what it can do for your home or small business. Now we're ready to move to Chapter 2, where I'll cover more networking concepts and terms.

2

Network Basics

Clients, servers, peer-to-peer, network operating systems. You may have heard these terms tossed around, along with names such as Unix and Linux, and wondered what they were. In this chapter, I'll introduce some of these terms and explain those that you need to know. If you're already familiar with the concept of a peer-to-peer network and want to get right into the nuts and bolts of planning and building one, I recommend that you skip this chapter and move to Chapter 3 to get started on your network. For those of you who want a little network background and definitions, here goes.

Peer-To-Peer Network

The most basic kind of network you can create is a *peer-to-peer network*. Peer-to-peer networks can use the features in Windows 95 and Windows 98 to build a network. With the right hardware, which I'll talk about in later chapters, Windows 95 and Windows 98 offer the easiest ways to build a network.

Definition, Please

peer-to-peer network—A type of network that links computers together, and for all practical purposes, the computers have equal status within the network. Each computer shares its resources, which can include files, printers, and more, and uses the resources found on other computers.

Because all the computers in a peer-to-peer network offer their resources to share and use the resources that are available on other computers, it's something like a computer commune—every computer shares the work and relies on the others. Thus, a printer may be attached to a single computer on the network, but it's used by all the other systems; another computer may house the office's only CD-ROM drive, which it shares with the other computers in the network. While a computer is sharing its resources or using the resources of other computers, you can still use it as a workstation (for example, to do word processing or work on databases). Keep in mind that if you or someone else is working on a computer that is sharing a resource with another system at the same time, the performance of the computer will slow down as it's trying to do several things at once. Figure 2.1 shows a peer-to-peer network.

Peer-to-peer networks are the easiest networks to set up; they don't require special networking software. You can connect several computers together into a network using the features in Windows 95 or Windows 98, along with some network hardware, which I'll discuss in later chapters.

If you build a peer-to-peer network, you can improve overall network performance by designating a single computer as one that exists solely to share resources (called a *server*—see the next section). If you think your network may need to expand in the future, you can install a peer-to-peer network and later upgrade it to a server system based around Windows NT Server. All of the hardware that you install—and which is explained

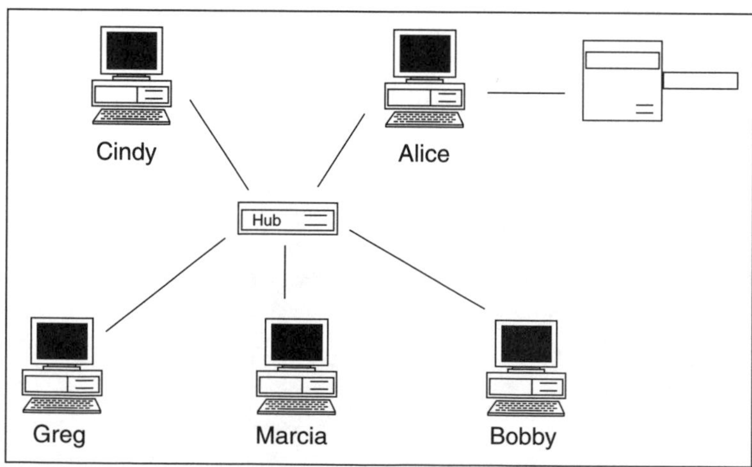

Figure 2.1 A peer-to-peer network.

in the following chapters—will work with either a Windows peer-to-peer or a server-based system.

Server-Based Network

The computer on your network that offers resources, drives, printers, modems, and more, is called the *server*. On the other hand, any computer that isn't a server and uses the resources that are available on the server is called a *client*. A client depends on the server for many things that it needs to work with and functions it performs. For example, if a client computer needs to print a document, it uses the printer that's connected to the server; if it needs to open and work with key files, it accesses them on one of the server's drives. Figure 2.2 shows a network with a server.

Definition, Please

server—1. The central system on a computer network that houses the drives and other resources. A server typically shares its resources, but it doesn't use the resources of other computers on the network. 2. Sometimes this term is used to refer to the computer that is connected to the printer or fax/modem in a peer-to-peer network. This usage is also correct in that the server is a computer that serves a specific purpose in the network.

client—A computer that is connected to a network and that uses the resources of the server, but doesn't share its resources with the other computers on the network.

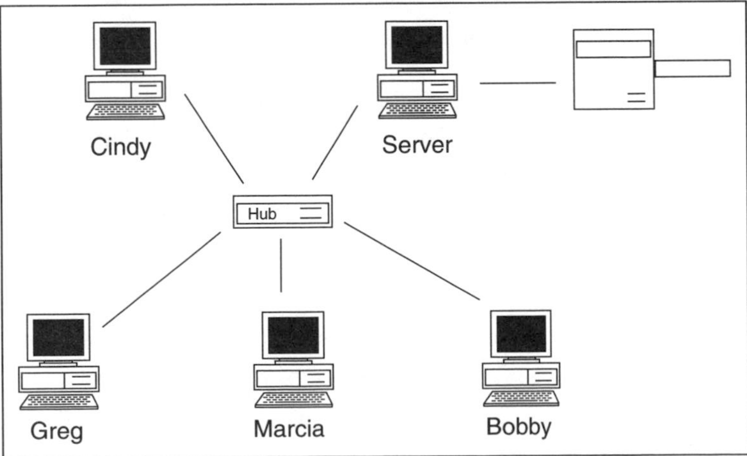

Figure 2.2 A server-based network.

I like to think of a server as a supply room, like those that exist in lots of companies. In such a room, you'll often find the notepads, staples, paperclips, Post-It notes, and other office supplies that everyone needs; you also might find copy machines, fax machines, and even printers. The supply room, in a sense, is a server that holds all the resources that all of the departments in a company use, and everything is found in one place to be shared with everyone. Taking this analogy a step further, the various departments are the clients that typically don't share their own resources with other departments or with the supply room.

Other aspects distinguish a server from a client. The server is often the most powerful computer on the network; after all, it's sharing its resources with lots of other computers and needs considerable processing power to fulfill all the requests that it must field. A network always has more clients than servers. After all, this is the whole point of a network—being able to share limited resources. Servers commonly support anywhere from five to hundreds of client computers.

Network Operating Systems

Unlike the peer-to-peer networks that I talk about building in this book, server-based networks run specialized networking software called a *network operating system*. Although lots of popular *network operating systems* exist, including Linux, Novell Netware, Unix, and Windows NT Server, Windows NT Server offers the most logical upgrade path for the Windows-based network that you will build while reading this book.

Definition, Please

network operating system (NOS)—An operating system that is designed to support a network. Popular network operating systems include Linux, Novell Netware, Unix, and Windows NT Server.

Windows NT Server

Rapidly gaining in popularity, Windows NT Server is best used in server-based networks where the client computers are running any version of Windows. Windows NT Workstation and Windows NT Server both look a lot like Windows 95 and Windows 98—they all feature similar desktops. Although the hardware drivers are different, the common desktop is an advantage—if you know Windows 95 or 98, Windows NT will immediately feel familiar. This doesn't mean that Windows NT is an absolute cinch to learn—it's not. For example, NT's domain structure can be confusing to understand and set up. But the Windows-style interface means that you have less to learn.

Besides offering powerful network features, Windows NT Server comes with Internet software, as well as tools that support remote access and virtual private networks. The Small Business Server package that supports up to 25 users bundles Windows NT Server with Microsoft's Exchange Server for email, SQL Server that supports databases, faxing software, and more. According to its specs, Windows NT Server can handle an unlimited number of users and an unlimited number of open files.

As I write this, Microsoft is developing Windows 2000, which will be the newest version of Windows NT (Microsoft originally had planned to call it "Windows NT 5"). Windows 2000 will offer a host of new features, including a directory of network resources that managers can modify using an application that resembles a Web browser, step-by-step wizards that walk users through various network configuration tasks, better means for users to manage documents in a specified folder, and more.

Windows NT is the logical upgrade for your Windows 95– or Windows 98–based network. Although we won't be covering its finer points here, Windows NT is the network operating system that can take you to the next step beyond the peer-to-peer network that you'll build with the help of this book.

Moving On

In this chapter, you learned basic definitions for network terms, including peer-to-peer, servers, clients, and network operating systems. In the next chapter, I'll talk about how to plan for your network.

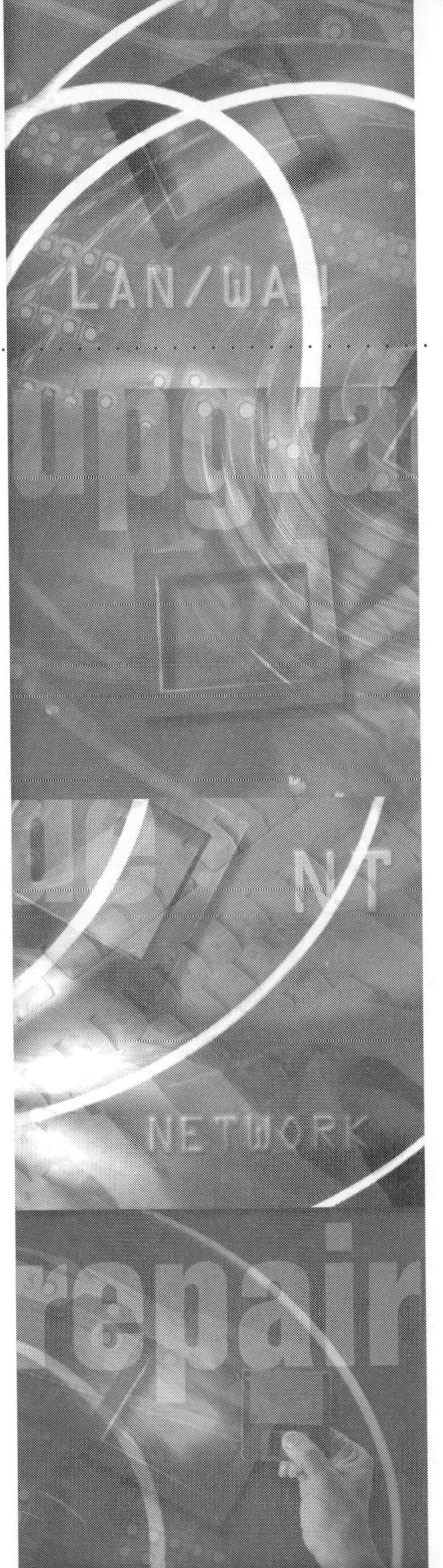

Part 2

Building Your Network

3

Planning For Your Network

To get to where you want to go, you should always have a plan. Even so, I'm like a lot of people who drive their cars around, never refer to maps, and won't ask gas station attendants for directions. But when it comes to building a network in your home or small business, it definitely makes sense to see what you have to work with and establish a goal for your network. This way, you'll have fewer surprises along the way, and you're far less likely to spend money on hardware or software that you don't need (the shoestring angle again).

Building a network out of two systems that happen to be in your home won't take much planning. But if you form a network made up of the six personal computers (PCs) in your office, a little planning at this stage will mean fewer adjustments to make later; you'll also save time in the long run. To make your plan, look at the computers that you currently have and assess how you can make the most of them in your new network. And whether you're building a network that has 5 workstations or 100, the general planning approach is much the same.

Inventory Everything

The first step in creating a network plan is to look at the existing systems that you want to connect in a network. Once you know what processors, hard drives, and other components each system in your network has to offer, you can decide which computers will fill each particular aspect of your network. For example, a computer with a large hard drive and lots of

RAM will work best as the *file server*, the system on your network that stores files and lets other computers access them.

Processors

The first aspect to consider is each system's processor. If you don't know what processor or CPU a system is running, you can usually tell by looking at the monitor as the computer boots. The information doesn't remain on screen for very long, so you have to watch carefully, but you can usually see some designation for the system's processor.

A fast way to review all information about a system's processor—as well as the installed RAM—is to use Microsoft Office or Windows 98 software, as specified in the following procedure. If your system has Microsoft Office, you can run Word or Excel and determine the system's processor and installed RAM by doing the following:

1. Start Word or Excel.
2. Select Choose from the Help menu, and then About from the submenu.
3. Click on System Info. You'll see the screen that appears in Figure 3.1.

If you're running Windows 98, you can find all of the system specifications on a single screen. Follow these steps:

1. Click on Start.
2. Select Programs|Accessories|System Tools|System Information.
3. Windows 98 displays the screen shown in Figure 3.2, which shows all of the system information on a single screen.

Hard Drives

You need to know how large the hard drive is for each system on your planned network. Within Windows 95 or 98, you can do the following:

1. Double-click on the My Computer icon on your Windows desktop.
2. Right-click on the hard drive (place the cursor on the hard drive icon and click the right mouse button).

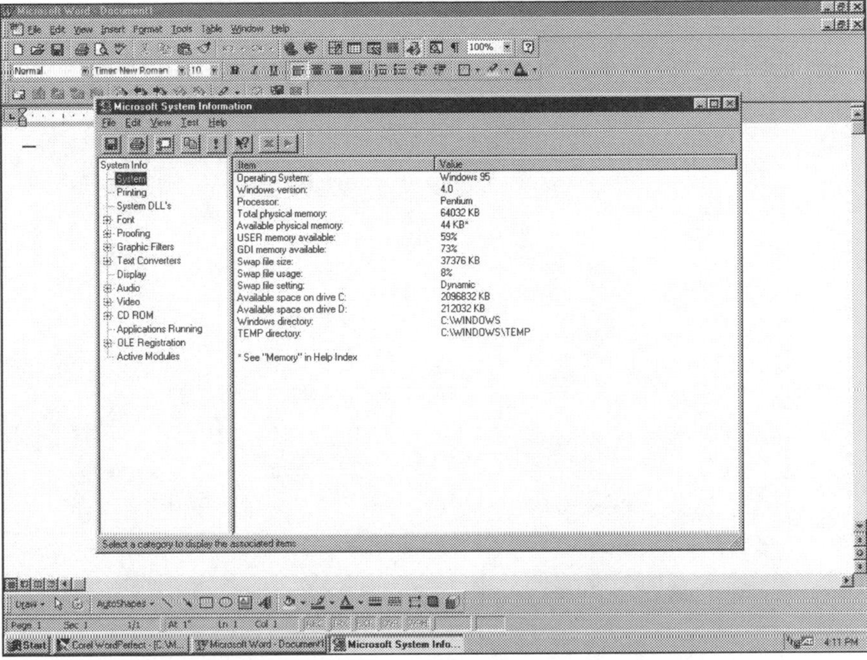

Figure 3.1 You can use Microsoft Word or Excel to find a system's specifications.

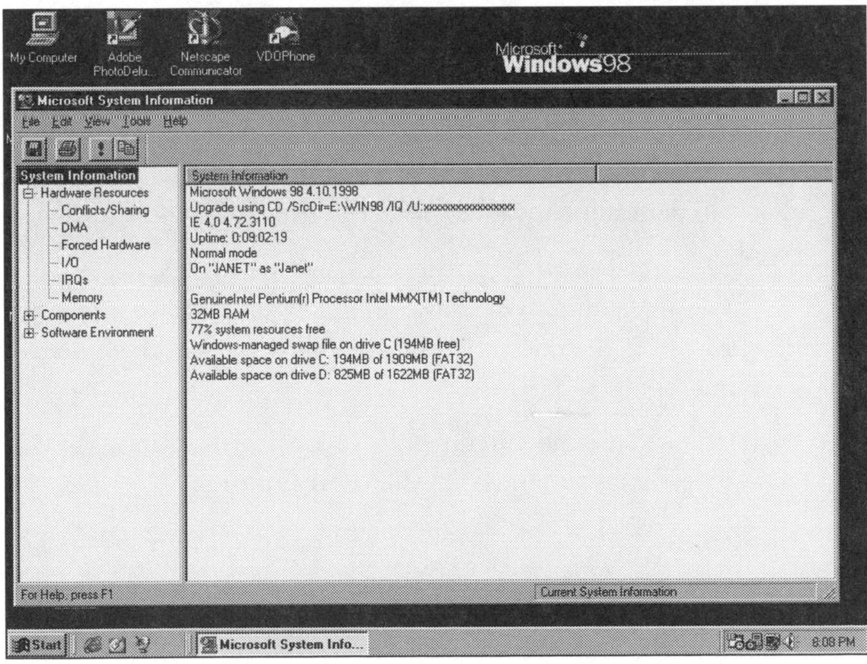

Figure 3.2 Windows System Information displays all pertinent system information on a single screen on computers running Windows 98.

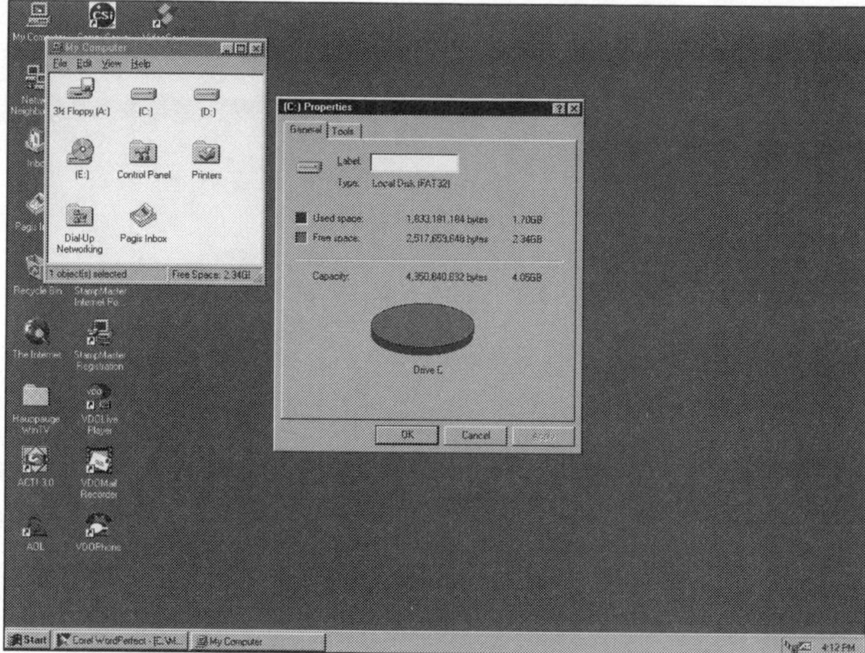

Figure 3.3 You can view the specifications on each system's hard drive by selecting its properties.

3. Select Properties. You'll see a screen (see Figure 3.3) that displays the size of the drive, as well as the free and used space.

Memory

You can determine the memory in each system by one of the following methods.

- If you are running Windows 98, follow the directions given in the "Processors" section earlier in this chapter to run the System Information program.
- If you are running Windows 95, follow the directions given in the "Processors" section to run Microsoft Office.

You can also:

1. Click on Start.
2. Select Settings|Control Panel.
3. Double-click on the System icon. Under the General tab (the default), you'll find the amount of RAM installed in the system, as well

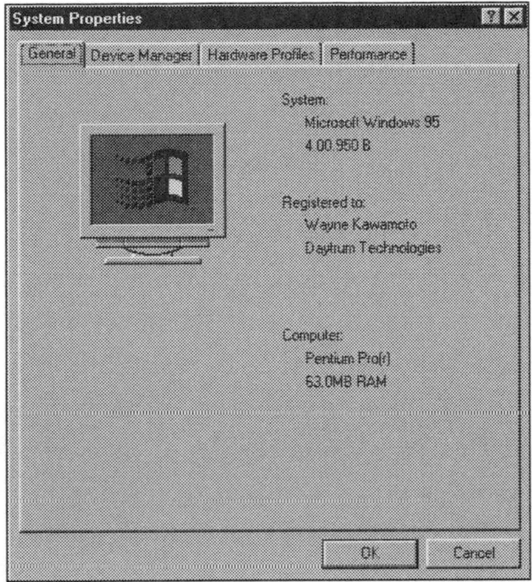

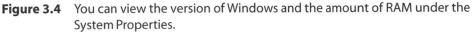

Figure 3.4 You can view the version of Windows and the amount of RAM under the System Properties.

as the version of Windows that is installed, as shown in Figure 3.4. (Note that I have edited the figure so that it doesn't display my Windows registration information.) It's a good idea to note the version of Windows you are using.

Another method you can use is as follows:

1. Right-click on the My Computer icon on your Windows desktop.
2. Select Properties.
3. Under the General tab (the default), you'll find the amount of RAM installed in the system, as well as the version of Windows (refer again to Figure 3.4). It's a good idea to note the version of Windows you are using.

You can also determine a system's memory by simply turning on the computer, which as part of its bootup routine counts and briefly displays the amount of RAM installed in the computer.

What Do You Want To Do With Your Network?

Chapter 1 talked about the many things that a network can do for your home or office. What you want to do with your network will determine how you set it up and which computers you select to perform particular network functions. The following sections describe tasks you might want to be able to accomplish with your network.

Sharing Files

You may want to use a single computer to store the data files of many users or to store key files—for example, database or accounting files—so others can access and use them from their own computers. For this purpose, you'll require the computer with the largest and roomiest hard drive. It also doesn't hurt to use a powerful system with a fast processor and lots of RAM to ensure that the system can adequately serve information to others. Keep in mind that you can also use a relatively slow system as a server; however, no one on the network will want to use it as a main work computer.

Sharing Printers

On a peer-to-peer network, you can connect a printer to a single computer and everyone on the network can print to it, just as if their computers were connected to it. However, the person whose workstation has the printer connected to it will find that each time someone uses the printer, it greatly slows down his or her computer, because that computer must receive and process commands.

For this reason, it's a good idea to have a fast system with lots of RAM for the computer that hosts the printer. On the other hand, if you have an extra system that no one will be using, this may be the perfect one to connect to the printer. In this case, you can use a very slow system, because no one will be irritated by its reduced performance.

Running Networkable Programs

In the networkable programs category, I place accounting packages—such as Peachtree Complete Accounting and Intuit's Quickbooks Pro—that let several users access accounting information from a single file. This group also includes contact managers and other programs that rely on databases. All users can access the same files and work with them from their systems. For example, in the case of the accounting packages, one person can take phone calls and enter orders, while another person runs the payroll. And because one computer will be serving the files to a lot of other systems, you should assign this duty to a computer that has a roomy hard drive, a fast processor, and lots of RAM.

Playing Games

If you're planning to build a network that lets you play head-to-head games such as Quake II and StarCraft, use your fastest and most powerful system as the main system or host. When you're playing games, not only does the host system need the horsepower to run the game itself, it also has to process the communications from the other computers. The more players that are connected to a single game, the greater the burden on the host system.

Keep in mind that if you want to beef up the performance of a system on your network, you can always follow the upgrade advice that is provided in later chapters in this book.

Do You Want To Dedicate One PC As A Server?

You can devote one PC in your network to the sole task of taking care of network functions. This dedicated PC—or *server*—offers the following advantages:

- A dedicated PC that acts as the server offers faster network performance.
- You don't have to use the fastest and most powerful machine that you have for a server, because no one will be working on it and become frustrated with its slower performance.
- No problems arise from someone shutting off his or her computer and preventing access to some network peripheral. For example, when the person whose system is connected to the printer shuts off that computer at the end of the day, it prevents anyone else from using the printer.

This discussion of servers logically leads to considering a standalone server and true network operating systems, such as Novell NetWare or Windows NT Server. These sophisticated network operating systems are used by large firms that have extensive networks of computers to support. These systems are beyond the scope of this book. Keep in mind that you can start with a simple, Windows-based peer-to-peer network that this book shows you how to build, and as your needs increase, you can add a server running Windows NT Server later, when you need the additional performance. Also, computer companies such as Compaq and Dell sell powerful systems, with lots of room for expansion, that are designed specifically for use as network servers. The networks that you'll be building by following the instructions in this book are relatively simple, but the sky is still the limit.

Moving On

In this chapter, I discussed how to plan for a network, evaluate the systems that you have to work with, and designate computers for specific network functions. In the next chapter, I'll discuss the components you'll need to build your network.

4

What You'll Need To Build A Network

Enough of all this background stuff on networks—let's talk about the nuts and bolts that will let you actually build your network. In past chapters, I've talked about what a network can do for you and how to plan your network. In this chapter—finally—we'll talk about the components that you'll need to build it.

Ether-What?

The key to linking computers together using Windows 95 or 98 comes in a network standard known as *Ethernet*.

Definition, Please

Ethernet is a standard for connecting computers together into a network. It defines the type of cables that you can use, the way computers send and receive data, and more. Right now, Ethernet is the most popular network standard and is the basis for connecting computers together with Windows. You may have heard of other standards, including token ring and ARCnet, but in this book, we will be working only with Ethernet.

Ethernet can send data at a rate of 10 million bits per second (10Mbps). A newer version of Ethernet exists that sends data some 10 times faster, at 100 million bits per second (100Mbps). This newer and faster standard is called *Fast Ethernet* and is more expensive than regular Ethernet. But if speed is a paramount consideration in your network, consider using Fast Ethernet.

Definition, Please

Fast Ethernet is a standard for connecting computers together into a network that is 10 times faster than standard Ethernet.

Network Interface Cards

To build a network, you'll need something called a *network interface card* (*NIC*) that you install in each of your computers.

Like modems and video expansion cards, network interface cards come in all types. The important kinds of NICs are described in the following sections.

Definition, Please

A *network interface card* is a special kind of expansion card that you install in your computer and connect to network cables so the computer can become part of a network. An *expansion card* is a specialized computer board that lets you add new functions to your computer. Examples of expansion cards, besides network interface cards, are internal modems and sound cards.

Expansion Bus

Over the years, network interface cards have come in versions that install in the 8-bit slots of old 8088 systems, 16-bit ISA versions that work with computers from the 80286 era to today's speed demons, and PCI versions, which are the most popular now.

Definition, Please

A *bus* is an internal data highway among key computer components that defines how fast data can travel. The larger or wider the bus, the more data can pass. All computers feature expansion slots or buses that accept expansion cards.

Industry Standard Architecture (*ISA*), a type of bus with a 16-bit data path, is found on most computers, from the old 80286-based ATs to most of today's Pentiums.

Peripheral Component Connect (PCI), a type of bus with a 64-bit data path, is found on most computers, from late 486s to today's Pentium II systems.

You'll need to purchase a network card that will fit into your computer's available slots. An ISA board can install only in an ISA slot, a PCI in a PCI slot, and so on. Before you buy a network interface card, be sure that your computer has an appropriate slot to accept it.

Connectors

Every network interface card comes with a connector, or more than one connector, that attaches to network cable. You'll need to purchase network cards that have connectors that will mate with the type of cables that you plan to use. Popular cables and corresponding connectors include *10BaseT* and *coaxial cable*. See the "Cables" section later in this chapter for more information.

Network Compatibility

The current standard for network cards is something called *NE2000*. For all practical purposes, if you're purchasing a new Ethernet network card, it will be compatible. Another item that I look for in a network interface card is *Plug and Play* compatibility. This standard works with Windows 95 and 98 and lets your computer perform most of the configuration of a board for you. Although Plug and Play isn't without its faults—sometimes, it simply doesn't work—it generally makes it easier to install network cards.

Definition, Please

NE2000 is a driver (software) standard for 16-bit network interface adapters (cards) that allows them to work with various network operating systems.

Cables

Deciding what cables to use may initially sound simple, but you need to consider several factors before making your choice. The type of cable that you select to use with your network will affect the arrangement of your network, as well as the connectors that you'll need on your network interface cards. Although other types of cables are available, we'll cover the two most popular kinds that you should consider for your Windows-based network.

Thin Coax

Coax (or *thinnet*) cable, as shown in Figure 4.1, is often what people are referring to when they mention coaxial cable. It's a popular way of connecting computers into networks.

Definition, Please

Thinnet cable, also called *coax cable,* is a common cable for connecting computers together to form networks; computers are connected in series.

Coaxial cable uses a connector called a *BNC connector*. If you've worked with antennas and radios, you've probably seen a BNC connector before. When you connect your network using thinnet cable, you have to connect your computers together in a specific way. Each network card has to have a T connector attached to its female BNC connector, as shown in Figure 4.2. You then connect your main network cable to one end of the T connector.

You can usually purchase thinnet in different lengths and with the connectors already on at various computer stores. If you'll be working with lots of thinnet cables, you can purchase a spool of bulk coax, cut it, and attach your own BNC connectors using a special crimping tool. However, for most small networks, this is not cost effective.

When you use coax to link a bunch of PCs together into a network, you have to connect them as you would a bunch of lights in series. Thus, the

Figure 4.1 Thinnet or coax cable.

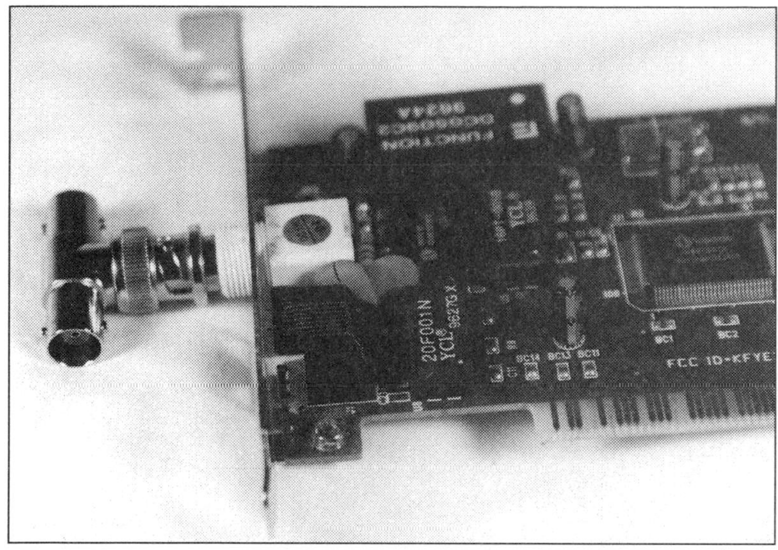

Figure 4.2 Each network card must have a T connector attached to its female BNC connector.

first computer connects to the second computer, the second computer connects to the third computer, the third computer connects to the fourth computer, and so on, as shown in Figure 4.3. An advantage of this arrangement is that if you have a row of computers to connect, you can easily connect one to the other (like a string of Christmas lights) and build your entire network. A down side of this arrangement, however, is that when one connection goes bad, the entire network connection is broken.

At the first and last computers in the network, you must install a device called a *terminator* at the opposite end of the T connector, as shown in Figure 4.4.

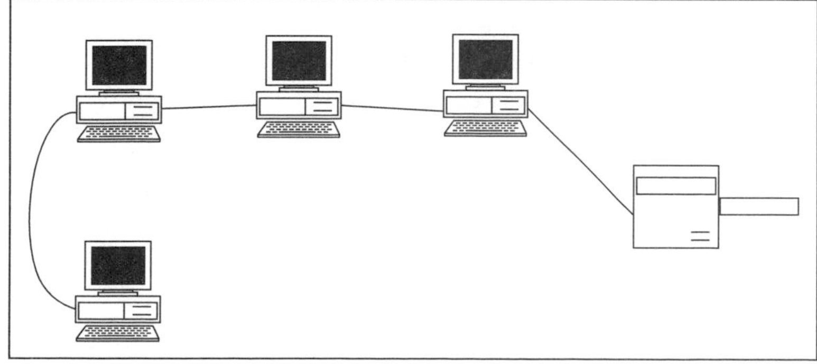

Figure 4.3 A network built with coaxial cable.

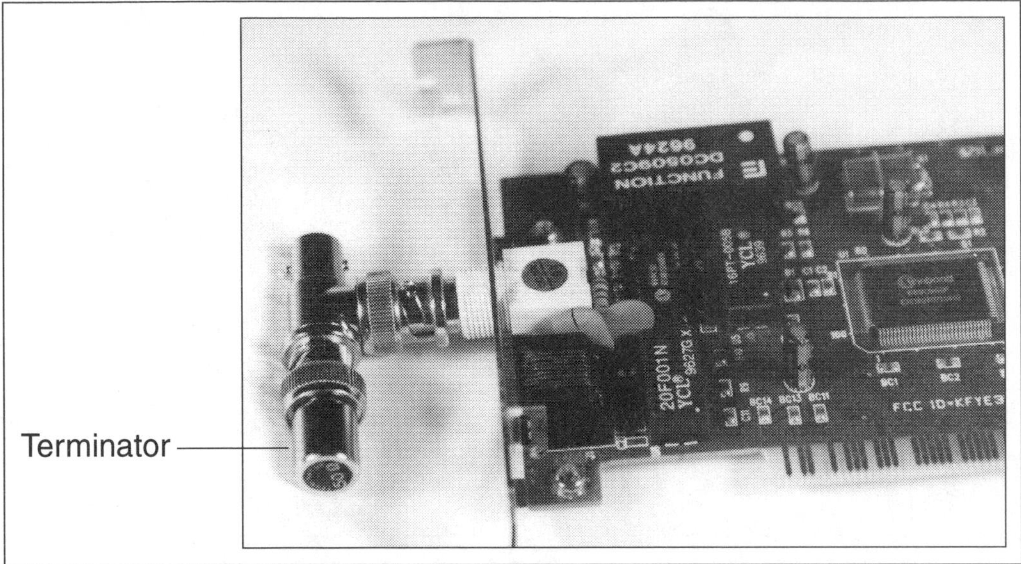

Figure 4.4 A terminator connected to a T connector.

If you decide to go with coax, you can use it to span distances up to 500 feet and connect up to 30 computers. You can extend this distance beyond 500 feet by using a device called a *repeater*.

Unshielded Twisted Pair

Unshielded twisted pair (*UTP*) cable—also known as *10BaseT* (pronounced “ten-base-tee”)—is a type of cable that is less expensive than coax; it uses a connector that looks like a bigger version of the one used to connect your telephone to a wall phone outlet. Figure 4.5 shows a 10BaseT cable.

Definition, Please

Unshielded twisted pair (*UTP*), also called *10BaseT*, is a common cable for connecting computers together to form networks; computers are joined at a central junction box.

When using 10BaseT to connect computers, you join them at a central junction box to a device called a *hub*. All of the computers connect at the hub. Figure 4.6 shows an arrangement of a hub-based network.

Using a hub, you can connect anywhere from 4 to 24 computers, depending on the number of outlets in the hub. An advantage of a hub arrangement

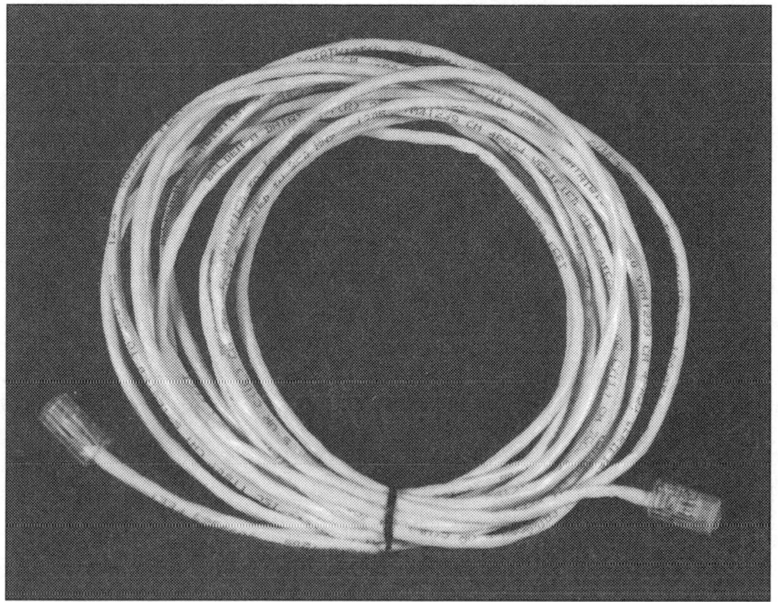

Figure 4.5 10BaseT cable.

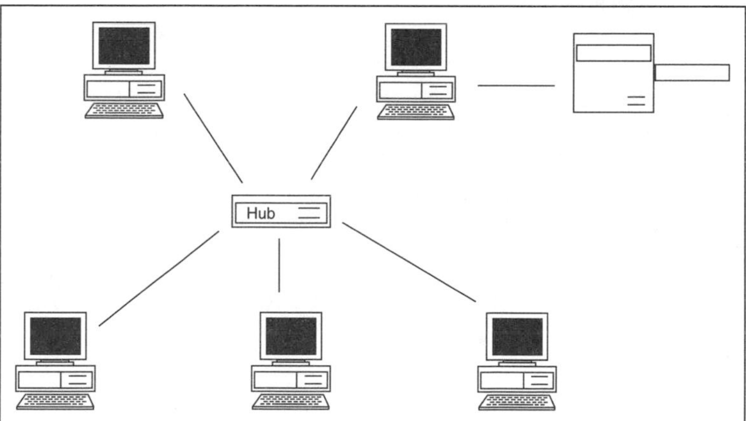

Figure 4.6 A network with a hub.

Definition, Please

A *hub* is a device that accepts 10BaseT cables from all of the computers on the network and joins them together.

is that if a connection to the hub goes bad, it only affects one computer. It's also usually easier to add more computers to a network than it is when you're working with thinnet—all you have to do is connect a

10BaseT cable to an open port in the hub. Another plus: If you outgrow the number of ports on your current hub, you can do something called *daisy chaining*: connecting hubs together to expand your network. You can also purchase hubs that support Fast Ethernet, or both Fast and standard Ethernet. After you decide what type of Ethernet you want to use, you should purchase your hub accordingly.

10BaseT cable comes in different grades called *categories*. Category 1 is the lowest quality and category 5 is the best. As you would expect, the better the quality, the higher the cost. Most experts recommend that you use category 3 or higher for your network. You can purchase 10BaseT cable in standard lengths from almost any computer store, or you can buy the cable in bulk and use a special crimping tool to attach your own BNC connectors. However, unless you'll be building a big network with 10 or more stations, it's probably best to buy the cable pre-cut and with connectors.

Tip—Cost

Unless you need sophisticated network managing features, avoid paying extra money for hubs that are equipped with something called *SNMP*. SNMP stands for Simple Network Management Protocol, which is a network standard for exchanging information between devices on a network. Despite the "simple" in the name, it's a complicated standard that is only for administrators who need these features to manage large networks.

Network Starter Kits

To create a network, you will need to install network interface cards in each PC and link them with either coaxial cable or with 10BaseT cable and a hub. You can go to your local computer store and purchase these components separately, of course, or you can buy a network starter kit that includes everything you need.

Network starter kits typically include enough hardware to join two or three computers; they also include network interface cards, coax or 10BaseT cable, and a hub (for 10BaseT) at reasonable prices. Without a doubt, these starter kits make it quite easy to build a network right out of the box, because you know that you have all the parts. You'll also find that these kits usually come with clear directions that help you install the network cards and hook up the hub and cables. Some kits even come with diagnostic network software that helps determine if something is wrong with your network setup; also, most companies offer tech support, so you can always call with your questions. And because you purchase the parts in a kit, you know that they should work together.

The only disadvantage of these kits is that they're put together with the idea that one size fits all. If you need cables of a longer length, you'll have to go out and buy them. Overall, I've been impressed with network starter kits, and in most cases, you usually don't spend much more on a kit than you do when you purchase your components separately.

Moving On

I've discussed the basic components that you'll need to build a network: the network interface cards, the cables, and the hub. In the next chapter, I'll discuss ways of purchasing your network components at the lowest prices—the meat of the shoestring angle.

5

Bargain Basement: Shopping For The Best Network Values

The key to building a network on a shoestring is to buy inexpensive parts and perform the work yourself. Most of this book talks about the hardware you need to buy and how to install it. In this chapter, I'll discuss where to buy parts and provide guidelines on getting the best deals, plus some warnings about potential pitfalls.

Network Hardware Shopping Options

Despite its popularity, network hardware is a specialty item. Although you can buy computers in department stores, you'll usually have to turn to specialized sources to get the parts you need to build your network. These sources include:

- Specialty computer stores
- Warehouse stores
- Computer and office superstores
- Mail order
- Computer swap meets
- Online shopping

Generally, the computer and office superstores have fairly competitive prices, while small computer stores vary in pricing. Some small computer shops are more expensive but provide excellent service. However, smaller stores may advertise great prices, especially if they carry specialty items.

Mail order and online businesses offer great prices as well, but you have to wait to receive your parts (although many companies will ship them to you by overnight express if you pay for it). If something doesn't work, it takes more effort to return it for an exchange or a refund. Without a doubt, computer swap meets offer the best deals. However, you have to be very careful when you buy network equipment at such an event.

As when purchasing anything, shop around and compare prices to get the best value for your hard-earned dollars; also, make sure that you thoroughly understand each vendor's return policy.

Let's look at each of these sources, what you can generally find at each, and where you're likely to find the best deals. Keep in mind that these are general guidelines and that there are always exceptions.

Specialty Computer Stores

These stores that spring up in convenient locations in your hometown are classic mom-and-pop outfits specializing in computers. Most of the time they offer repair services along with new computer systems, parts, and software, and many offer networking consulting services to build, configure, and service networks, mainly in small businesses.

Generally, these small stores have the highest prices, mainly because they can't (and don't) buy parts in enough quantity to get their stock at a lower cost. They sometimes won't have the part you need in stock and will have to order it, which can take a day or two.

The best time to opt for a small computer store is when you need expert advice or one-on-one attention and you're willing to pay for the service. Watch out, though; some smaller computer stores don't want you to install your own components and will only test them for you before you buy—after that, you're on your own. If something goes wrong with a part, these stores won't want to accept returns or exchanges. For this reason, be sure you understand the return policy and get it in writing. When I've shopped at small stores, I've generally paid top dollar; however, they do sometimes offer special deals that can match the mail order houses.

For a summary of advantages and disadvantages of specialty computer stores, refer to Table 5.1.

Table 5.1 Pros and cons of specialty computer stores.

Advantages	Disadvantages
Good service	High prices (usually)
Convenient location	Don't stock most items
Expert advice	Have to order parts

Warehouse Stores

Warehouse stores have changed how we buy (and store) products. Most of these stores sell food and other goods in bulk quantities (such as three-gallon jugs of maple syrup or three-pound blocks of cheddar cheese). You'll also find computers and a limited selection of accessories. Stores of this kind include Costco and Sam's Club.

Although warehouse stores often carry a decent supply of printers, scanners, floppy disks, modems, and software, they don't carry network hardware such as hubs or network interface cards. However, you may purchase components such as hard drives, RAM chips, and the occasional CPU upgrade chips. Their prices are usually competitive, but you have to know exactly what you want to buy.

If you have any questions, you'll have a hard time finding anyone who knows anything about computers, let alone the components. The person selling car wax or serving frozen pizza in the next aisle probably is not a reliable source for computer information. And the warehouse store's return policy often requires you to go back to the manufacturer if you want to return the item after you open the package. For this reason, be very sure of your purchase. (Also, if you go to one of these places, try to walk out without extra books and CDs that you never intended to buy, but that are such great deals.)

For a summary of advantages and disadvantages of warehouse stores, refer to Table 5.2.

Table 5.2 Pros and cons of warehouse stores.

Advantages	Disadvantages
Competitive prices	Little selection and few parts
	No expert advice
	Limited return policies

Computer And Office Superstores

For any computer enthusiast, a computer superstore is a high-tech candy shop, stuffed with the latest and greatest cutting-edge PCs, hardware, and software. In these stores, you'll also find a good selection of network hardware at decent prices. Well-known computer superstores include Computer City, CompUSA, and Fry's Electronics.

The best thing about a computer superstore is that it combines knowledgeable salespeople with the great selection of an established dealer. Because most of these stores have repair departments, their staff has a lot of technical expertise, and you'll find that most of these people know what they're talking about. I've had good experience buying components from these stores, although they don't have the absolute lowest prices.

A subset of the computer superstores is office superstores, such as Staples, Office Depot, and OfficeMax. In these establishments, you'll find everything you need for an office, including furniture, pens, and copy machines, along with computers and software at competitive prices. You can find some network components at these stores, but the selection isn't as large as at a dedicated computer superstore.

For a summary of advantages and disadvantages of computer superstores, refer to Table 5.3.

Mail Order

Like clothing, food, and just about anything else you can name, computer and network parts are available by mail order. All you have to do is peruse the ads in any computer magazine to find lots of mail order companies that will sell you components. Often you can find companies that specialize in a single item—network interface cards, for example—at excellent

Table 5.3 Pros and cons of computer superstores.

Advantages	Disadvantages
Great selection	Not available in some areas
Decent prices	
Expert advice	
Established store	
Lots of stock	

prices. I've done my share of buying by mail order and have never had a problem. In fact, my experiences have been downright pleasant.

All computer magazines have mail order ads, but the king is *Computer Shopper* magazine. This weighty tome is easy to find at any newsstand—it's twice as large and twice as thick as the others. When you open an issue, you'll find evaluations, articles with a mail order/direct purchase slant, and lots of ads. In fact, if you can't find something in *Computer Shopper*, it probably doesn't exist. If you want to make life hard for your mail carrier, you can order a subscription to this behemoth (it dominates my mailbox the same way that it dominates the newsstand).

Buying anything by mail order has pluses and minuses. Prices vary, but you can usually find great deals. You don't have to pay sales tax on your purchase (unless the mail order firm has a retail outlet in your state), which can mean significant savings, even if the local computer store can match the price. On the other hand, you do have to pay shipping charges, which vary according to the size of the package and how fast you want the product in your hands. If you don't have your purchase sent by overnight mail, it may be a week or more before you get it.

While shopping by mail may seem risky, most vendors who advertise in the major publications are reputable. You can't tell if a firm is reputable just by reading an ad, but you can find out in other ways. You can go back a few issues to see if the firm is placing ads consistently. Also, you can call the firm's home city government to ask about it and contact that city's Better Business Bureau. In addition, it's wise to avoid companies with only a post office box address. As long as you use a credit card, which is the preferred form of payment, you'll probably do just fine. (I'll talk about credit card issues later in this chapter.)

Most firms have established return policies and some offer technical advice hotlines. If the installation isn't going exactly the way you want, expert advice is a phone call away—a plus. Many mail order houses have Web sites where you can get up-to-date prices for quick comparison shopping, look up daily bargains, and order your parts. Most companies have toll-free numbers, so calling and comparing prices won't cost you a dime.

For a summary of advantages and disadvantages of mail order, refer to Table 5.4.

Table 5.4 Pros and cons of mail order houses.

Advantages	Disadvantages
Competitive prices	Must wait for product delivery
Expert advice	Must pay for shipping and handling
Save on sales tax	Can't see the product before purchase
Huge selection	
Easy to comparison shop	

Computer Swap Meets

Computer swap meets aren't available in every part of the country, but their popularity is spreading. They're like the swap meets held in parking lots and drive-in theaters, but they offer for sale only computers and computer software, accessories, and parts. You'll find tables set up by vendors who will sell you anything related to a computer at prices that can't be beat by any of the other sources I've discussed previously. You might even be able to wheel and deal to get a vendor to cut a price in order to match or beat swap meet competitors' prices. To clinch the sale, sometimes a dealer will pay the sales tax for you.

On the other hand, while you'll find the best prices at swap meets, you really have to know what you're buying; it's also hard to pick out the reputable dealers. When shopping this way, more than any other, the rule is caveat emptor—"Let the buyer beware." At the largest swap meets, you may be charged for parking and admission and could be out $10 before you walk in the door.

Most of the booths are staffed by dealers and vendors who also sell from storefront or factory locations. It's a good idea to attend a swap meet and pick up the fliers for deals that interest you; then, between swap meets, you can check out the stores or factories to make sure that they are legitimate businesses (although this isn't always practical, because some sellers come from a long distance). At the next swap meet, you can make your purchases. In this way, you can get the special show price; many of the sellers offer their best prices as swap meet specials. Occasionally, I've found a vendor who will give me the swap meet price at the store.

Another thing you'll find is that the vendors at swap meets want to deal in either cash or checks—very few will accept credit cards. This makes it extra important to know whether you're dealing with a reputable business.

When buying at a swap meet, be sure that you understand the seller's return policy; get it in writing if possible. Unfortunately, you'll find that some sellers hand-write their invoices, and dealings at swap meets generally are not very formal or businesslike. You also want to make sure that you actually see the component before it goes into the bag, to ensure that you are getting the right part (sellers can make mistakes).

For a summary of advantages and disadvantages of swap meets, refer to Table 5.5.

Online Shopping

Another shopping option is open 24 hours a day, 7 days a week: the Web and major online services such as America Online. You can conveniently peruse online shopping areas and sites any time of the day (or night) to browse for products (as you would with a catalog) and find out information on available hardware and software, including specifications; you can sometimes even view product pictures.

When shopping online, the sky is the limit. You can find and purchase almost any kind of hardware, including major or lesser-known brands of hubs, network interface cards, video cards, monitors, sound boards, and anything else that you may want to buy for your system. When you're online, you can even read reviews at other sites to help you with your decision. Another advantage—one that catalogs lack—is that you can check out hot bargains of the day. If you're into getting great deals, you can find them when you shop online.

For the most part, shopping online has many of the same advantages and disadvantages as shopping by mail order. Online stores are open 24 hours a day, you can easily make your purchase with a credit card, and you save

Table 5.5 Pros and cons of computer swap meets.

Advantages	Disadvantages
Lowest prices anywhere	Hard to determine firms' reputability
Expert advice	Returns might be difficult
Ready stock	Few accept credit cards

on sales tax. However, you can't actually see a product before you buy it, you have to wait for delivery (although most will overnight products to you if you pay for it), and you must pay for shipping and handling. As with stores and mail order catalogs, some aggressive price-cutting sites offer products at bargain basement prices; others emphasize their service and return policies.

Most mail order houses have online sites that you can check. To verify that a Web-based business is legitimate, you can try some of the strategies mentioned previously in the "Mail Order" section of this chapter. Most Web businesses clearly state their return policies somewhere on their sites.

For a summary of advantages and disadvantages of online shopping, refer to Table 5.6.

Making Your Decision

Where you buy your components is up to you. If you don't feel too confident about wheeling and dealing and making spot decisions, computer superstores, online shopping, and mail order probably are the best options. You'll save money over other sources and shop in a comfortable place with information available from online specs, knowledgeable salespersons, and written materials.

On the other hand, if you're looking for the absolutely lowest prices, you're not going to beat the swap meet. However, you have to know exactly what you're buying and be certain that you understand the return

Table 5.6 Pros and cons of online shopping.

Advantages	Disadvantages
Available 24 hours a day	Must pay for shipping and handling
Carries name brands	Can't see the product before purchase
Huge selection	Have to wait for product delivery
Save on sales tax	
Competitive prices	
Easy to comparison shop and use other online resources for more information	

policies. Swap meets involve more legwork, but the savings are worth it. If you're one of those people who thrive in a wheeling-dealing environment, head for the swap meet and enjoy.

To aid you in making your decision, a summary of the characteristics of each type of store can be found in Table 5.7.

General Buying Tips

When buying computer components, whether you're dealing with a store, a mail order firm, or a vendor at a swap meet, be sure that you clearly understand the seller's policies and get them in writing whenever possible. If you're purchasing by mail order or through an online site, you'll usually find the seller's policies clearly stated in the ad.

While shopping, besides looking for things like fair prices and quality products, keep these tips in mind:

- *Understand the return policy.* First, check and understand the return policy. Can you return the part in its original condition and get your money back? Does the firm charge a restocking fee? In that case, they will give you your money back but deduct a percentage, sometimes as high as 15 percent. Some firms will accept only a defective product for a cash refund. Because you usually can't bring your computer to the store to see if a part will fit and work, you need to have a clear understanding of this policy, just in case the installation doesn't go smoothly.

Table 5.7 Comparison of computer-shopping alternatives.

Store Type	Selection	Service	Price	Notes
Specialty computer store	Good	Excellent	High	Usually emphasizes service
Warehouse store	Fair	Poor	Fair	No expertise
Computer superstore	Excellent	Excellent	Low	Knowledgeable staff
Office superstore	Good	Excellent	Low	Few network products
Mail order/online	Excellent	Excellent	Low	Must wait for deliveries; no sales tax on out-of-state purchases
Swap meet	Excellent	Fair	Lowest	Must know what you are buying

Most vendors should give you 30 days to return parts, and they should return your money as long as you return the part in saleable condition, regardless of the reason (whether you have problems or just decide that you don't want the part).

- *Verify availability of tech support.* Make sure that the vendor will provide you with tech support if you encounter any problems.
- *Double-check whether you're getting an installation kit.* Be sure that you understand whether you are buying just a part or an installation kit. This is particularly important when you're purchasing a hard drive. Unless you have lots of spare parts lying around, plus experience installing a particular part, you'll want to buy the kit so that everything you need—rails, adapters, cables, and connectors—is included.
- *Make sure you're getting the correct part.* Be sure to double-check the manufacturer, model, and part number to make sure you're getting the correct part. If you can, get these facts in writing by fax or mail. Sometimes, unscrupulous vendors will sell reconditioned parts as new, so beware. If a price sounds too good to be true, it probably is.
- *Make sure you're not charged until the product ships.* When you purchase by mail order or through a Web site, the vendor shouldn't bill you until the product is shipped. You can call your credit card company to see if you've been charged. If it sounds like you've been charged but no product has been shipped, you can call the vendor and ask for a shipping bill number. If the vendor can't come up with one, call your credit card company and ask for a charge-back (that is, have the charge removed from your bill).
- *Always pay with a credit card.* When purchasing, it's best to use your credit card so that you have a way to stop payment if a seller refuses to accept a return or exchange for a defective product; avoid paying by check or money order. Problems like this aren't too common but do occasionally happen. A firm might charge your credit card, then go out of business before delivering the product to you. Or, more likely, you may not receive what you thought you ordered. If you have a disagreement with a vendor, you can contact your credit card company to perform a charge-back. To do this, report your complaint to your credit card company within 60 days of the billing statement. While it

investigates the problem, the credit card company holds the payment and charges no interest. If the vendor is at fault, you won't be charged. Be sure to always keep good records—dated notes of any related phone calls, as well as every scrap of correspondence. Before you make a major purchase, you might want to check with your credit card company to confirm its policies, your options, and what proof you would need to hold a vendor at fault.

- *Check out the reputations of companies you buy from.* If you're not sure of a company's reputation or stability, check with the Better Business Bureau in the company's area to see if any complaints have been lodged against the firm. It's probably a long shot, but it is one more thing you can do to protect your interests.
- *Compare warranties.* Consider and compare warranties. You can rely on extended coverage if you have the right kind of credit card. This extra coverage is usually automatic when you use your card, but exclusions and exceptions always exist. Again, you need to keep detailed records, including the shipping bill, credit card receipt, and written warranty. If your warranty terminates and you run into problems, inform your credit card company within 45 days of the malfunction. Company representatives will send you a form to fill out, and they'll probably direct you to a service provider (again, double-check with your credit card company).
- *Listen to friends' recommendations.* Finally, recommendations from satisfied customers are an excellent way to help you find a good dealer. Check with friends, relatives, and acquaintances who might recommend an excellent source for parts. If you work in an office with a network, you might talk with the network administrator, who has a lot of experience buying and assembling parts.

Moving On

Most of the time, you should have decent luck with shopping for parts. In this chapter, I've given you a good idea of what you should be looking for; if you keep my comments in mind, you should do quite well. Price isn't everything, but with some investigation and comparisons, you can save some serious money. I've also offered suggestions on ways to protect yourself as you make your purchases. Now, with network components in hand, you're ready to proceed to the next chapter, in which I'll discuss the tools you'll use to assemble your network.

6

The Tools

You can't beat having the right tools for a job. As you build and set up your network, you'll have to open the computers to install network cards and perform other tasks. Having the right tools will make the job a lot easier. In this chapter, I'll talk about the essential tools you'll need, plus a few extras.

Setting up a network doesn't take very specialized tools. In fact, you can probably get almost all the tools you'll need to build your network for less than $30. You probably already have some of them in your garage. On the other hand, if you are planning to do some serious work as a network administrator, you'll need some specialized tools; I'll talk about these later.

If you invest in the right tools, they'll come in handy whenever you need to work on your computer and they'll be well worth the investment. I've used the same tools (a small $30 set that I bought years ago) for almost everything that I've done, and I've never been without the right tool (if anything's missing, it's always a connector or cable). My kit includes some tools that I've never even used.

Having the right tools reduces the frustration of working on your computer and makes it safer for both you and your machine. For example, you could use a knife to turn a screw, but the knife could slip and injure you or damage the screw or nearby components. I can't overemphasize the need for the right tools.

Tools For All Your Needs

I'm going to discuss the basic, minimum tool set and then talk about tools that are nice to own—but not essential.

As a minimum, you should have at least the tools described in the following sections.

A Basic Set Of Screwdrivers

You'll need both standard and Phillips screwdrivers in a variety of sizes (as shown in Figure 6.1), all of which you can find at any hardware store. The tip of the standard screwdriver has a flat edge, and the tip of the Phillips forms an X. You probably have some of each in your toolbox already. I've also had good luck with a *switching screwdriver*, which has several interchangeable tips that fit on a single handle. Just avoid anything that costs $2.99 at the grocery market; such ultra-cheap tools will be worthless in the long run.

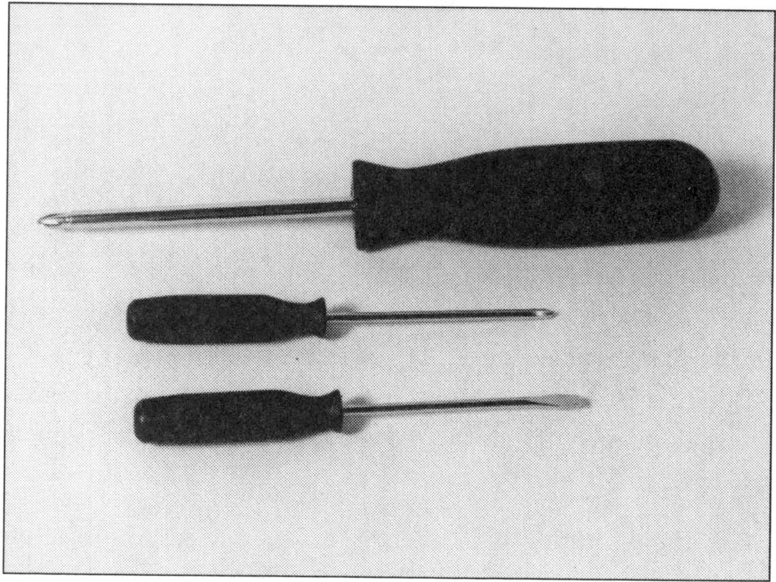

Figure 6.1 Standard and Phillips screwdrivers.

Caution

Although magnetized screwdrivers may be convenient for picking up small screws that you drop, don't use them around your computer equipment. Because computers store data magnetically, placing any magnetized tool or magnet near the internal components of a PC or near a disk might erase information.

Needle-Nose Pliers

You probably have these if you have a home toolbox. You'll find that needle-nose pliers are handy when you need to pinch and remove *stand-offs* (screws and little plastic fasteners) on some motherboards, as well as for numerous other applications. Figure 6.2 shows a pair of needle-nose pliers.

Tweezers

Tweezers are invaluable for picking up small objects and are particularly good for setting jumpers on a board. You can buy plastic versions for use on computers to minimize the possibility of shorting a circuit as you use them.

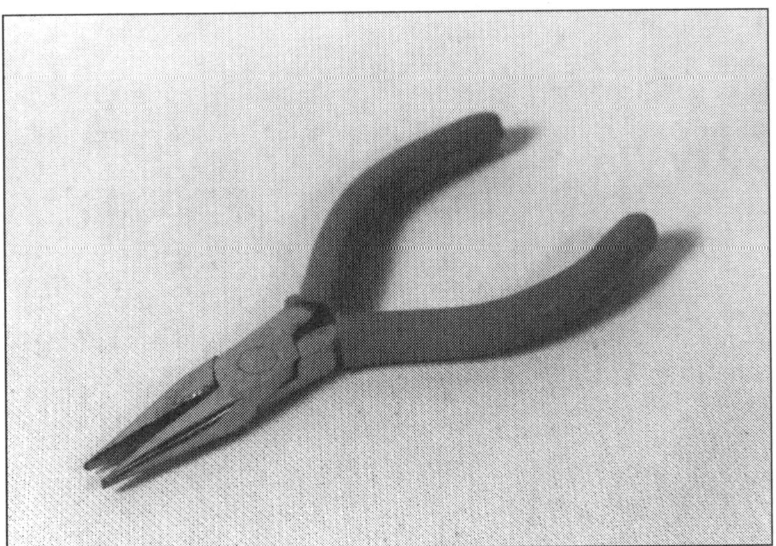

Figure 6.2 Needle-nose pliers.

Three-Prong Extractor

A *three-prong extractor* may not be familiar to you. It looks something like the claw in those machines you see at the local arcade or pizza parlor—you know, that glass box of enticing stuffed animals. You put in a quarter and manipulate the claw to see if you can pluck a prize. The difference is that a true three-prong extractor—unlike the one at the pizza parlor—has real gripping power and is invaluable for picking up screws and small items that fall into your computer case. When I didn't have an extractor, I often had to turn my entire computer upside down to retrieve tiny objects (usually screws) that I lost in the case. Figure 6.3 shows a three-prong extractor.

Caution

Do not use a magnetized device in place of the extractor; doing so might cause you to lose data or damage computer components.

Flashlight

Another tool that comes in handy is a flashlight. You might have trouble seeing into the depths of your case at times, or your head may cast a shadow that obscures what you're looking at.

Flashlights come in different types and styles, of course. Some people like to use those flashlights that mount on your head so you can easily direct

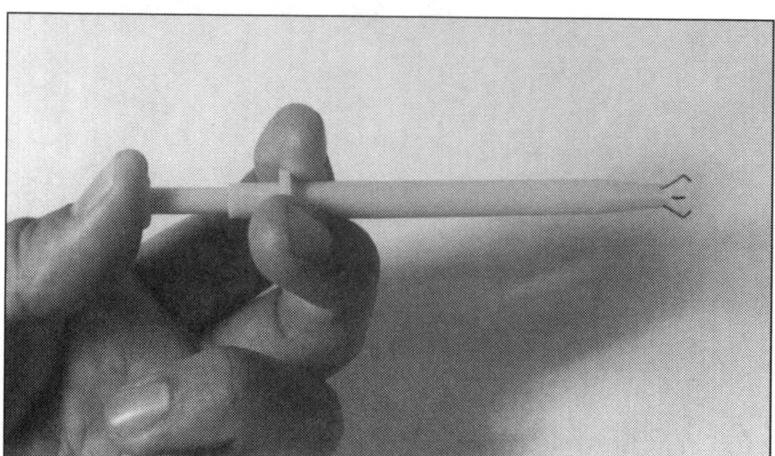

Figure 6.3 A three-prong extractor used for picking up tiny objects.

the light where you need it and keep your hands free. I've had good luck with one of those snake-style flashlights that can bend in different ways. The kind of flashlight you need will depend on your work area and available lighting.

Fine-Point Permanent Marker

This type of marker is useful for labeling parts of your computer. No one else will be looking inside your case, so a little graffiti there is no problem and can save you hours when you're trying to put things back together.

DOS Boot Disk

Although a DOS boot disk isn't a piece of hardware, it's a primary tool in any computer worker's troubleshooting arsenal.

Definition, Please

A *DOS boot disk* is a floppy disk that contains the necessary information to boot—or start—a computer. You can create one of these disks by formatting a floppy and telling the computer to add system files.

It doesn't hurt to have key files, such as Fdisk.exe and Format.exe, on this boot floppy for use as diagnostic tools. If you own Norton Utilities or a similar program that helps make your system run at its peak and comes with tools to "rescue" your data in a catastrophe, by all means use it.

Foam Padding

Nonconducting foam padding is a good surface to use as a resting place for expansion boards while you work on your computer. A foam surface is also a safeguard that will prevent damage to a board or component that might fall or get dropped.

Small Adhesive Labels

Labels are good for marking cables so that you can find what you need when it's time to put everything back together. Also, it doesn't hurt to label your internal components with information, such as the date you purchased or replaced them.

Antistatic Wrist Strap

An antistatic wrist strap will ground you so you won't build up static electricity. It consists of a strap that goes around your wrist and is connected to a cable. At the other end of the cable is a clamp that attaches to a ground, usually your computer's case. I admit that I don't know anybody who uses one of these all the time, and the repairmen in the shops I've been in never seem to use them at all. But you should consider using one to minimize your chances of frying your boards with static electricity, although it will literally tie you to your computer.

Workspace

Finally, you'll need a good work area. Obviously, you need to be close to an electrical outlet so that after you make an installation you can immediately plug in and power up to see the results. You'll also want a large surface on which to spread out your tools and components. I've worked on meeting room tables, kitchen tables, coffee tables—and sometimes I've just cleared a space on the floor. The best setup is a big workbench.

Make sure you have adequate lighting—it's easy to lose small parts, and you might have to refer to poorly written instructions (written in tiny fonts) that come with components. If you run a multiple-outlet power strip from the nearest outlet, it'll minimize the number of electrical cords dangling from your work area, so you won't trip over them or get them tangled up.

Also, work in an area that is free from things that can fall onto and into your open system. It doesn't hurt to clean the area so it's relatively free from dust (which can more easily collect in your system as you're working on it).

Additional Tools You Might Need

A few other tools might come in handy from time to time. Of course, because I say they're optional, chances are good that you'll absolutely have to have one of them one Sunday night when all the stores are closed and you need to be back up and running on Monday morning at eight A.M. for your most important client (computer users are especially subject to Murphy's Law). With that caveat in mind, these are tools that you might need. Sometimes they're included in the inexpensive tool kits I mentioned earlier.

Nut (Hex) Drivers

Nut drivers (also called *hex drivers*) look much like screwdrivers, but they are designed to turn nuts, as shown in Figure 6.4. You can get away with using a Phillips screwdriver to turn most hex nuts (the hex nut has a slot that accepts a Phillips screwdriver), so although nut drivers are nice to have, it's probably not absolutely necessary.

Torx Screwdriver

Another type of screwdriver, called a *Torx screwdriver*, is shown in Figure 6.5. Only a handful of manufacturers—one of them is Compaq—use these oddball screws, so your need for this screwdriver depends on your system.

Containers

Whether you use paper cups, Tupperware containers, or those little plastic boxes that hold fishing lures, you will want to have a few places to

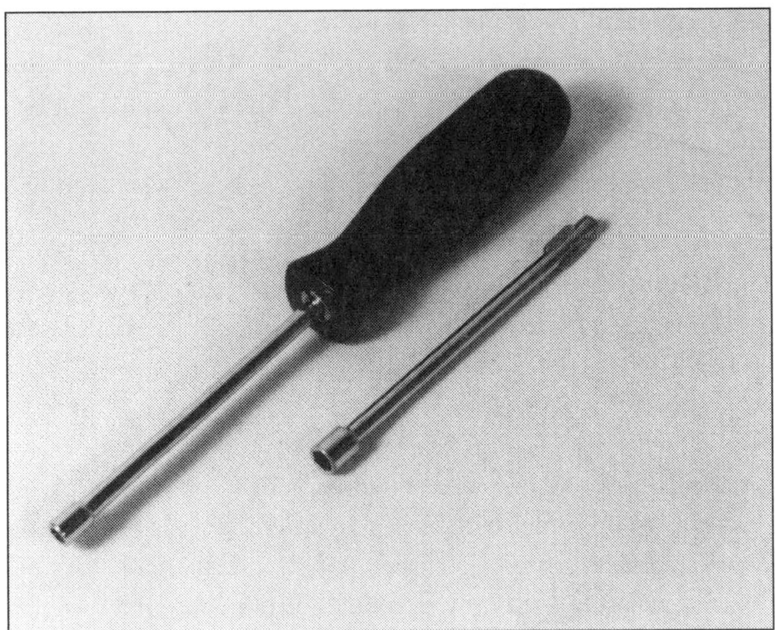

Figure 6.4 Nut drivers.

Figure 6.5 Torx screwdriver.

store small parts. In particular, containers come in quite handy when you're removing screws from your computer. And instead of simply setting them down where they can fall off the workbench, roll around, or get lost, you can keep them organized in compartments or containers so you don't lose them and can easily find them when you need to.

You may even want containers with lids so items won't fall out if you knock them over. You don't necessarily have to go out and buy containers; a quick trip through your kitchen can yield all the containers you could ever need.

Crimp Tool

This specialized tool attaches network connectors to networking cables. If you plan to build network cables on a regular basis or if you're planning to work as a network administrator, you'll find this tool absolutely invaluable. In this case, I definitely recommend that you purchase a crimp tool.

However, if you're planning to build a network with only a few stations and will probably stop after that, a crimp tool is an unnecessary expense, because you can purchase the cable you need with the connectors already attached from a variety of sources. Yes, you'll pay more for the cable than if you had purchased an entire coil of cable and attached connectors with your own crimp tool. But if you're only going to build a few cables, the cost of bulk cable and a crimp tool are not worth it.

Moving On

In this chapter, I've talked about the basic and optional tools you need to build your network and work on your computers. Once you have these tools, you're ready to learn how to open up your computers and add network cards, as I'll explain in Chapter 7.

7

Installing And Configuring Network Cards

The first step in building your network is installing network cards. I hope that Chapters 3 and 4 gave you a feel for what type of network card you need. Also, Chapter 5 gave you tips on purchasing your network cards on a shoestring budget. At this point, you should have your network cards in hand and be ready to install them.

Installing A Network Card

Your network card is an expansion board that you add to your computer. And just as you can't work on a car with the hood closed, you will have to open your computer case so you can get inside and install the board. You'll find that although these tasks initially sound daunting, they're actually quite easy to perform. Here goes.

Opening The Case

You'll find that most cases are designed so you can remove some screws and slide the top cover off, but covers fit in different ways.

Caution—Data

Back up all the important data on your computer before you begin any kind of work on its innards. I can't overemphasize how important this is. Although you probably won't, it's possible to lose data when you make an upgrade, and it's only sensible to back up data and have it in a safe place in case something goes awry.

Also, before you open your PC and begin any installation, take the time to record the information on your hard drive—the type, cylinders, and so forth. You'll find this information in your computer's setup, which you usually can see by booting up your PC and then holding down a key to view a menu screen (computers vary; check your manual). Write this information down and keep it somewhere. If you have the hard drive documentation, it will include this information.

Caution—Safety

Before you open your PC, turn it off. I always unplug my PC as well, although some experts will tell you to leave it plugged in (just as long as it's turned off). When working on your system, don't probe screwdrivers in areas that you're not working on, particularly the power supply.

To open the case:

1. Disconnect all of the cables and connectors attached to your computer—power, printer cables, speakers, telephone line, keyboard, mouse, video connections, and so on. Then you're ready to remove the screws, which you'll usually find along the back side of the computer case, as shown in Figure 7.1.

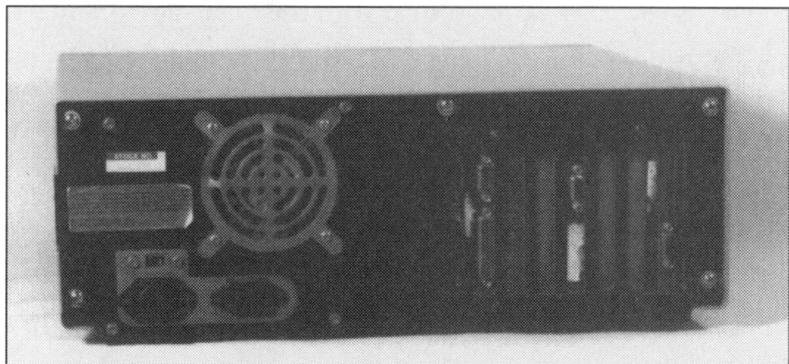

Figure 7.1 The screws that hold the case on are usually on the back of the computer.

Caution

When removing screws from the back of the case, be sure to remove only those that appear to hold the case. If you go overboard and remove all the screws, you may hear internal components—the power supply, for example—drop loose and fall down inside your computer. Be conservative. Remove the obvious screws first and then see if the case cover budges.

2. Gently push the cover to see if it moves. If it does, slide the cover off the case. If it doesn't, you probably missed a screw. Check for any errant screws and then try to budge the cover again. On a desktop machine, as shown in Figure 7.2, the cover usually is removed by sliding the chassis backward, away from the front of the computer. On a tower case, the cover can slide either forward or backward, as shown in Figure 7.3. Your case may not fall into any of these categories. Some cases swivel, others lift off, and still others don't even use screws; you simply depress a couple of buttons to open the case. Please refer to your system's documentation for more on how to open the case.

Inserting The Network Card

With your PC's cover off, you're ready to install your new card.

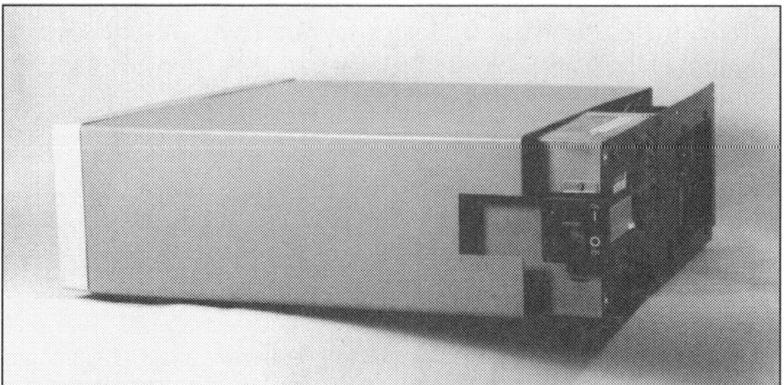

Figure 7.2 A typical desktop case cover opens by sliding the chassis back from the front of the computer.

Figure 7.3 A typical tower case cover opens by sliding either forward or backward off the case.

Caution

Always hold a board by its edges. The static electricity in your body can fry a component on the board. Also, never touch the connectors on the bottom of the board. It is essential that they make good contact in the future.

Follow these steps:

1. Find a slot that's appropriate for your board (PCI to PCI, 16-bit ISA to 16-bit ISA, and so on). For an examination of the types of boards and their matching slots, refer to Figure 7.4.
2. Remove the retaining screw and cover, as shown in Figure 7.5.
3. Hold the expansion board by its edges and gently push it into its slot. You may have to rock the board a bit to make it connect properly, as shown in Figure 7.6. Be sure that the network card is not touching any other expansion board. In fact, you should keep some room between expansion boards when you can to allow air to circulate between them and to help them stay cooler.

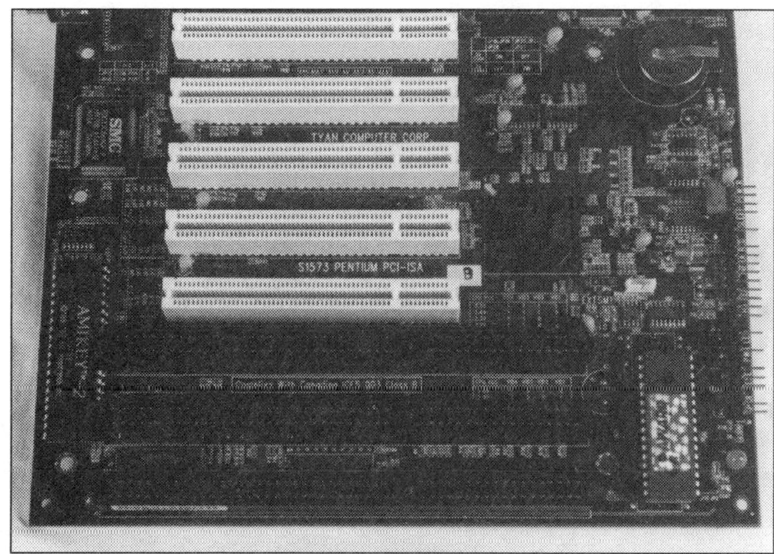

Figure 7.4 Matching different boards with their slots.

Figure 7.5 Prepare a slot by removing its retaining screw and cover.

Figure 7.6 Gently rock the board in place to gradually seat it in its slot.

4. After the board is firmly seated, replace the retaining screws.
5. Before you replace the system's cover, connect the monitor to the PC card and reconnect power to the system so you can test it.

Caution

Don't forget that you have a live machine. Under no circumstance should you probe your PC or touch any internal component when your system is running. Always shut off power before doing any work on your PC or before removing or adjusting any component. Not only could you get a dangerous shock, you could also fry your components.

6. Turn on your PC and ensure that your system appears to be working correctly. If it's not, check the installation of your network card.
7. At this point, you need to install the drivers for your new network card. Look for one or more disks that came with your new network card. Place the first disk into your system's drive. If you're running Windows 95/98, use Microsoft Explorer or My Computer. See the following sections for an explanation of the basic instructions for each scenario.

If You Have Installed A Plug And Play Network Card

If you are running Windows 95/98 and have installed a Plug and Play network card, follow these steps to install the drivers for your new network card:

1. Reboot your computer. Windows 95 or 98 should boot up and immediately recognize that a new network card is installed in your system.
2. At this point, the program will ask for a disk that contains your network card drivers; you can usually follow the instructions on the screen, which will tell you to insert your driver disk. Windows 95/98 will perform most of the configuration for you.

If You Have Installed A Non–Plug And Play Network Card

If you are running Windows 95/98 and have installed a non–Plug and Play network card, you can use either Windows Explorer or My Computer to install the drivers for your new network card:

If you are using Windows Explorer:

1. Right-click on the Start button on the left side of the Taskbar.
2. Select Explore to open Windows Explorer.
3. Select the A: drive by double-clicking on it (assuming A: is the drive holding the disk). If your setup is different, your drive may be a different letter.
4. In the file list to the right, look for the setup file or whatever file the network board's manual says needs to be executed to install network driver files. Double-click on this file to start the program, then follow the on-screen directions.

If you are using My Computer:

1. Double-click on the My Computer icon on the desktop.
2. Double-click on the A: folder. If your setup is different, your drive may be a different letter.
3. Look for the Setup file or whatever file the network board's manual says needs to be executed to install the network driver files. Double-click on this file to start the program, then follow the on-screen directions.

Checking To See That Your Network Card Is Correctly Installed

To see if your network card is correctly installed and working properly within Windows 95/98, click on Start|Settings and then click on Control Panel. Double-click on the System icon and then click on the Device Manager tab. Double-click on the Network Adapters icon; you should see an icon that represents your new network card. If this icon does not appear, something in your installation went wrong. Or if you see a yellow circle containing an exclamation point next to your network card's listing, your new card is conflicting with another peripheral or not working properly. If this is the case, follow the suggestions in the next section to resolve the problem.

Troubleshooting Your Network Card Installation

If your card does not work or is not recognized by your system, try the following remedies:

- Check your network card installation once again to be sure that the board is properly seated in its socket. (Be sure to shut off your PC and disconnect power before removing the cover.)
- Make sure that the card is installed in the correct type of expansion slot (ISA, PCI, VESA, and so forth).
- Consult the motherboard's manufacturer to confirm that the bus is indeed a true PCI or VESA and ask about any known problems with certain network cards. You can also check with the network card manufacturer for known problems or conflicts with certain systems.
- Refer to the documentation that came with your network card for any troubleshooting suggestions and potential problems that are too specific to cover here.
- Try moving the network card to a different slot.
- Your network card may not be working correctly because it is conflicting with another computer peripheral. Consult the documentation for your various other cards to see if conflicts exist. To resolve this problem:
  - In Windows 95, click on Start|Help|Troubleshooting and select If You Have A Hardware Conflict. Then, follow the on-screen instructions to resolve the conflict.

    - In Windows 98, click on Start|Help|Troubleshooting|Windows 98 Troubleshooters|Hardware Conflicts. Then, follow the on-screen instructions to resolve the conflict. If you're not sure whether you have installed your network card correctly, click on Start|Help|Troubleshooting|Windows 98 Troubleshooters and select I Am Unable To Install A Network Adapter.
- Call tech support for the network card's manufacturer for further help.

Moving On

We have gone through the steps necessary to install a new network card. In the next chapter, I'll talk about installing cables and hubs. You'll be well on your way to building that network.

8

Making Network Connections With Cables

With network interface cards installed in your computers, you're now ready to run network cables to connect them together. Some of you will probably be running cables from one computer to another on the very same desk; others will be running cables all around an office or home from room to room, and even floor to floor.

In many ways, network cables are much like other cables in your office and home—for example, telephone wires and extension cables. And although you can route cables every which way as you connect them, a little planning ahead of time on your part will make for a more orderly setup. In this chapter, I'll try to present the basic things you should keep in mind. For our purposes here, I'll assume that you have your PCs with network interface cards in place, and now you want to wire those systems together.

General Cable Guidelines

Here are some general guidelines for installing cable, whether you are using *coaxial* or *10BaseT* (for background information on these cables, refer to Chapter 4):

- Always buy and use more cable than you'll actually need. It's easier to coil up some extra cable than it is to have to buy a longer piece of cable or have someone splice an extension onto it.

- When routing cable around your office or home, try to keep the cable free of kinks. It's okay to bend the cable around corners, but try and keep the turns somewhat gradual. In a sense, you can think of network cable as being similar to a garden hose: You can curve a garden hose and keep the flow of water moving, but if you kink it or turn it too sharply, the water shuts off.
- As you route cable, try to avoid sources of magnetic interference that can influence and even corrupt the electrical signals that pass through the network cable. Potential sources of magnetic interference include: fluorescent lights (a significant problem in many offices), electric motors, microwave ovens (hey, computer users have to eat microwave pizza), power cords, and more.
- Try to avoid running a cable across a floor where you or others walk; this creates a tripping hazard. In addition, the cable could be damaged by people stepping on it. If you can't avoid running cable in places people will be walking, you can solve these problems by purchasing cable protection devices at an office supply store.
- When you have several cables that are running parallel to each other or coming together in a single place, you can use twist ties (the kind that come with new electronic products, plastic trash bags, or bags of bread), or you can buy special cable ties (they're quite inexpensive—usually just a couple of bucks). You can use masking tape or duct tape to bind cables together and hold them in place, but after some time the glue on the tape—particularly the glue from duct tape—becomes a sticky mess. For this reason, I recommend that you use twist or cable ties.
- If you can, route your cables through walls and ceilings and try to keep them from routing every which way along floors. If you are using 10BaseT, you can install wall jacks. These allow you to plug your computer into a network outlet using a short length of 10BaseT. I realize that this is a lot of work—and my own network in my home office doesn't have this polished routing—but it is the neatest, most professional way to go.

Making The Connection

To physically connect your computers to the network, all you have to do is connect the cables. The following sections explain how to connect coax and 10BaseT.

Coax

When installing coax, you have to connect the cable from one computer to the next, and then to the next, and the first and last computers must have terminators. Thus, the first computer will feature a T connector with a terminator in one end and the cable on the other; the second computer will have a T connector that accepts the cable from the first computer and a second cable that goes to the next computer; and the last computer will have a T that accepts the final cable and receives a terminator.

Here are the general steps to install coax:

1. You'll need to install a T connector into the female BNC connector of each computer's network interface card. The BNC connector installs with a twist—simply line up the slot on the male BNC connector with the nubs on the female connector, as shown in Figure 8.1, and then press down and twist, as shown in Figure 8.2.

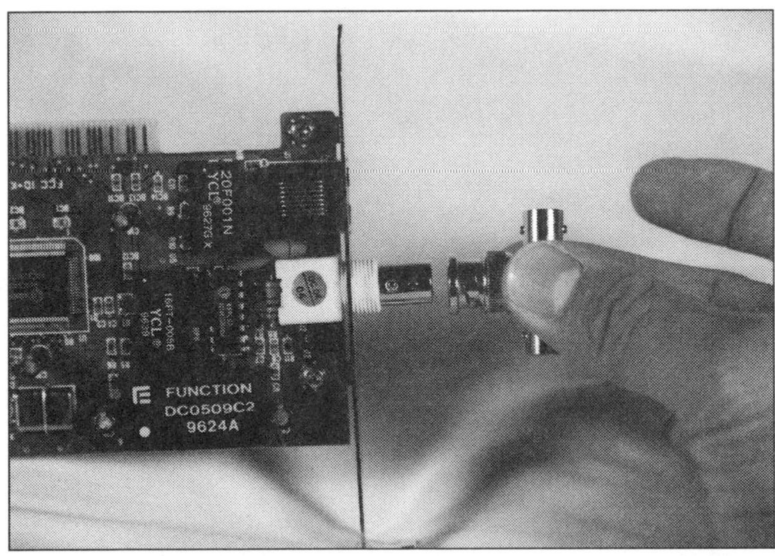

Figure 8.1 Hooking up coax.

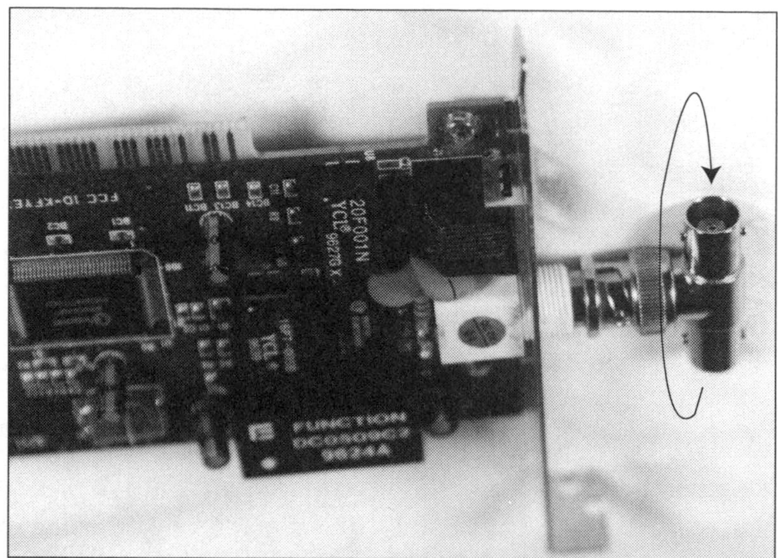

Figure 8.2 Twist the male BNC connector onto the female BNC connector that's on the network card.

2. If you are working on a computer that will be the first or last in the network, install a terminator into one end of the T connector.
3. Route the coax cable to the next computer and connect it to the T connector that you've attached to the system's network interface card.
4. Repeat the process until you are working on the last computer. After connecting the last coax cable, install a terminator at the other (final) end of the T connector.

10BaseT

When installing 10BaseT cable, you route the cable from each computer to a central junction box called a *hub*. Simply connect each cable to the connector on each computer's network interface card and connect the other end into an open port in the hub (be sure that it's off). The connector (called an *RJ-45*) at the end of a 10BaseT cable is easy to use.

To install 10BaseT:

1. Match the front profile of the connector with its mate on the network interface card (you'll see a rectangle with a little notch).

2. Press your finger on the tab on top of the RJ-45 and slide the tab into the notch.
3. Release the tab.

Hubba, Hubba: Installing Hubs

In the case of installing 10BaseT and a hub, physically place the hub in a central location where all of the computers can conveniently connect with it. Also, be sure that an electrical outlet is nearby, because all hubs require power.

As you route the various cables from your computers to your hub, it's a good idea to label each end to identify which computer it comes from. This way, you'll always know which cable goes to which computer. This can be particularly important when you have a hub that supports both Ethernet and Fast Ethernet and you want to make sure that you are plugging the cable into the correct port. For a label, use a marker to write on a little strip of masking tape. If you like (if you're one of those people with a neat desk), you can buy nice little labels for the job that will look more professional.

Most hubs have a port that lets them connect to other hubs (a process called *daisy chaining*). To avoid plugging the 10BaseT into this port, check the documentation that came with your port to double-check which port to avoid. Many hubs indicate on the front which is the daisy chaining port.

Moving On

In this chapter, I talked about routing and connecting network cabling. In the next chapter, I'll discuss new technologies that let you make network connections through existing wiring in your home, or with no wiring at all.

9

Other Network Connections

In this book, we talk about making network connections across cables. However, new technologies are just coming to the market that will let you make network connections through wiring that already exists in your home or office, or with no wiring at all. In this chapter, we'll briefly discuss some of these new technologies that may change the way you build a network.

If you can use wires that already run in your house or no cables at all, the bottom line is that you don't need to buy and route cables, no unsightly cables will wrap around your desk and on the floor and walls, and you won't have to drill holes in the walls and feed those cables through. Good riddance. The wireless concept has lots of potential.

Wireless Networks

Just as the name implies, a *wireless connection* is one that requires no cable or wiring, but uses radio waves to transmit data. As I write this, two companies—Diamond Multimedia and Proxim—are bringing wireless network products to market.

Both companies offer specialized *network interface cards* (*NICs*) that don't accept a 10BaseT or coaxial BNC connector as conventional NICs do, but instead house a wireless transceiver that sends and receives data. Both companies also sell a similar PC card device that you can use on notebook computers.

After installing a wireless network expansion card or PC card device, you'll have a conventional Windows network that lets you copy and share files, share printers, modems, and Internet connections on computers that may be as far apart as 150 feet, according to the manufacturers. Also, according to the vendors, you can easily add new PCs to your wireless network by simply installing more expansion cards.

One downside of these wireless networks is that they don't tie into existing networks—they basically form their own networks and won't plug into existing hubs. However, Proxim promises an upcoming Ethernet bridge card that will plug into a hub and let it communicate with the wireless adapters. The company expects the device to be available sometime in mid-1999, and it estimates the price between $400 and $500.

Another disadvantage is that the performance of these wireless networks is significantly less than a conventional 10Mbps network, and they will only transmit and receive data at 1.6Mbps, 16 percent of the speed of conventional network hardware. However, if you can live with the slower performance, and have a situation that can use a wireless connection, either of these solutions may be worth considering.

Proxim offers its Symphony ISA Card and Symphony PC cards, shown in Figures 9.1 and 9.2. The ISA card for desktop computers sells for $149 and the PC card device sells for $199. According to Proxim, you can link up to 10 computers together.

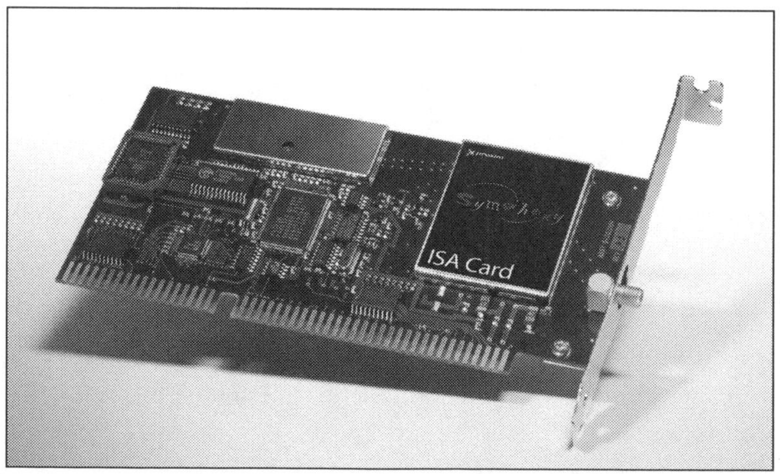

Figure 9.1 Proxim's Symphony ISA card for wireless network communications.

Figure 9.2 Proxim's Symphony PC card device for wireless network communications.

Diamond Multimedia sells its HomeFree system in a $199 Desktop Pac, as shown in Figure 9.3; it includes a PCI network interface card and an ISA interface card. The Combo Pac, shown in Figure 9.4, comes with one network interface card and one wireless PC Card device and sells for $299.

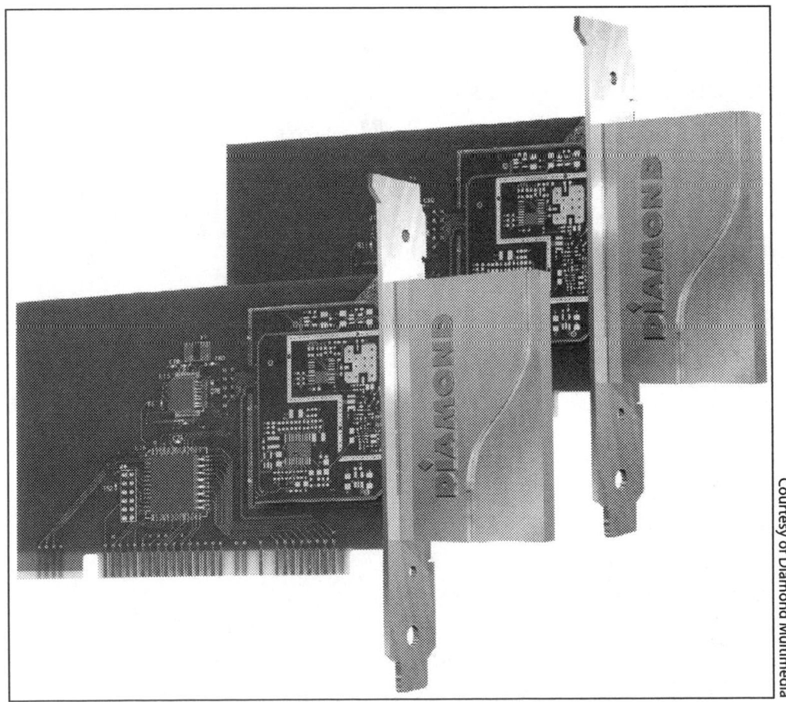

Figure 9.3 Diamond Multimedia's HomeFree Desktop Pac for wireless network communications.

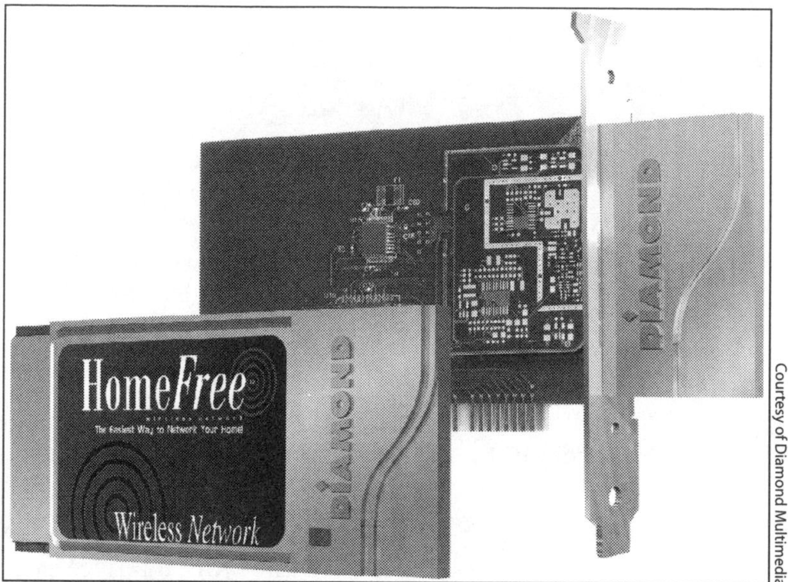

Courtesy of Diamond Multimedia

Figure 9.4 Diamond Multimedia's Combo Pac for wireless network communications.

Networks Using Existing Wiring

Instead of routing new cable or relying on airwaves for your network connections, how about using wiring that already exists in most homes and businesses? A company called Epigram is developing technology that will let you route network connections through existing phone lines in homes or businesses, and the company claims that this network will not interfere with normal voice and data calls.

Epigram says that the performance will be equivalent to a 10Mbps network, and the company has struck agreements with companies such as 3Com and NETGEAR, which are building products that will make use of the technology.

Moving On

Although the technologies for making wireless network connections and using existing wiring in a business or home are in their infancy, a non-cable network connection could be in your future. As for all cutting-edge technologies, you can expect to pay more to obtain the latest and greatest capability.

In this chapter, I covered up-and-coming technologies for making network connections that don't use conventional coaxial or 10BaseT cables. In the next chapter, you'll learn how to begin configuring your new network.

Part 3

Using Your Network

10

Basic Network Concepts

With your installed network hardware, which includes network interface cards, cables, and a hub, you're ready to configure the network capabilities within Windows 95 or 98 to get your network up and running. In this chapter, I'll discuss how to set up Windows 95 or 98 to share the files on one computer with others and how to use files that reside on other networked computers. If you have any problems with sharing files, you can refer to the troubleshooting tips found in Chapter 18 for more help.

Verifying That Your Network Card Is Installed Correctly

Before we begin configuring Windows, we should first check to make sure that your network hardware—your network interface cards, in particular—are installed correctly. To do this:

1. Click on Start.
2. Select Settings|Control Panel, then double-click on the System icon.
3. Click on the Device Manager tab and then double-click on the Network Adapters icon. Underneath, you should see an icon that represents the network card. If the network card has no listing, Windows 95/98 is not recognizing the network interface card. And if the Device Manager lists the network interface card, but a yellow circle with an exclamation point next to it displays, as shown in Figure 10.1, the card is conflicting with another peripheral or not working properly. If this is the case, follow the

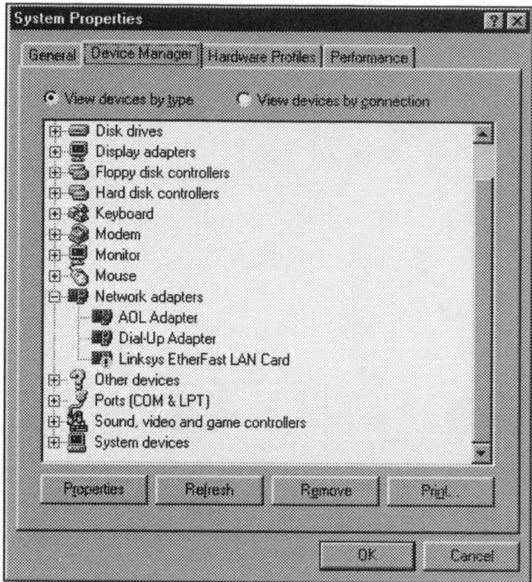

Figure 10.1 A network interface card that is not working properly within Windows.

suggestions in the "Troubleshooting Your Network Card Installation" section of Chapter 7 to resolve the problem.

If you see a listing for the network card along with a network icon, as shown in Figure 10.2, all should be well and you can proceed to the next section.

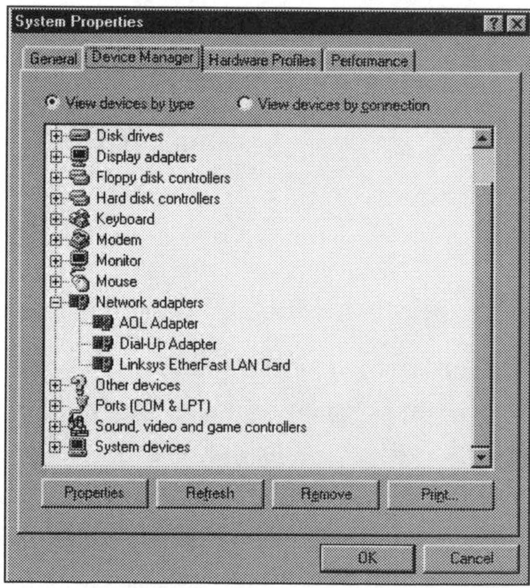

Figure 10.2 A network interface card that is working properly within Windows.

Time To Share

When you share files on systems that use Windows 95 or 98, drives on other computers will look as if they are on your own system. In the same way that you open folders on the drives on your own computer, you can open folders on other PCs across the network (provided you have the correct access) and copy, open, and use the files that reside there. And if the files you access are programs, you can execute them.

What a user actually does with a file will depend on the access rights that you set. Access rights can vary, from allowing users to only look at files, to allowing them to work with files or change them. For more on setting access rights, please refer to the "Rights" section later in this chapter, as well as the discussion in Chapter 13. And if you ever install a full-fledged Windows NT Server, the process of using and accessing files is much the same, but the access rights and security are far more sophisticated.

To share the files on any computer in your network, you first have to enable file sharing on that computer.

Enabling File Sharing

To enable file sharing, perform the following:

1. Click on Start.
2. Select Settings|Control Panel, then double-click on the Network icon.
3. On the Configuration tab, as shown in Figure 10.3, click on the File And Print Sharing button, then check the box that's labeled I Want To Be Able To Give Others Access To My Files.
4. Click on the Identification tab, as shown in Figure 10.4, and type in a name in the Computer Name field to give the computer a name on the network. This will be the designation that others will see and refer to when they access your computer across the network.
5. Click on OK.

Perform theses steps on each computer that contains folders that you wish to share. Also, if you would like to configure a drive so you can

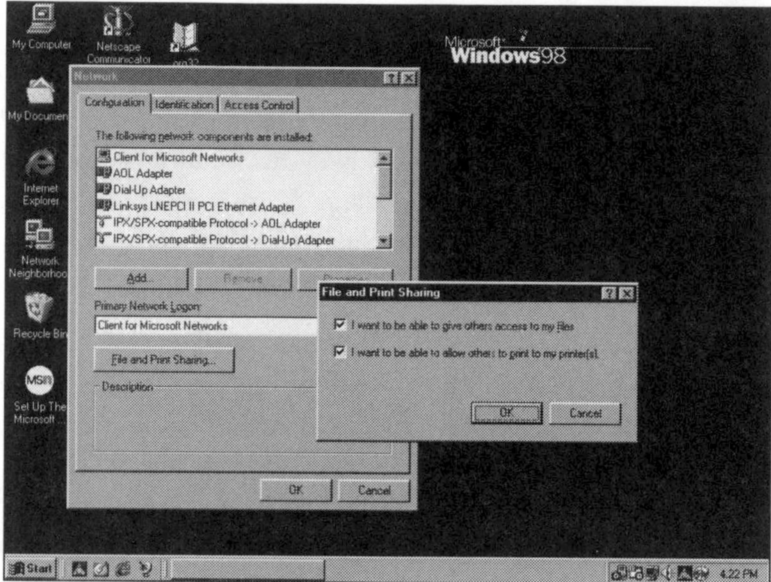

Figure 10.3 Configuring a PC to share its files.

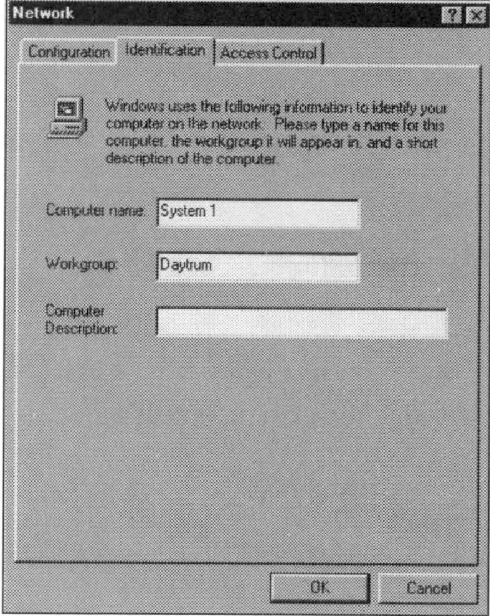

Figure 10.4 Giving a computer a name that others will refer to on the network.

restrict how others access the drive and its folders, as well as what they can do (read files or modify them), please refer to the instructions in Chapter 13.

To check that a computer can share files, you can click on My Computer and view the drives. Each shared drive icon appears with a hand underneath it, as shown in Figure 10.5.

Now that your network is configured with computers that can share their files, you're ready to access the files from another networked computer. Say goodbye to floppy disks. From now on, when you need to transfer files from one system to another, you can quickly do this across your network by using the Network Neighborhood, explained next.

Using The Network Neighborhood

When you want to use files on another computer that's on the network, you'll find that the *Network Neighborhood* is your ticket to all of the resources that are available on network computers.

Definition, Please

Network Neighborhood represents the network resources that you can work with.

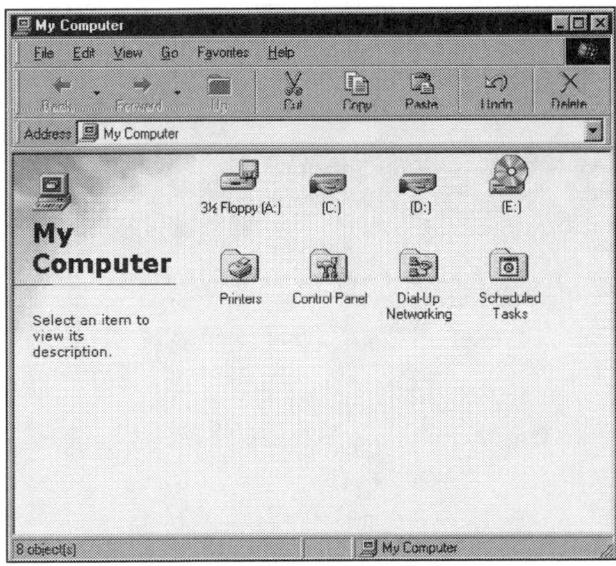

Figure 10.5 A shared drive appears with a hand underneath it.

You can get to the Network Neighborhood in one of two ways. The first method is as follows:

1. Double-click on the Network Neighborhood icon on your desktop. You'll see all of the available computers and servers (if you have them) that are on the network.
2. To access the files on a particular computer on the network, simply double-click on a computer's icon to view its available drives and folders—just as you would view drives and folders on your own computer.

The second method is as follows:

1. Use Windows Explorer by right-clicking on Start and selecting Explore.
2. Scroll through Windows Explorer until you see the Network Neighborhood icon, which is usually near the bottom of the window.
3. Double-click on Network Neighborhood and then click on Entire Network to see all of the available computers and servers (if you have them) that are on the network. Figure 10.6 shows Network Neighborhood as it displays when accessed by Windows Explorer in Windows 98.

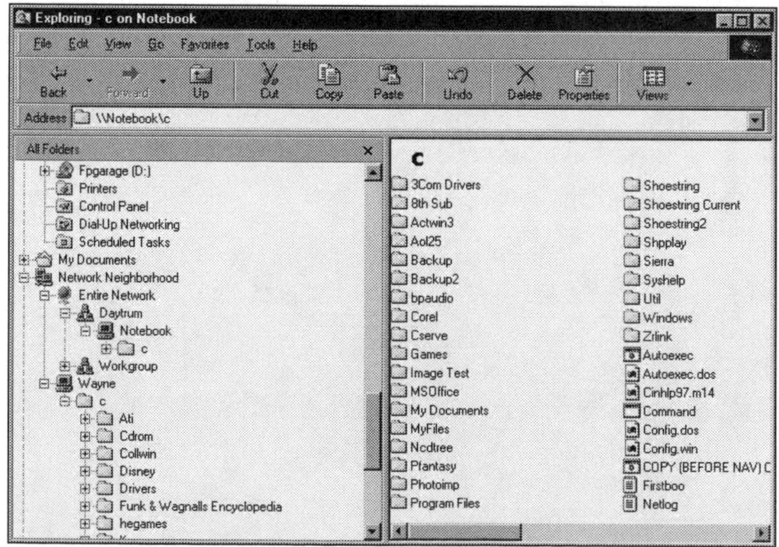

Figure 10.6 Network Neighborhood as displayed by Windows Explorer.

4. To access the files on a particular computer on the network, simply double-click on its icon to view its available drives and folders—just as you would view drives and folders on your own computer.

You'll notice that Network Neighborhood also offers a listing for your computer. Using this, you can see what drives and folders on your computer are available to others (that is, you can see how others see your system).

Using Network Neighborhood each time you want to access a folder on another PC that's on the network can become rather cumbersome. To speed up this access, you can create something called a *desktop shortcut*. This will display as an icon on your desktop; all you have to do is double-click on it to gain immediate access to the folder.

Creating A Desktop Shortcut

To create a desktop shortcut:

1. Navigate to the folder by going through Network Neighborhood, as explained previously.
2. Right-drag the folder (place the cursor on the folder's icon, hold down the right mouse button, and drag it) onto your desktop.
3. Choose Create Shortcut(s) to create the desktop shortcut.
4. To give the shortcut a different name, right-click on it, and select Rename. Type in a new name to identify the shortcut.

Another way to quickly access a folder on another network is to use a process called *mapping*, which is explained later in this chapter in the "Mapping" section.

Rights

What you are allowed to do with a file or folder depends on the access *rights* that you are given.

Definition, Please

Rights are rules that specify whether others have access to your files; they also determine if others can read or change your files.

If you have *read-only rights*, you can work with the files in a folder, but you won't be able to save any files in that folder. With *full access*, you can do all of the things that you can do with a file that is on a drive on your computer, including copying, deleting, moving, renaming, and opening. Some folders and files may require you to input a password for access. For more on how to set restrictions on drives and folders, please refer to the instructions in Chapter 13.

Mapping

Mapping is a process that makes a folder on another PC appear as if it were one that is on the PC that you are working on.

Definition, Please

Mapping makes a drive that's on another PC look like one that is on your own hard drive. It's a slick networking trick.

Mapping offers many benefits:

- A folder on another networked PC is immediately available through My Computer and looks like a drive that's part of your PC.
- Windows automatically connects with your mapped folders so they're always available. You don't have to take the time to navigate to them and open them.
- You can use Windows' search tools to look for files on mapped drives.

To map a drive:

1. Navigate to the folder that you wish to map (one that is on another computer that's on the network) via Network Neighborhood using either Windows Explorer or My Computer.
2. Right-click on the folder's icon and select Map Network Drive from the menu.
3. In the Map Network Drive dialog box, as shown in Figure 10.7, select a drive letter from the Drive drop-down list. Windows will suggest a letter, but you can choose any letter of the alphabet that isn't already used by your system.

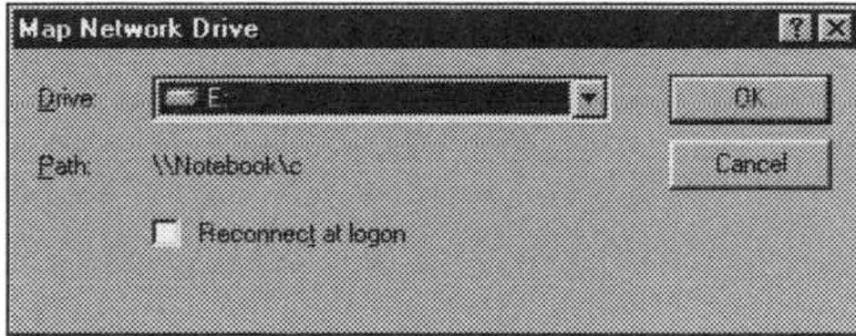

Figure 10.7 Mapping a folder on another networked PC so it appears as a virtual drive on your own computer.

If you change your mind and no longer want a folder mapped to your computer, you can unmap the drive, as follows:

1. Right-click on the mapped drive.
2. Select the Disconnect command, as shown in Figure 10.8.

Basic Troubleshooting

If you can't share files, check the following items:

- Make sure that the computers are on, and double-check all of those network connections that include hubs and cables. If you are using a hub, you should see a light on the hub next to a computer's cable connection that indicates that the hub recognizes your computer on the network.

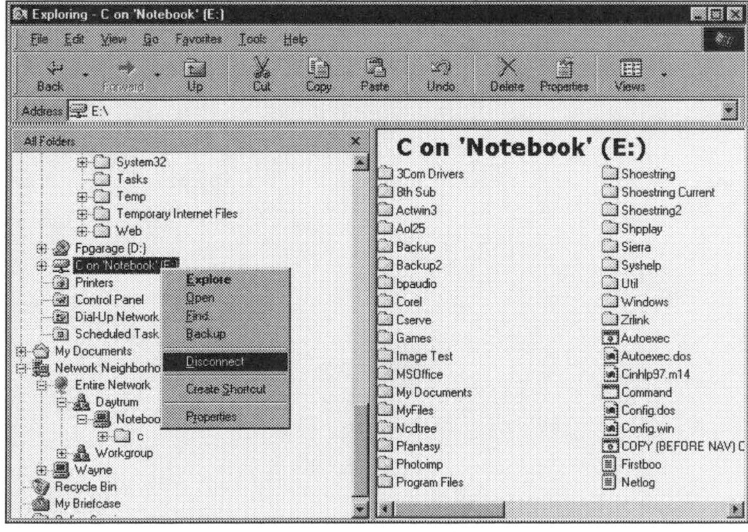

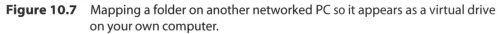

Figure 10.8 Use the Disconnect command to stop mapping a drive to your computer.

- Verify that your network hardware—in particular, your network interface cards—are correctly installed, and that Windows recognizes them. To do so, refer to the "Verifying That Your Network Card Is Installed Correctly" section at the beginning of this chapter.
- Look for error messages. These can provide important clues.
- Try shutting your computer off and then turning it back on.
- Try shutting off the other computers on the network and turning them back on.

For more troubleshooting tips, refer to Chapter 18.

Moving On

You have now configured Windows so you can share files across a network. In the next chapter, I'll discuss how you can share a printer across your new network.

11

Sharing Printers

In addition to sharing files, many homes and small businesses build networks so they can share printers. With a network in place, you can print from any computer. This means that as long as your computer is on a network, you can print to (or view the status of) any printer that's connected to another networked PC. For example, if the color inkjet is connected to the computer in the art department, or the eldest kid's bedroom, or if you want to output crisp black and white text on a laser jet that's linked to a computer in the finance department, or in the home office, you can do so. No need for copying your file onto a floppy, carrying the disk, and loading the file into the computer that's connected to the printer. In fact, not only can you print to any printer on the network, but you can also perform other print functions. You can view print queues on an individual printer to see how many people are using it and waiting for their documents to print. You can see if a delay might be in store if you choose to print to one printer, or you might find another printer with lighter traffic that has less wait time.

Definition, Please

A *print queue* is a line of documents that is waiting to be output onto a printer. When you look at a print queue, you see a list of jobs. In an office, for example, a marketing report from the sales department might be waiting to print, soon to be followed by the quarterly statements from the finance department. In a home, the queue may include Jimmy's school report on dinosaurs, followed by Susie's certificate that she is printing from Math Blasters for completing a significant level.

You can not only view the jobs in a print queue, you can actually control the order of jobs, or even remove print jobs—the electronic equivalent of butting in line (now, if we only could do this at Walt Disney World and at our local Department of Motor Vehicles). If you have any problems with your network printers, refer to the troubleshooting tips in Chapter 18.

Setting Up A Shared Printer

Before you can configure a printer to be used on a network, you first have to install it onto a system that is on the network. If you already have a printer that is installed and working on a computer, you can skip this section and go to the next section, "Sharing a Printer," which shows you how to configure a printer so it can be shared across a network.

To install a Plug and Play printer (usually a newer printer):

1. Follow the instructions that came with your printer to physically connect the printer to the computer. This usually includes connecting power, installing toner or an ink cartridge, and linking the printer to a PC with a parallel cable.
2. With the printer connected to the computer and turned on, activate your computer. Your computer should immediately recognize and identify your printer and begin the process of walking you through the Add Printer Wizard. This wizard will ask you several questions. When the wizard asks, "How is this printer attached to your computer?" select Local Printer, as shown in Figure 11.1. The wizard may also request that you insert a driver disk (a floppy or CD-ROM that came with your printer) to load the printer's driver and install the printer to the PC.

Definition, Please

A *local printer* is one that is actually connected to the computer that you're working on.

To install a non–Plug and Play printer:

1. Follow the instructions that came with your printer to physically connect the printer to the computer. This usually includes connecting

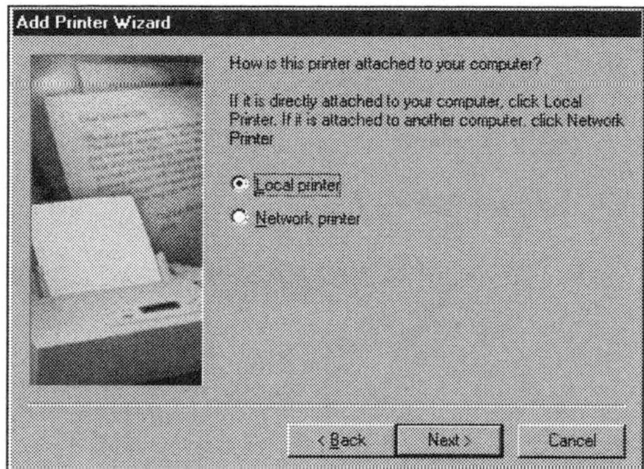

Figure 11.1 When installing a printer that's physically connected to a PC, install it as a local printer.

power, installing toner or an ink cartridge, and linking the printer to a PC with a parallel cable.

2. Double-click on My Computer.
3. Double-click on the Printers folder.
4. Double-click on Add Printer. Windows starts the Add Printer Wizard.
5. When the wizard asks, "How is this printer attached to your computer?" click on Local Printer. Then, click on Next.
6. The wizard then displays a list of printers that you can choose from by scrolling through the list of manufacturers on the left side of the window and printer models on the right. You can select a printer from the list or, if you have the printer driver disk, click on Have Disk. This lets you install the correct printer driver for your printer and configure it so it can be used by the computer that is connected to it. If your printer is not on the list and you don't have the printer driver—either on a floppy, CD-ROM, or on the hard drive—you'll have to contact your vendor to get it. Most printer vendors have Web sites that you can visit to download the correct drivers.
7. The next screen, shown in Figure 11.2, asks you which port your printer is connected to. Unless you've got a special printer, select LPT1.

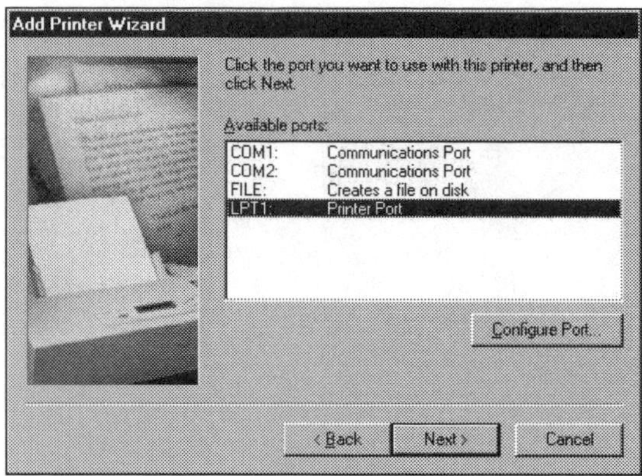

Figure 11.2 The wizard asks which port your printer is connected to.

Definition, Please

A *port* is the connection on your computer that provides the physical link between a computer and a printer. LPT1 is just another name for a computer's parallel, or printer, port.

8. The next screen will ask you to name your printer. You can choose to accept the default name, or you can get creative. Just remember that this name is the one that you will see whenever you select a printer from within an application.
9. If you like, you can print a test page to see if the installation is working correctly.

Sharing A Printer

Now that you have installed a printer that's connected to a computer on a network, you have to configure it so it can be shared and used by other computers across the network. Before you can share a printer, you must have enabled sharing, as described in Chapter 10.

To enable file sharing on a computer (skip this if you have already enabled file and printer sharing, as described in Chapter 10):

1. Click on Start.
2. Select Settings|Control Panel and then double-click on the Network icon.

3. Double-click on the Printers folder.
4. Right-click on the printer that you wish to share and select Properties.
5. Select the Shared As option.
6. On the Configuration tab, as shown in Figure 11.3, click on the File And Print Sharing button, and then check the box that's labeled I Want To Be Able To Allow Others To Print To My Printer(s).

To share a printer, perform the following:

1. Double-click on My Computer.
2. Double-click on the name of the printer that you wish to share across the network.
3. Click on the Sharing tab to display the Sharing portion of the printer's Properties dialog box, as shown in Figure 11.4.
4. If you like, you can add a comment to further identify the printer, and you can define a password so others can use the printer only if they know the password.

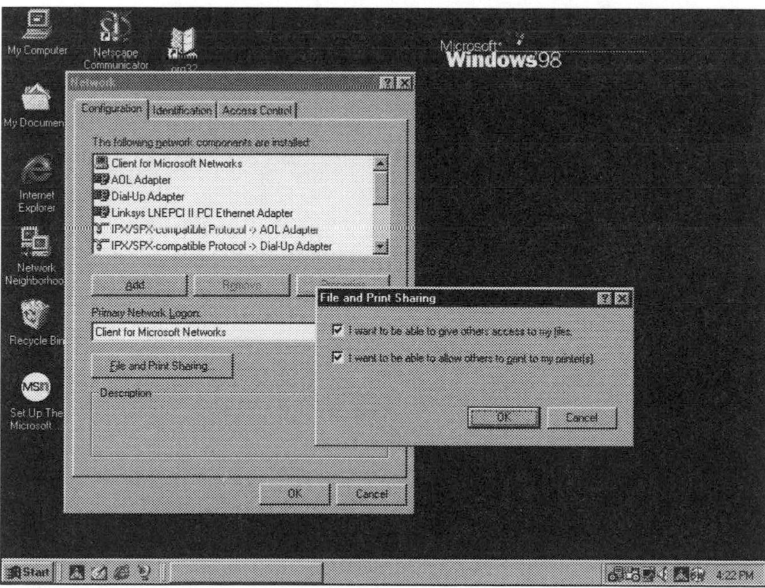

Figure 11.3 Configuring a PC to share a printer.

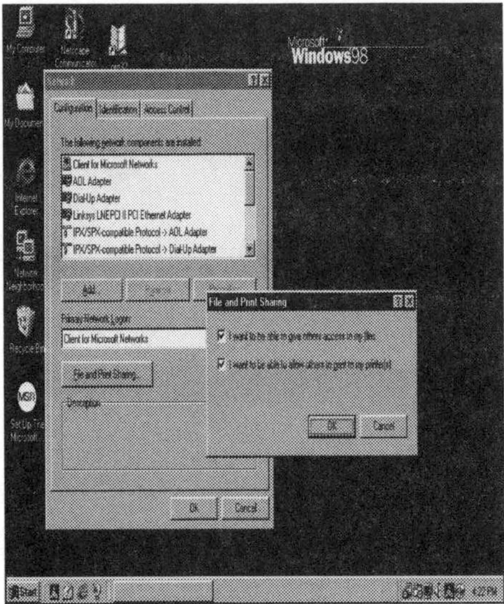

Figure 11.4 Use the printer's Properties dialog box to share the printer.

Configuring A Printer Across A Network

Before you can print to a printer that's connected to another computer across the network, you have to install it onto your computer as a network printer. To do this, perform the following:

1. Double-click on My Computer.
2. Double-click on the Printers folder.
3. Double-click on Add Printer. Windows starts the Add Printer Wizard.
4. When the wizard asks, "How is this printer attached to your computer?" click on Network Printer. Then, click on Next.

Definition, Please

A *network printer* is one that is physically connected to another computer that's on the same network.

5. The wizard will ask for the location of the network printer. You can click on the Browse button and locate the printer in a diagram. After entering this information, Windows will install the printer driver for the network printer.

A faster way to install the printer onto your computer as a network printer is to simply drag and drop a printer's icon from the Network Neighborhood folder to your Printers folder:

1. Double-click on the Network Neighborhood icon on your desktop.
2. Navigate through the Network Neighborhood to find the printer that you want to use.
3. Double-click on My Computer on your desktop.
4. Place the cursor on the printer's icon. Holding down the left mouse button, drag the printer's icon from the Network Neighborhood and drop it on top of the Printers folder in My Computer. Then, release the mouse button.

Using A Network Printer

Using a network printer is almost the same as using a printer that's physically connected to your PC. If you have followed the steps for installing and configuring a network printer, given earlier in the chapter, you should be ready to roll. In the same way that you would print from any application, such as Microsoft Word, you simply select the network printer and print away.

Working With Print Queues

As mentioned earlier in the chapter, a print queue is a line of documents (print jobs) that are waiting to be printed on a printer. Windows gives you several print queue options. You can view the print queue, pause and resume printing for the entire queue or for individual documents, remove documents from the queue, or delete all of the jobs that are waiting in the queue.

Viewing A Print Queue

You can easily view the print queue to see what's waiting to be printed on a printer. To do so:

1. Double-click on My Computer.
2. Double-click on the Printers folder.
3. Double-click on the printer's icon. The printer's print queue displays, as shown in Figure 11.5.

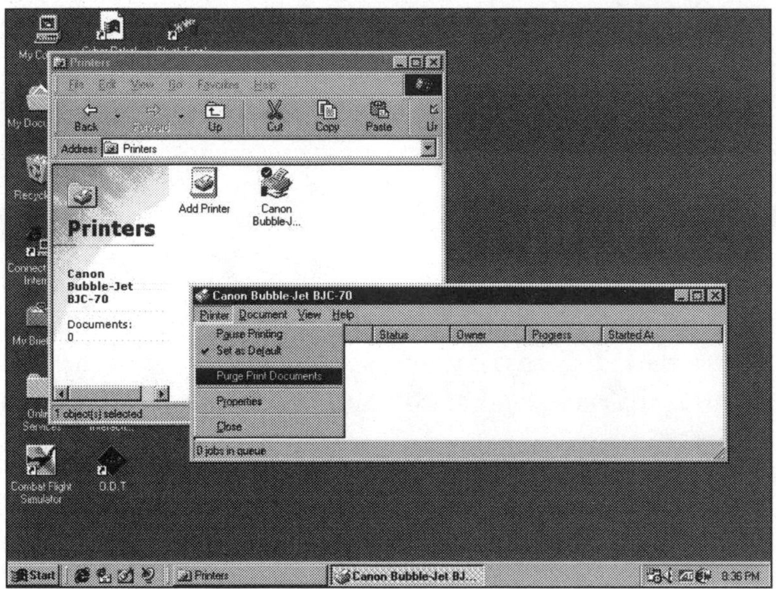

Figure 11.5 A printer's print queue displays the jobs that are waiting to be printed.

Pausing And Resuming Printing The Entire Print Queue

Use the following procedure to stop and restart printing a print queue:

1. Open the printer's print queue.
2. Select Printer|Pause Printing.
3. Choose the Pause Printing command a second time to resume printing.

A faster way to pause a local printer is to right-click on the printer's icon from within the Printers folder, then choose Pause Printing.

Pausing And Resuming Printing A Document

Sometimes you may find it convenient to pause and resume printing a document in the queue:

1. Open the printer's print queue.
2. Select the document in the print queue window by clicking on it.
3. Select Document|Pause Printing.
4. Choose the Pause Printing command a second time to resume printing the document.

Removing Documents From The Print Queue

You can remove one or all documents from the print queue.

To remove one document from the queue:

1. Open the printer's print queue.
2. Select Document|Cancel Printing.

To remove all documents from the queue:

1. Open the printer's print queue.
2. Select Printer|Purge Print Documents.

A faster way to remove all of the documents from the queue is to right-click on the printer's icon from within the Printers folder and choose Purge Print Documents.

Basic Troubleshooting

If you are unable to use a network printer, you can try the following:

- Make sure the network printer is powered up and online.
- Make sure that the computers are on and double-check all of those network connections that include hubs and cables. If you are using a hub, you should see a light on the hub next to a computer's cable connection that indicates that the hub recognizes your computer on the network. Also, check the printer cables.
- Verify that your network hardware—in particular, your network interface cards—is correctly installed, and that Windows recognizes this. For instructions, see the "Verifying That Your Network Card Is Installed Correctly" section in Chapter 10.
- Look for error messages. These can provide important clues.
- Try shutting your computer off and then turning it back on.
- Try shutting off the other computers on the network and turning them back on.

For more troubleshooting tips, refer to Chapter 18.

Moving On

You now know how to install a printer, configure it so it may be shared, and print from it across a network. In the next chapter, I'll talk about how you can get email on your network.

12

Email

After you install a network, you may want to use it to support an email system that lets you send messages from one computer to another, either across the office or home network, or through the Internet. If this is something that you want to do, read on to learn what's involved in bringing email into your network equation.

The Benefits Of Email

Email has many advantages over paper notes and phone calls:

- When you send an email message, the other person is alerted when it arrives, and if the recipient is too busy to read it at that time, he or she can read it later when time allows.
- If you have a document that you want someone else to review or you want to pass on a cool shareware utility, you can attach it to an email message. All the recipient has to do is open the attached file.
- You can keep an electronic list of people you often send messages to. This is convenient for sending messages to individuals, but it's even more helpful when sending messages to people in a particular group (if you've set up your email so that if you type in a group name, every member of that group will receive the message). For example, if you need to send an update to everyone working on a project, you can simply type in the group name to send your message to everyone in that group.

Definition, Please

email—A means of communicating through computers that's similar to writing a letter or fax, but instead of the message appearing on paper, it appears electronically on the recipient's computer screen.

attachment—A file sent along with an email message; the recipient simply has to open it.

Email System Components

The two main components of an office email system are:

- *Mail client*—Software that runs on a PC and lets people access and read their own email
- *Mail server*—Software that runs on the server to send email and retrieve it from the Internet

Both components are generally available as part of email system software.

Definition, Please

mail client—The software that runs on a PC and lets recipients retrieve their email. You use this software to compose messages, add attachments, and tell the computer where to send them.

mail server—The software that runs on a server and sends and retrieves email, sending email to others on the network or routing it via the Internet.

Types Of Email Systems

On a very small network, you may choose to forego the mail server software and use the Internet to handle your email, essentially using the services of your Internet Service Provider (ISP) to act as your mail server. If each user is connected to the Internet via a telephone line and modem, each can send email to others in the office. Although this isn't an efficient way of routing email, it's workable. But for a true email system that lets users send email within an office, you'll want to consider buying an email system.

Email systems generally come in two different types: those for large organizations and those for small ones. As you'd expect, the systems for large corporations are powerful, very expensive, and support hundreds of users; they even add features that support groups to help them maintain schedules, work on documents, and perform other tasks. These systems are also customizable so programmers can create applications. Meanwhile, those for smaller organizations and networks cost less and eschew the fancy features.

Some of the email systems that you may want to consider for a smaller organization include:

- QuickMail Pro Mail Server
- QUALCOMM Eudora WorldMail
- SoftArc First Class

The powerful email systems include:

- Lotus Notes/Lotus Domino
- Microsoft Exchange
- Netscape SuiteSpot Messaging Server
- Novell GroupWise

Microsoft Exchange Server 5.0 comes as part of Microsoft BackOffice Small Business Server and supports up to five users. This is a logical upgrade for a Windows-based network, because Small Business Server also includes Microsoft SQL Server, Microsoft Proxy Server, Shared Network Model Capability, and more. If your network grows to the point where it needs these services, BackOffice is a worthy consideration. For most of you, this will probably be well down the road.

Factors To Consider Before Purchase

Before you choose an email system, here are some options you may wish to consider:

- *Filtering*—Some email systems come with features that let you *filter* email, which is particularly helpful for keeping junk email ("spam") to a minimum. This is particularly useful for offices to minimize unnecessary email.

- *Virus protection*—Some email systems can automatically *scan* files attached to incoming email for viruses, which can give you some added security. As a general rule, you should always scan any file before you open it.
- *MIME support*—If your email system supports the Multipurpose Internet Mail Extensions (MIME) standard, you'll be able to handle file attachments from the Internet that comply with it. Because messages using this format are quite common, MIME support is good to have. Also, Secure MIME (S/MIME) encryption can encrypt file attachments for security purposes.
- *POP3 and IMAP compatibility*—Nearly all email systems support *Post Office Protocol version 3 (POP3)*, a standard that email clients and servers conform to so they can talk with each other. The up and coming standard is *Internet Message Access Protocol (IMAP)*, which is probably something you should look for in an email system.
- *Ease of use*—I can't emphasize enough that an email system should be easy to understand and use. It's a good idea to evaluate a trial version of the software you're thinking about buying to see how difficult it is to use and configure, and to make sure that your users will be able to understand and use the client software to send and receive their email. You might also look for something called *remote management* that lets you work with your email server from another location.
- *Scalability*—Your system should be the right size to meet your needs. For a network with only a few users, don't pay for a sophisticated system that is more than you will need. On the other hand, if your network later grows to many users, you can upgrade to a more powerful email system that can accommodate everyone.

Keep in mind that Windows 95 comes with Microsoft Exchange, an electronic email client, and Windows 98 comes with Outlook Express, a program that compiles mail from both your network and the Internet. Windows NT Server 4 and Workstation both come with Microsoft Exchange.

Moving On

In this chapter, I discussed the basic components of an email system and provided some tips on what to look for when purchasing an email system. In the next chapter, I'll talk about network security.

13

Network Security

Once you install a network to share computer resources with others, you'll often find that you don't necessarily want to share everything with everybody. Think about all the files on your computer; would you feel comfortable if others were to see the data that is in all of them? Some files contain financial and personal data. And if you run a business, files hold personnel and pay information, as well as data that is crucial to your business and that competitors would love to get their hands on. Not all unauthorized access on a network is malicious; at times, users simply stumble into files that they shouldn't see. However, there's no reason to take chances with sensitive files, and setting up network security is a fairly straightforward process.

To establish different levels of access, you can use the security features built into Windows 95 and Windows 98. It would be great if configuring security on a network were as easy as simply sticking a big lock on each computer; however, it's not quite that simple. This chapter discusses how you can control access on your network and protect key folders and files from prying eyes.

Levels Of Access Control

For security, Windows 95 and 98 come with two levels of access control: share-level access and user-level access.

Definition, Please

Share-level access control lets you assign passwords to shared folders so only the users who know the passwords will be able to access the files in those folders.

User-level access control, which lets you assign access rights to users or groups, is more sophisticated than share-level access. However, this feature can only be used when the Windows 95 or Windows 98 system is part of a network that is running Windows NT.

Sharing Folders

To share folders using the share-level access features in Windows 95 and Windows 98, you must first enable file sharing with your system. You can do this by performing the following steps (for more details on this procedure, refer to Chapter 10):

1. Click on Start|Settings|Control Panel, and then double-click on the Network icon.
2. On the Configuration tab, as shown in Figure 13.1, click on the File And Print Sharing button, and then check the box that's labeled I Want To Be Able To Give Others Access To My Files.
3. Click on OK.

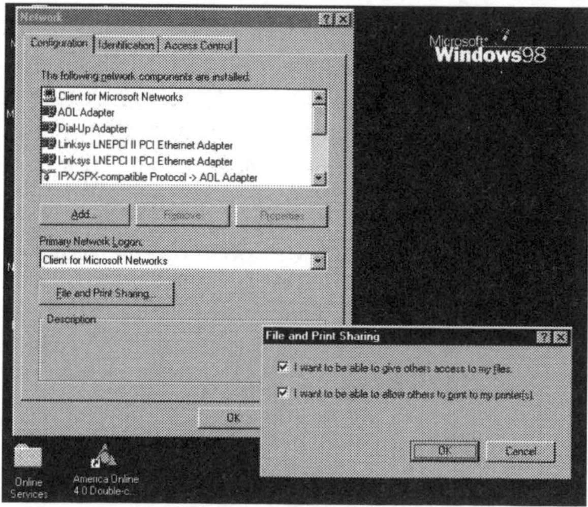

Figure 13.1 Sharing folders in Windows 98.

Setting The Share-Level Access Of A Folder

To set the share-level access of a folder, follow these steps:

1. Click on Start|Settings|Control Panel, and then double-click on the Network icon.
2. In the Network dialog box, click on the Access Control tab, and then select Share Level Access.
3. Click on OK.
4. For these settings to be in effect, you'll need to restart your computer.
5. Call up Windows Explorer by right-clicking on Start, then selecting Explore.
6. Right-click on the folder that you wish to control access to and select Sharing from the menu. This brings up the dialog box shown in Figure 13.2.
7. Select the Shared As option button, and then change the Share Name if you wish or accept it as it is. The Share Name will be the

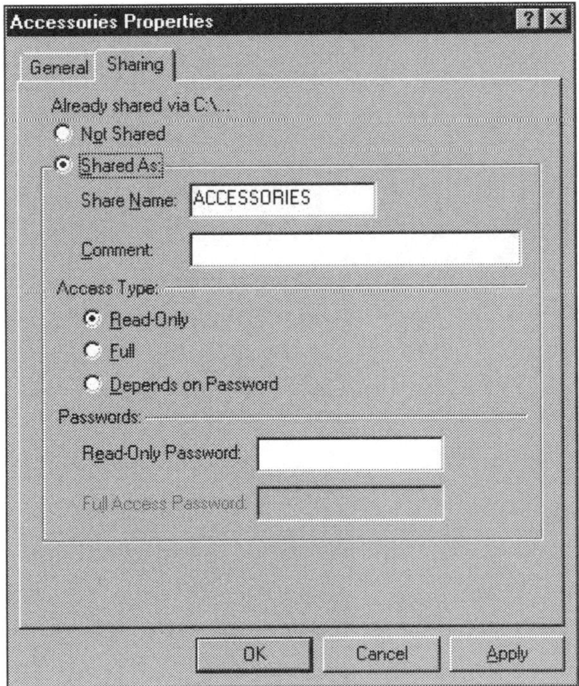

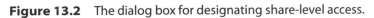

Figure 13.2 The dialog box for designating share-level access.

name that appears when others on the network access the folder, and it will appear as the folder's network path. Windows presents, by default, the folder's name as the shared name, which will probably work in most situations.

8. Optionally, you can also change the comment line. Others will see this comment when they view the folder in a details view.

Types Of Access Rights

To each folder, you can assign one of two access rights: Read-Only, Full, and Depends On Password.

Definition, Please

Read-Only—You share a folder, but users can only open and read the files within the folder—they can't make changes to them.

Full—Users have full access to the files in a folder and can open, read, modify, and delete the files.

Depends On Password—You need to define two passwords: one to control read-only access and one for full access. With one password, users can read the file. With another, users have full access to make modifications and save the file in the network folder.

As an example of different access levels, let's say that a single word processing file is stored in a shared folder. With Read-Only rights, users would be able to open the file with their word processors and view the contents of the file, but they couldn't modify or save it. (They can, however, save a version of the file in another location, such as their local hard drives.) Users with Full access could open and read the file, and then make changes and save it in the network folder where it resides.

Setting Share-Level Rights

To set share-level rights along with passwords, perform the following:

1. In the Program Files Properties dialog box, select an access type: Read-Only, Full, or Depends On Password.
2. If you select Read-Only or Full, you have the option of defining a password. After selecting Share-Level Access, simply type a password

in the field. If you select Depends On Password, define passwords for both Read-Only and Full Access. This controls users' access according to their password.

Passwords

A few notes on passwords:

- Don't use passwords that are obvious. If you use your street name, company name, the names of your kids, or other such choices, your passwords will be easy to figure out. The most difficult passwords to guess are those with combinations of numbers and letters. Although these are the hardest to remember, they are also the most difficult to break.
- Don't write a password down and display it in an obvious place (like taped to your computer).
- Don't automate your login process to include your password. This is as bad as having no password at all. Anyone can use your automation procedure and gain access to your system.

Keep in mind that you don't necessarily have to use passwords. You can simply limit access to certain folders so no one has access to them; also, you can make sure that the folders that everyone can access contain data that is not sensitive.

Using Net Watcher To Monitor The Network

A valuable tool to help you monitor your network is a utility called *Net Watcher*. This tool comes with Windows and shows you who is connected to which network system; it also lets you add and delete shared drives and disconnect users. To use Net Watcher, you must have it installed. If you need to install Net Watcher, follow these steps:

1. Click on Start|Settings|Control Panel.
2. Double-click on Add/Remove Programs.
3. Click on the Windows Setup tab.
4. Select Accessories and click on Details.
5. Select Net Watcher and click on OK.

To use Net Watcher once it's installed, perform the following:

1. Click on Start|Programs.
2. Select Accessories|System Tools|Net Watcher (this is the default location).
3. Net Watcher provides a "by Connections" view, which shows the users who are accessing shared resources (see Figure 13.3). The default view shows the connection by users; however, you can also view this information by shared folders and open files by clicking on the tools on Net Watcher's toolbar, or by choosing commands from Net Watcher's View menu.

Disconnecting A User

If you want to disconnect a user, select Administration|Disconnect User. If you want to close a file so no one can access it, select View|By Open Files, then select the file you want to close. Next, select Administration|Close File.

Creating A New Shared Folder

To create a new shared folder using Net Watcher:

1. Select Administration|Add Shared Folder.
2. Define the network folder that you want to share, then specify access rights and passwords, as discussed earlier in this chapter.

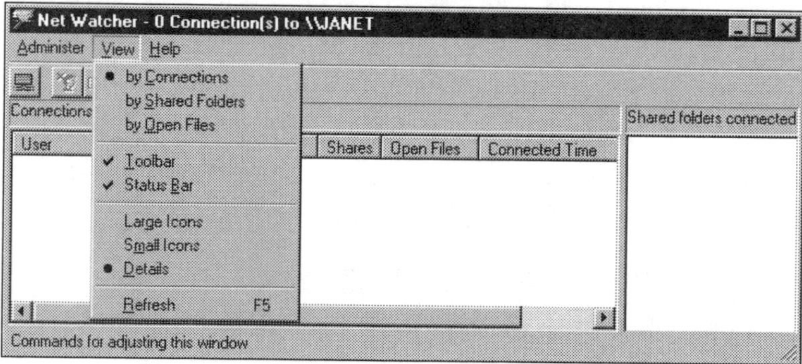

Figure 13.3 Net Watcher's "by Connections" view.

Stopping File Sharing

To use Net Watcher to stop sharing a folder:

1. Select View|By Shared Folders.
2. Select the folder.
3. Select Administration|Stop Sharing Folder.

Monitoring Another Computer

You can also configure computers so you can monitor them using Net Watcher from a different computer on the network. First, you have to configure a computer so it allows for remote administration. To do this:

1. On the system that you want to configure for remote administration, click on Start|Settings.
2. Select Control Panel|Passwords.
3. Click on the Remote Administration tab, as shown in Figure 13.4, and check Enable Remote Administration Of This Server.
4. Supply and verify a password (optional).

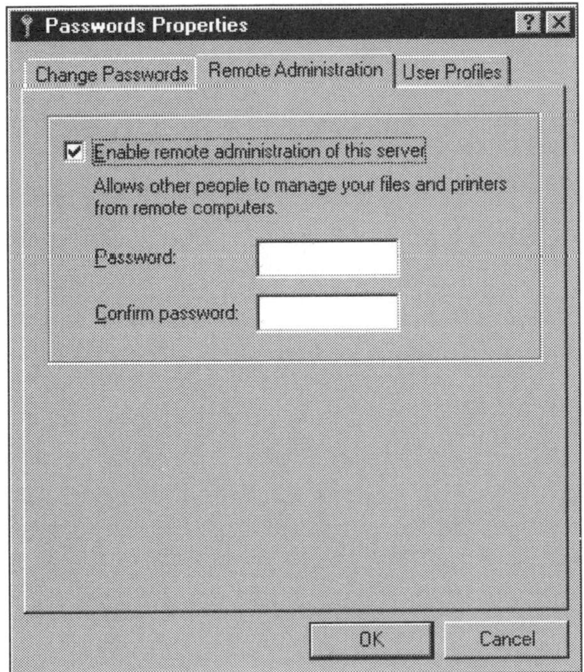

Figure 13.4 Configuring a system for Remote Administration.

To use Net Watcher to monitor another computer:

1. Bring up Net Watcher.
2. Select Administration|Select Server.
3. Browse to the server that you wish to monitor. Provide a password if the other server requires it.

Moving On

In this chapter, I discussed security techniques that you can use to limit access to the resources on your network. In the next chapter, I'll discuss other network issues, including backups, virus protection, and checking the integrity of your network's hard drives.

14

Backups, Viruses, And Drive Maintenance

Service every 3 months or 3,000 miles is great advice for keeping your automobile in good shape, but what about your computer or network? Although your computer or network does not have a mileage counter, you can do certain things to help it work at its peak performance and to ensure that your data always stays intact. In this chapter, I'll discuss how you can keep your data safe, and I'll explain some things you can do to keep your network drives in top shape, including backing up your data, checking for viruses, and maintaining your drives.

Backups

When a computer or network is part of your life, you'll find that you store a lot of important information on it. If you're like me, you're using your computer to store financial and tax information, crucial business records, client data, various contracts and proposals, resumes, and other personal documents. But computers aren't perfect, of course, and any act of man or God can cause computer glitches that make your system lose data. Other factors, such as computer viruses, can deliberately or inadvertently erase data. And if you're tired or not thinking, it's easy to accidentally erase important files.

I have experienced major hard drive crashes on my computers, and if I hadn't had backups for my important data, I would have lost all of it. Fortunately, I'm pretty good about keeping backups. I even go so far as to keep copies of all my data in my briefcase, which goes wherever I go. I

Definition, Please

Backing up your data means making a copy of the data on your hard drive—or everything on your entire hard drive—onto another hard drive, tape, removable drive, series of floppies, or on special backup services available on the Internet.

always knew it was a good idea to carefully back up all my data, but it wasn't until I had a serious hard drive crash and my backups saved the day that I fully realized why.

If you have a hard drive crash, you can contact a company that can retrieve lost data from the damaged drive. But this service is extremely expensive (the last time I checked, it was in the thousands of dollars). At these prices, only rich corporations can probably afford it. Your data may be important enough that you resort to paying for such a service, but a little expense and thought beforehand will make it a lot easier—and cheaper—to get through a disaster. Because virtually everything that you do with your computer resides on your drives, you need to back up your data. I can't overemphasize the importance of this.

Back in the old days, when a 20MB hard drive was state of the art, it was feasible to back up your hard drive onto a series of floppies. You could get most of that 20MB drive onto eight or nine 1.2MB floppy disks (with disk compression).

These days, however, 6.4GB and larger hard drives are the norm. If you tried to use floppies to back up these monstrous drives, you'd end up with a stack of thousands of disks, depending on the data. Not only would you have to store that stack of floppies somewhere, but during the backup process, you would have to feed these disks, one by one, into the drive—a tedious process that would take hours (maybe days). The bottom line is that floppies are no longer a reasonable way to back up large amounts of data and today's hard drives.

Fortunately, as you would expect, several hardware alternatives are available for backing up data. We'll explore some options that can be excellent upgrades to your current system. But first, I'll give you a little background on backup software.

Regardless of the backup hardware you buy for your computer or network, you'll need an adequate *backup program*. This will allow you to configure a backup so that it copies the files and directories that you need to preserve, and you can schedule backups to occur at any time. This way, you can have a computer copy files at a time when you're away from your desk—late at night or during lunch, for example. And in addition to copying programs and data, a backup program compresses your data so you can fit more data into the same space. Both Windows 95 and Windows 98 come with adequate backup utilities, and almost any hardware backup device you buy comes with its own backup software.

Generally, the more data you have to back up and the bigger your network, the more you need to use backup software. However, if you have only a few data files on a workstation that you need to back up, you may be able to get by with a simple copy command (I've often used *DOS batch files*—small programs that you can write to copy files and perform other basic tasks—to do this).

Backup Options: Data Only Vs. Entire Drive

Personally, I back up only my data, but I know many people who back up their entire drives, so if something happens they can restore the programs as well as the files. I find that it's not worth my time to back up my applications. First of all, applications like Microsoft Office are huge, and because they come on CD-ROM anyway, installation is not a major task. Of course, if you installed a huge application from a stack of 35 floppy disks, you might think otherwise. But a CD-ROM installation is fairly painless, and I usually don't have that many macros or templates to lose (I back those up, anyway).

If you take my approach and don't back up your applications and operating system, you also could lose your settings in Windows, including wallpapers, arrangements of groups, icons, and other aspects. If you have Windows set up in a particular way and it would take you days to reconfigure a fresh installation, by all means, back up the entire hard drive. (I'm just not all that attached to my screen savers and desktop.)

When you're backing up lots of important data, say for a business, you have to get serious about your backups. Although some of the methods may seem downright paranoid, they'll be invaluable should your systems ever crash. First of all, you should always have more than one backup. For example, if you back up your data to a tape drive, consider saving all your data daily on at least two tapes. This way, if one tape fails, you have one or two other recent backups. It's not unusual for businesses to use different tapes for every day of the week (Monday, Tuesday, etc.) and archive data onto backups for permanent storage at weekly and monthly intervals. If your data is important, you should consider doing this.

Backup Methods

Regardless of the method that you choose to perform your backup, just be sure that you regularly create backups of your crucial data. I can't emphasize this enough.

Two Hard Drives

One backup solution involves installing a second hard drive in your computer. At the end of each day, you simply copy all of your data files to it. Then if you have a crash on your main drive, you'll have a backup of data already on your system.

The advantage to this relatively cheap solution is that you also get more hard drive space, which you can use to store more applications. The down side is that you can't take the data with you. If someone steals your computer, or a fire or flood occurs, both your main and backup data will be gone. That's why, in addition to storing data twice on my computer's hard drive, I also store data on another medium, usually a Zip drive. I'll cover Zip drives later.

Caution

Be sure that you back up data onto a second drive that is a different physical drive. If you simply partition a large hard drive into two smaller ones, these are physically still the same drive. If a crash occurs, both of your drives will be knocked out and all your data will be irretrievable. To make the hard drive backup scheme work, you must have two physically different drives installed in your PC.

Tape Backup Drive

An excellent backup choice is a tape backup drive. You can find these at fairly low prices (under $100 for a 450MB drive) and they can store a lot

Definition, Please

Tape backup refers to a technology that saves digital computer data onto special cassette tapes. Because tape drives are very slow, most of them come with software that lets you schedule automatic backups at times you will not be using the computer. This lets you have your system perform the backup on its own, outside your normal working hours.

of data (up to 8GB). Most experts consider tape drives to be very reliable for storing data. The downside is that these devices are slow at reading and writing data, and backing up a large amount of data can take hours.

If you do want to perform unattended backups, you'll need to make sure that the tape cassette has enough space to store all of the data (a tape backup drive can't swap tapes for you when one tape gets filled). Recording data on a tape drive is much like using a VCR to tape your favorite television show while you're away. If the VCR tape runs out just before the detective in the movie dramatically reveals the killer, you're going to have to wait for reruns or call your friends to fill you in. In the case of a tape that runs out during a backup, you must perform the entire backup again on a longer tape.

I talked earlier about backing up data on two different media. For the same reason, I recommend that if you use a tape drive, you should rotate at least two tapes for each of your daily backups. It is possible that some force of nature could destroy your main hard drive, and only then would you discover that the backup tape you've been using for weeks is faulty. If you switch tapes each time you back up, you'll have your data on two tapes and lessen your chance of losing anything important.

When it comes to losing data, I can speak from personal experience. I once had a hard drive crash, and one of the backups of that data failed. As I brought out my second backup, I was literally holding my breath—some three weeks of work plus nine months of financial data were riding on this. Fortunately, the second backup worked just fine and I was immediately up and running. I have friends who laugh at me for my "paranoid" backups, but in this one case it definitely saved me. I can't overemphasize the importance of backing up your files.

Recordable CD-ROM

Another medium that is gaining in popularity is recordable CD-ROM. Devices are now on the market that let you make a single and even rewriteable recording to a CD-ROM disk. Both recordable and rewriteable CD-ROM drives will function adequately as CD-ROM players as well. If you're thinking about buying a new CD-ROM drive, this may weigh into your decision. For more information on the various types of CD-ROM drives, please refer to the "CD-ROM Drives" section in Chapter 15.

Removable Drives: Zip Drives And High-Capacity Floppy Drives

Another technology gaining in popularity is removable hard and floppy drives. Until recently, these drives were extremely pricey. Although they are still a bit expensive, removable drives offer many advantages.

Definition, Please

A *removable* hard or floppy drive is one that lets you store large amounts of data—usually from 100MB to 2GB—on a disk that you can easily remove from the computer.

The obvious advantage is that a removable hard drive can hold lots of data, sometimes as much as 1GB. As with a floppy, you can take this data with you wherever you go—in fact, most of these removable drives look much like floppies. If you need more space to store data, all you have to do is buy another disk, the same way that you would buy more floppy disks. Therefore, your ultimate storage backup space on a removable drive is virtually unlimited.

A popular high-capacity floppy drive is the Iomega Zip Drive, which uses 100MB 3.5-inch cartridges. I've been pleased with most aspects of the Zip drive, which comes in two versions: a SCSI version that attaches to a SCSI port, and a parallel version that connects with your system's printer, LPT1, or parallel port. The beauty of the parallel port model is that you can easily use the Zip drive on different machines by simply attaching it to a system's parallel port. You don't have to open the case and install the drive. I use the Zip drive as a second backup to my second hard drive.

If you have visions of using a Zip drive as a hard drive from which to run programs, you'll find that the parallel version is far too slow. However, the SCSI version runs more quickly and will give you acceptable performance. Also, Zip cartridges are a good choice when you need to mail a lot of data to someone, because Zip cartridges are fairly inexpensive and an increasing number of people own Zip drives. I have used Zip cartridges to send large presentations to others.

You can gain more backup space and faster performance using removable hard drives that use 1GB and 2GB cartridges, such as the Iomega Jaz Drive, but these are rather expensive. If speed is an issue, definitely go with one of the removable hard drives.

And more high-capacity floppies are coming to market to challenge the Zip drive. Among the most intriguing in this category is the 120MB SuperDisk, an internal drive from various manufacturers that reads and writes to 3.5-inch Imation SuperDisks. These disks look like regular floppy disks, but each disk can store up to 120MB of data. The advantage of this system is that the drive connects to your system's EIDE controller, and the same drive that reads the 120MB SuperDisks can still read standard 1.44MB floppies (something a Zip drive can't do). At the time of this writing, Sony and Fujifilm "HIFD" floppy technology is just hitting the market, and it promises 200MB of capacity on a special 3.5-inch disk.

Another option is a *magneto optical* (*MO*) drive—a compact 3.5-inch drive that can store at least 230MB. Optical drives are known for being rather slow, but they are also recognized as a reliable medium for storing data for long periods. Most rewriteable optical discs are rated to maintain data for up to 10 years. On the other hand, most magnetic media, such as floppies and tapes, are rated to last only five years. Also, optical drives are less sensitive to shock, so they can take more abuse than a removable hard drive or other media.

Popular MO models include the Olympus Sys.230 and the Fujitsu DynaMO 230, both of which can store 230MB, and the Panasonic PD/CD drives, which can store up to 650MB and come in two versions: parallel and SCSI.

Viruses

You also need to protect your computer from viruses. *Viruses*, of course, are those infamous programs that surreptitiously alter your computer's operation. At the least, they're mild annoyances that attach themselves to files and reproduce, gradually slowing your computer's performance. Some display irritating or obscene messages when activated. At their worst, viruses can make your computer unable to boot, crash your applications, destroy your data, or even trash your hard drive. If you're unfortunate enough to contract an aggressive virus, you may find that it has run rampant, infecting many of your disks, as well as the disks and hard drives of co-workers and friends you share files with.

Definition, Please

virus—A malicious computer program that is designed to infiltrate your computer system and replicate itself. It can try to erase data, post obnoxious messages, or slow down the performance of your system.

Like their biological brethren and namesakes, computer viruses spread by latching onto files, usually programs, and modifying their codes. When you run an infected file, the virus activates itself in the memory of your computer and tries to spread to other programs. You can get viruses through shared floppies, networks, and files downloaded from the Internet. You never know where you may have picked up a virus: It could come from a Zip disk that you used to get a file to your print house, a consultant may have inadvertently introduced a virus by using an infected disk, or you may have downloaded an infected program or file from the Internet.

Today, with the Internet's far-reaching influence and ability to quickly distribute information via Web sites and email, and with company networks that let large numbers of employees share programs and data, the ability for viruses to spread is even greater. Where do viruses come from? Talented computer programmers waste their time creating viruses for their own amusement or to prove how clever they are.

Until a few years ago, most viruses only attacked key PC files, such as those in the crucial areas of your hard drive that affect how it starts and boots; they would also invade executable files for applications. These viruses would cause your system to be unable to boot, prevent applications from running, or cause them to crash. For the most part, data files, such as those from word processors or spreadsheets, were relatively safe. However, a new breed of viruses, called *macro viruses*, changed everything.

A New Breed Of Viruses

Macro viruses are built out of the macro scripting languages found in popular applications, such as Microsoft Word, Microsoft Excel, and Corel WordPerfect. In these applications, you can build macros that will automate and perform a series of steps with a single command. For example, in a word processor, you can create macros that quickly reformat pages, add text, and replace words, and these can save you lots of time. But hackers have found ways of using macro languages so they change the spelling of words, print obscene messages, modify documents, and even erase hard drives. These days, macro viruses are the most common type of virus out there, and they are spreading faster than any other type of virus because data files are what most of us share.

As technology evolves, so do—unfortunately—the related viruses. New Internet technologies such as Java and ActiveX are introducing a new breed of viruses. Also, sophisticated viruses called *polymorphic viruses* can change their characteristics each time they infect a different file, making them more difficult to identify and catch.

Virus Detection Programs

Fortunately, virus detection programs are on the market that can hunt down viruses and minimize their damage. These programs identify viruses by their *signatures*—combinations of bytes unique to each virus. Once the detection program locates a virus, it alerts you, destroys the virus, and tries to repair the file. Sometimes a file is too far gone, and in this case, it's best to delete the file and replace it from your backups. Popular virus utilities include Norton AntiVirus and TouchStone's PC-Cillan.

The best way to deal with viruses is to prevent getting them in the first place. Any time someone sends you a new file or disk, you can use an anti-virus program to scan for known viruses. Keep in mind that macro and program viruses activate themselves only as you open or activate the infected files. Thus, viruses can reside on your hard drive in contaminated data, program files, or compressed Zip files, and never activate themselves.

When you scan your drive, the anti-virus programs can find the viruses before they have a chance to cause damage. By the way, any commercial software that you buy should be free from viruses. There have been instances of viruses arriving on commercial software, but these incidents happened years ago, and all software companies take extraordinary measures to make sure that their systems and distributed software are virus-free.

When you use an anti-virus program, you have to let it periodically scan your drives, which takes time. You can set a program to scan your drives each time you boot up, but you'll have to wait for the program to finish its scan before you can use your computer. Depending on the size of your hard drive and the speed of your processor, a scan can take three minutes or more.

Most anti-virus programs will let you schedule scans at times that are convenient for you. If you leave your computer on at all hours of the night, you can have your anti-virus software scan your drives after work hours. To do so, most programs offer simple interfaces with which you can select drives, folders, and files, and designate a time to perform the scan. Also, anti-virus programs will scan any disk that you attempt to copy and every file that you execute—a convenience that protects you if you get behind in your periodic scans.

To recognize viruses during a scan, a program has to know what it is looking for. And because new viruses are constantly hitting the streets, anti-virus programs have to be frequently updated with new signature files so they can identify the newest crop. To stay up to date, all anti-virus programs let you regularly update the software with new signature files across Internet connections. All you have to do is click on a button while connected to the Internet and these programs perform the update for you. Most programs provide free signature updates for as long as you use the software.

Most people I know who use computers have run into a virus at one time or another. It's a shame that we all have to be concerned with these mean-spirited pranks, but they are a reality. Virus detection software is an excellent addition to your digital toolbox, particularly if you have lots of crucial data. The following list summarizes some anti-virus measures that you can take:

- Scan your hard drives regularly with anti-virus software.
- Always scan any floppy disk before you copy files from it.
- Always scan any files that you download from the Internet before you open or uncompress them, or set your virus scanning software to automatically scan files as you download them.
- Never open a file before you have scanned it.
- Always consider the source of a file you download (or otherwise receive).

Drive Maintenance

Just as tune-ups cause a car to run at optimal performance, regular maintenance ensures that your computer's drives work at their best. Although the steps set out here won't stop a hard drive from crashing, they can check for errors on and optimize the performance of your system's hard drives.

Defragmentation

When you're grasping for any speed enhancement for your servers and workstations, you may want to consider defragmentation software, which will provide some performance gains by optimally aligning data so a hard drive's head has to move only a short distance to read files.

Consider using a defragger periodically, especially if your computer seems a bit sluggish. Depending on how far the clusters are distributed across

Definition, Please

Fragmentation occurs during normal computer operation and describes the process in which files are broken into segments and distributed across a hard drive, which slows the drive's performance. This process occurs naturally over time.

A *defragger* or *defragmenter* is a special software program that rearranges a hard drive's clusters so a drive can operate as efficiently as possible.

the drive, you should see some performance improvement. In my experience, however, I've never seen anything better than a 10 percent increase in speed. Thus, using a defragger is more of a system maintenance process than an upgrade. To defrag your hard drive, you can use the utilities that come in Windows 95 and 98. Special network defraggers, such as Executive Software's Diskeeper, let you schedule and perform remote defragmentation across a network.

Check Your Drives

It also makes sense to perform periodic diagnostics on your hard drive, using software such as Norton Utilities to check for and correct minor drive problems. Also, in both Windows 95 and 98, you can run ScanDisk, a program that will check your drive. Follow these steps:

1. Choose Start|Programs.
2. Select Accessories (this is the default, your system may be different)|System Tools|ScanDisk.
3. Within ScanDisk, highlight the hard drive in question, check Thorough and Automatically Fix Errors, and then click on the Start button.

ScanDisk evaluates your hard drive and repairs any problems that it finds.

Removing Extra Files—For Advanced Users Only

After a while, particularly after you add lots of Windows programs, your system begins to accumulate extra files, some of which you may no longer need. Even after you delete a Windows program, it probably has left some files on your drive that just take up space. These files occupy valuable hard drive real estate and system resources, because they load every time you run Windows.

For this reason, advanced users can examine their Windows system files periodically and check and delete excess files.

Moving On

In this chapter, I talked about backing up your data, protecting your system from viruses, and optimizing the performance of your hard drives. In the next chapter, I'll cover how to install peripherals.

15

Adding And Configuring Peripherals

Networks don't live on files and printouts alone. I've spent a lot of time in earlier chapters talking about how you can share files and printers across a network. But you can share lots of other devices and peripherals—such as CD-ROM drives, modems, and scanners—as well. In this chapter, you'll find that network resources other than files and printers are abundant.

CD-ROM Drives

CD-ROM drives are standard on any computer that you purchase today. But when you have a network installed, you can share a CD-ROM drive just as you can any floppy or hard drive. So if a CD-ROM drive breaks on one machine, you can use a CD-ROM drive on another system that's on the network. And when you use a CD-ROM drive on another network machine, you can remotely install programs, read files, and run programs that require that a CD be in the drive.

This ability to share a drive probably comes in most handy in situations where you buy a specialty CD-ROM drive, such as a *recordable* (*CD-R*) or *rewriteable* (*CD-RW*) drive, or one of those new *Digital Versatile Disc* (*DVD-ROM*) drives. Because these drives cost significantly more than conventional CD-ROM drives, you can buy one, install it on a single system, and then any computer on the network will be able to use it. This allows different people to record CD-ROM disks or read programs from a DVD-ROM drive without your having to invest in new drives for everyone. For more on CD-ROM, CD-R, CD-RW, and DVD drives, refer to Chapter 25.

Definition, Please

compact disc-recordable (CD-R) drives—Specialized CD drives that let you burn, or record your own CDs by copying files from a hard drive. You can also copy audio CDs or commercial CD-ROMs. Once you burn a CD, you can read it with just about any computer that's equipped with a CD-ROM drive or play it in your stereo's CD player (if you burn an audio CD). Most of the drives on the market are CD-R drives that write to a blank CD that only accepts data a single time and cannot be erased or reused.

compact disc-rewriteable (CD-RW) drives—Specialized CD drives that let you reuse and rewrite information to a special CD, almost as you would to a floppy disk. According to the manufacturers, you can overwrite a rewriteable CD some 1,000 times.

digital versatile disk (DVD) drives—CD drives that accept a disk that looks like a CD but holds 4.7GB (about seven times the amount that a conventional CD holds) and has the potential to hold up to 17GB.

You share a system's CD-ROM drive the same way you share a hard drive. For more on sharing files, refer to Chapter 10. One word of advice: If users need to constantly use a certain CD across a network (for example, a reference CD), it's usually best to dedicate a CD-ROM drive to support the disk. Otherwise, someone trying to work on the system will have to swap disks frequently. For high-end applications, large companies often purchase devices called *CD-ROM servers*, as shown in Figure 15.1, which are computers that connect to your network and house multiple CD-ROM drives. Devices called *jukeboxes* serve the same purpose, but they swap several disks in a single CD-ROM drive, much as a carousel in an audio CD player does.

Modems

If you want to surf the Net, send and receive faxes from a PC, communicate with other computers, obtain information through the telephone line, or use a computer to answer the phone and record messages, you'll find that you can do all of these things by buying a modem and connecting it to your computer. As you can see in Figure 15.2, modems act as translators between two computers so they can connect over telephone lines.

Figure 15.1 A CD-ROM server that a company might use to make CDs available to those on the network.

Definition, Please

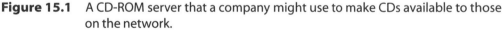

At its simplest, a *modem* is a device that lets your PC talk with another computer over a telephone line. A modem (short for modulator/demodulator) converts signals from your PC into a form that can be sent across a telephone line. At the other end of the phone line, a receiving modem converts the signal back to its original form so that a computer can read and use the information.

When you buy a new modem, your first consideration, besides the type (fax or fax/voice), is the modem's speed. The fastest modems you can buy today are rated at a speed of 56 *kilobits per second* (*Kbps*).

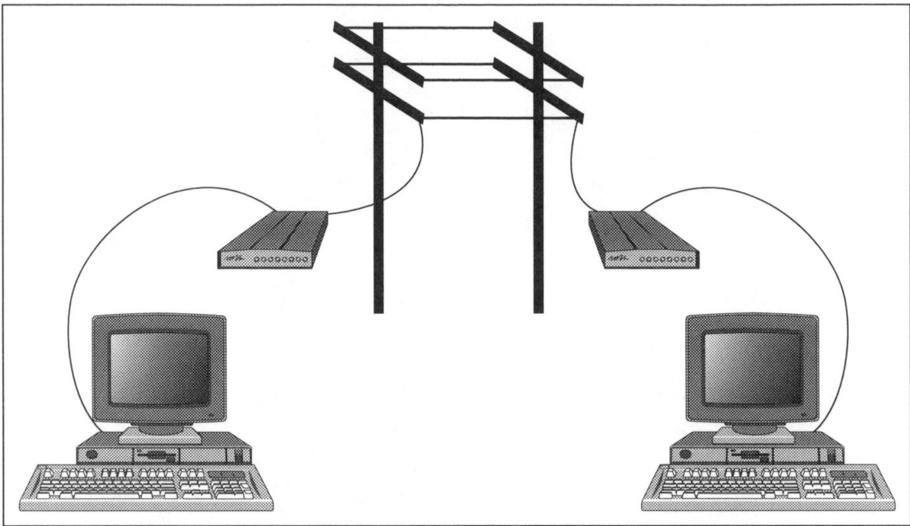

Figure 15.2 A modem converts information from a PC into a form that can be transmitted across telephone lines.

Definition, Please

Kilobits per second (Kbps) is a measure of the amount of information, in thousands of bits, that a modem can send and receive in a second. (For example, 56,000 bits per second equals 56Kbps.) The more bits it can send, the faster you can exchange information.

A modem lets your PC work through telephone lines to connect with other computers to obtain information. When you *go online*, you get copies of (or download) program files, find information to help your kids with their homework, check stock prices and news, review current happenings, reserve airline tickets, investigate a company's site or join its *forum* (an online area set up by a company to distribute information about

Definition, Please

Going online is a generic computer term that refers to using your computer and a modem to connect with other computers across a telephone line, usually to obtain information or communicate with other computer users. You can go online and connect to the Internet, World Wide Web, or any commercial Internet/online service, such as America Online or CompuServe.

its products), or participate in groups that exist to explore a particular interest: pets, movies, computer games, chat with other users, and so on.

Today, the most popular online destination—and the one that has received the most attention—is the *World Wide Web* (*WWW*), a portion of the Internet that works with graphics. The Internet is a worldwide network of computers that can readily communicate with one another. Usually, when anyone talks about the Internet, Web, or *information superhighway*, they are referring to the World Wide Web.

To connect with the Internet and online services, you must have a modem and the right software. Many Internet service providers and major online services will provide you with a disk of software that you install on your computer so you can use your modem to connect with their computers. For more on how to share modems for Internet access, refer to Chapter 16.

Fax/Modems

If you equip your PC with a *fax/modem*, which includes almost any modem that you buy today, you can send and receive faxes right from your computer, a capability that can replace your standalone fax machine.

Pros Of Using Your Computer As A Fax

Using your computer as a fax machine has many advantages. You can fax documents directly from your computer (where you're probably creating them), instead of printing pages out and then feeding them into a separate fax machine (you'll save paper as well). The quality of your sent fax will be higher because the document doesn't have to be scanned and translated into computer code by the fax machine before it's sent. When a fax is sent directly from your PC, it's already in the computer code in which you created it, so it looks cleaner when it's read at the receiving end.

Another advantage is that fax software can display a list of all received faxes. You can choose the ones that you want to print out (again, saving paper if you don't need to print them) and delete those that don't interest you, particularly junk faxes.

Finally, when you use your own printer, you can print your faxes to plain, dry paper. You don't have to deal with expensive, greasy paper—the kind used in inexpensive fax machines—that curls and smudges in your hands.

All fax programs install a *driver* for your application, which allows you to send a fax from any Windows application on your computer by simply using the Print menu. For example, if you're working in a word processor—let's say, Microsoft Word—you simply "print" the document to your fax/modem. The program asks you for the name and number of the person you want to send it to, and off it goes. Fax software allows you to perform more complex tasks, such as sending one fax to several locations or even scheduling them to be sent at a later time (when phone rates are lower).

Cons Of Using Your Computer As A Fax

On the downside, if you use your computer to receive faxes, you'll have to leave it on and connected to the phone. In fact, you might have to leave your computer on 24 hours a day, because it's not uncommon for businesses to send faxes late at night. If you don't leave your computer on, you can be jolted out of a restful slumber by a phone call that plays that irritating, high-pitched fax tone. If you distribute your fax number, others will assume that your fax machine is on night and day and that you have a dedicated line.

When fax calls come in, they usually take control of your computer and interrupt what you're doing. So if you're working—in your word processor, for instance—you may have to wait for the entire transmission to finish before you can continue. Some Windows fax packages now promise *background processing*, which allows you to receive faxes without interrupting the work you are doing in another application. From what I've seen, this background processing isn't entirely invisible, but it is a big help.

Another downside is that if you don't have a scanner attached to your computer, you'll have no way to fax a document that's already on paper (unlike a standalone fax machine, which lets you feed in and send the paper).

Sharing A Fax/Modem

Today, most modems on the market are fax/modems, which means that you can use them to send and receive faxes, as well as connect to other computers to transfer data. Most of the modems come with fax software so you can immediately try out these capabilities.

Windows 95 and 98 come with built-in features that let you share a fax/ modem on a networked computer. To do this, follow these steps:

1. Click on Start|Settings.
2. Select Control Panel and double-click on the Mail icon. The Settings Properties dialog box appears, as shown in Figure 15.3.

To set the Mail option, you must have installed it during your initial Windows installation. To install it, insert your original Windows CD-ROM disk, go through its installation, and select and install the Mail option in the process.

3. Double-click on Microsoft Fax in the list of information services.
4. Click on the Modem tab in the Microsoft Fax Properties dialog box, as shown in Figure 15.4.
5. Check the box labeled Let Other People On The Network Use My Modem To Send Faxes. A dialog box will ask you what drive and

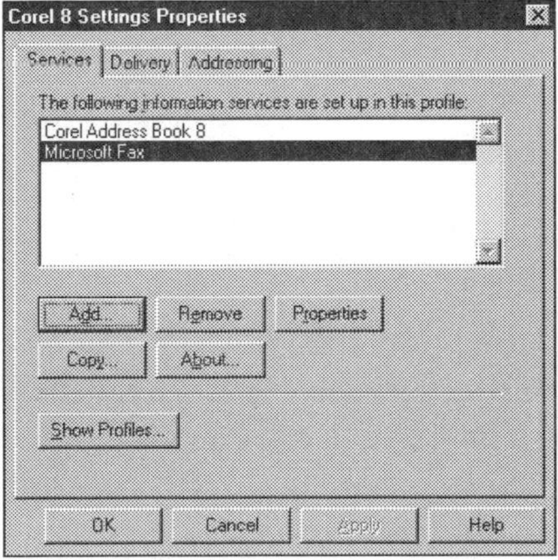

Figure 15.3 The Settings Properties dialog box.

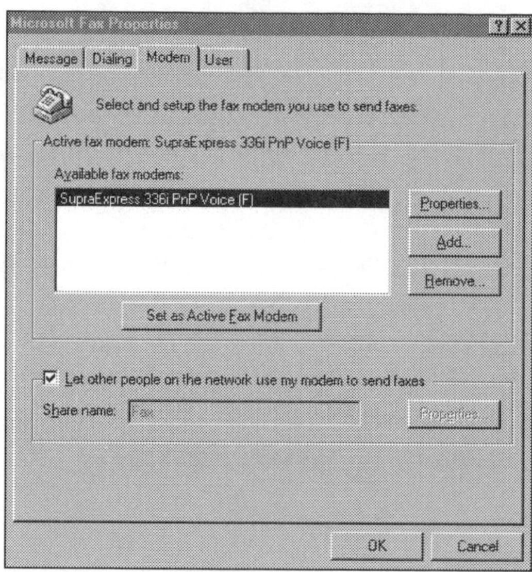

Figure 15.4 The Microsoft Fax Properties dialog box.

folder you wish to use for the fax service. Click on OK, unless you want to change the drive and folder.

6. Click on the Properties button next to the list of Available Fax Modems.
7. Depending on how you have set up Windows security, you can use this dialog box to assign rights to users who need to use the fax/modem.
8. Click on OK through the various levels to quit the program.

When other users on the network want to send a fax, they simply select the network fax/modem as their printer and print their documents to it.

Voice Modems

If you buy and install a special kind of modem, called a *voice modem*, you can use your computer as a sophisticated answering machine. When you're not at your desk, your computer can answer your phone, play your greeting, and record the caller's message. When you get back to your desk, your computer will tell you that you have a message waiting and play it for you.

Definition, Please

A *voice modem* is a special modem that supports voice capabilities.

A voice modem's capabilities go well beyond those of a simple answering machine. Your PC can work much like the sophisticated (and aggravating) voice mail systems that you often encounter when you call a business. Your PC can answer your phone, route calls to individual mailboxes ("press 1 for sales, 2 for customer service," and so on), and record messages in these separate boxes. When you get back to your computer, you can open your mailbox and read the list of all recorded voice messages so you can choose to play, save, or delete them.

Voice systems are useful if you're running a business, because you can create a system that sends callers to separate mailboxes to leave messages. The other advantage is that these systems make it sound as if you are a big company with an expensive phone system. Keep in mind, though, that large recorded voice files can occupy considerable space on your hard drive.

Any voice modem on the market today will have fax capabilities built right in and will come with fax and voice message software. Theoretically, this means that your PC can answer the phone, determine if the call is a fax or voice call, and then either receive the fax or record the voice message. However, I've never gotten this to work perfectly.

Setting up a networked voice-mailbox system requires specialized hardware and software and is an expensive proposition. And if you want a company voice mail system to accommodate several incoming telephone lines, you're looking at a project that probably requires an expert.

Scanners

Just a few years ago, an entry-level scanner would set you back at least $600. These days, you can find entry-level scanners with far more capability for under $150. If you put together presentations or need images for your desktop-published or word-processed documents, scanners offer the easiest way of getting existing photographs, illustrations, charts, and tables from printed materials into your computer. Until now, sharing a scanner across a network meant that you had to purchase a network scanner for thousands of dollars. Just recently, however, Hewlett-Packard's ScanJet 6200C broke this price barrier and costs just a little over $300.

The ScanJet 6200C is a competent 600-dpi, 36-bit flatbed that costs more than the cheapest scanners (which cost about $100), but its ability to be shared across a network makes it a clear office standout. When you connect the 6200C to a single computer, other workstations can use the device across a network, just as if they were attached to the scanner. The network-sharing software also comes with features for limiting access to the scanner with the use of passwords. If you've been looking for a scanner for your office and want one that could be shared across a network, the 6200C is one to consider, and more will undoubtedly follow in its footsteps.

Moving On

In this chapter, I talked about different devices beyond hard drives and printers that can be shared in a network. In the next chapter, I'll talk about how to obtain Internet access for network users and what it takes to build a Web site.

16

Connecting To The Internet

The *Internet*—our present-day information superhighway that politicians like to tout and newscasters love to babble about—may be overhyped, but it's a reality. Today, business cards feature email addresses, companies advertise their Web addresses in television commercials, and a wealth of information and downloadable files (usually via FTP) can be found on the Web. Once you connect your network to the Internet, everyone on your network can access its resources. You can also post a page to advertise your business.

Definition, Please

Internet—A huge network that connects thousands of commercial, academic, private, and government computers and networks in almost 100 countries. Originally developed by the military, the Internet has grown to be used by millions of users to exchange and share information.

electronic mail (email)—A way to communicate through computers. It's similar to writing a letter or fax, but you don't send any paper—the messages appear electronically on a recipient's computer screen. With the right equipment on your own network, you can send email from one network user to another. And if you connect your network to the Internet (the subject of this chapter), your network users can send email to anyone on the Internet and receive it as well.

Web—A part of the Internet that emphasizes graphics. The Web is the most popular aspect of the Internet, and it's what most people have in mind when they say "cruising" or "surfing" the Internet. On the Web, you'll find an endless amount of information in pages that are created by companies, educational organizations, clubs, and individuals. Mail-order catalogs, movie ads and reviews, and information on fly-fishing, gardening, raising pets, and more—they're all available on the Web. You view Web pages with software called a Web browser. The two most popular *Web browsers* are Netscape Communicator and Microsoft Internet Explorer.

File Transfer Protocol (FTP)—The Internet's method of making files available to users for download. Major companies, government agencies, and organizations usually have FTP sites that offer programs and files for download.

When considering how the Internet relates to your network, you need to think about three things:

- How to connect to the Internet so you can provide network users with access
- How to build a Web site and create a presence on the Internet
- How to offer other Internet-based services, such as an intranet

Making Connections

This section discusses common ways to allow your network's users to access the Internet, send and receive email, and cruise the Web.

Modems

Without a doubt, a modem is the most common way that most users access the Internet, and it's the least expensive. You need only a telephone line and a dial-up account with an *Internet Service Provider (ISP)* to obtain Internet access. On the downside, a modem connection across a telephone line is slow compared to other technologies that you may choose from, and a modem ties up your telephone line so you can't make voice calls while you're surfing the Web. (For more information on modems, see Chapter 15.)

Definition, Please

Internet Service Provider (ISP)—A company that provides Internet access services. When you open an account with one of these companies, you typically obtain an email address, and can use your modem to dial a modem at the ISP to access the Internet.

Sharing Modems

From a network perspective, the simplest way to give several users Internet access is to install a modem in each computer and dedicate a telephone line to each computer. This approach gives each user individual access, and you can easily make arrangements with an ISP to set up individual accounts for each user. However, this method bypasses the LAN completely, and you'll probably find that paying for all those individual phone lines will add up.

A more cost-effective solution is to install a single modem on one computer (a server) and use software that lets network users share this modem. To do this, you have to purchase special modem-sharing software, because Windows 95/98 and Windows NT don't come with this feature. Popular software for sharing modems includes Artisoft Modem Sharei and LanSource WINport.

The plus side of using a modem server is that you'll pay for fewer telephone lines, but because your users have to share modems, not everyone will be able access the Internet at the same time—they're limited to the number of modems that you have installed on the server. Another thing to keep in mind is that the computer that's connected to the modem will take a performance hit and slow down whenever someone uses its modem. For this reason, it's often a good idea to dedicate a machine to serving and sharing the modems. You can also connect up to four computers and three modems to devices such as Ramp Networks' WebRamp M3 and then share modems on a network.

As you might expect, the faster the modem that you install on your network, the better the performance and the higher the price. And although you can save some money by purchasing a slower modem (for example, 28.8 or 33.6Kbps) and live with slower performance, you will probably become quickly frustrated with slow performance. Because the price difference isn't large, it's worth buying a 56Kbps modem (keeping in mind the issues with 56Kbps that I mention in the following section). These modems promise faster connections for your Internet sessions. However, to actually obtain optimal performance, you need to consider a number of factors that clearly affect it.

First, your ISP and online services have to be using 56Kbps modems on their end. For more information, check with your ISP or online service. And not only does the modem have to match speeds, but the 56Kbps standard that the modem uses—US Robotics' x2, Motorola's K56flex, or the latest ITU V.90 (V.90)—has to be the same as yours. As I write this, the contest between the two competing standards, US Robotics' X2 and Motorola's K56flex, is largely over. Most of the modems on the market are accepting the new V.90 as the current industry standard.

If you are buying a 56Kbps modem, definitely buy one that supports V.90. If you purchase an X2 or K56flex modem (your ISP may still support only one of these), make sure that you can upgrade it for free with a download to V.90 (some modem manufacturers want to make you pay for this). And if you currently own an X2 or K56flex modem and want it to conform to V.90, many such modems can be upgraded. Check with your modem manufacturer to determine your options and to get instructions on how you may accomplish this upgrade.

Another factor has to do with the quality of your telephone line. To receive data at 56Kbps, your telephone line has to be clean and free of any "noise." This includes static that you hear as you talk on the phone; this can bring 56Kbps transmissions to a grinding halt. When considering your phone line, you also have to consider the number of times that the signal is converted along the way from your ISP or online service to you. If too many conversions take place, 56Kbps will be impossible and your actual performance will be far slower.

To test your line, many of the major ISPs and modem manufacturers have online testers that can determine if your phone line can support 56Kbps. (For the test, you don't need a 56Kbps modem; a 28.8Kbps or 33.6Kbps modem will do). Check with your ISP or modem manufacturer to see if this service is available on its Web site, or simply visit its home page.

Still another factor is cost. Some ISPs will charge you extra—about $5 more each month—to dial a special 56Kbps telephone line, and you'll want to consider this in your budget. You should also check to see if your ISP has a local number; the closer the access number, the better. In my experience, I have phone lines that are supposed to meet the 56Kbps standards, but I have never seen performance better than 40Kbps. This is faster performance than what I get with my other systems equipped with 33.6Kbps modems, but not by much.

If you are upgrading from a 28.8Kbps or slower modem, by all means purchase a 56Kbps V.90 modem, particularly if your phone lines can handle the speed. Another important thing to remember is to make sure that the modem that you buy is memory-upgradeable. This type of modem uses a technology called *flash memory* that lets you later upgrade the modem's software to support any future standards (or versions of V.90). Because the standards for 56Kbps transmissions will probably evolve over time, this is like buying insurance.

If you find that your phone lines are too noisy to handle 56Kbps, you may consider upgrading to a 33.6Kbps modem; however, be warned that you won't save a lot of money. On the other hand, if you currently own a 28.8Kbps or 33.6Kbps modem, you could forego the upgrade and save the money that you would spend to purchase a 56Kbps modem. This decision is entirely up to you.

ISDN

You can gain faster Internet performance through an *Integrated Services Digital Network* (*ISDN*) connection.

Definition, Please

ISDN is a digital telephone line that can communicate at speeds up to 128Kbps—approximately twice that of a 56Kbps modem.

An ISDN digital line consists of two *bearer* channels that can each carry up to 64Kbps of data or voice. You can use these as two distinct telephone lines—for example, you can download files on one line while you talk or fax on the other. With a process called *Bandwidth on Demand Internet Working Group (BONDING)*, you can use both channels together to send data at up to 128Kbps (your Internet Service Provider has to support this). In addition to faster Web page updates and downloads, ISDN negotiates online connections faster, typically in seconds, and the digital line isn't affected by the noise that plagues modem connections.

Getting ISDN takes some effort. First you have to arrange for your phone provider to install a special ISDN line. Then you will need to buy an ISDN adapter (also called an *ISDN modem* or *terminal adapter*) and subscribe to an ISP that supports ISDN. Of course, every step requires that you pull out your checkbook or credit card, so be prepared to make some phone calls and shop around.

If you're not sure who your provider is, you can find out by looking at your phone bill. Call your telephone provider to find out the availability of ISDN in your particular area, or check out the telephone provider's Web page. ISDN pricing is complicated. Most companies charge a monthly fee for the service, usually between $30 and $50, and then charge you for use by the minute. These per minute rates are usually complicated because the rate varies with the time of the day and the day of the week. Also, with many providers, the charges apply only when you use a single channel. If you connect at 128Kbps, the cost doubles.

After you've had an ISDN line installed, the next step is to find an ISP that supports ISDN. If your current ISP offers ISDN support, you can stay with it; however, expect to pay more for ISDN—approximately twice as much. In general, look for BONDING support, which lets you connect at speeds up to 128Kbps, and Multilink PPP+, which lets you use channels as your connection requires them. Also, make sure that your ISP has local access lines that are toll-free calls (you can obtain the numbers from your ISP and then call the operator to see if the number is a toll-free local call).

Finally, you'll need to buy an ISDN adapter. If you plan to use an external adapter, make sure that your system has a 16550 *universal asynchronous receiver/transmitter (UART)*. If you have a Pentium or higher system, you probably have the 16550 UART. If your PC doesn't have one, it will only communicate at speeds up to 57.6Kbps, well below maximum ISDN speeds. In this case, you'll want to install a new I/O card with the 16550 UART (you can get one for about $30 or less from your local computer dealer) or install an internal ISDN adapter.

And before you lay down money for an ISDN adapter, contact your ISP and see if it recommends a modem. An *ISDN U interface* ensures that you can connect your adapter directly to the ISDN line. You'll want *RJ-11 jacks* (conventional phone jacks) to connect with phones and fax machines (some don't provide these), and *Flash ROM* to accept future software upgrades as they become available. I also recommend that you look for an ISDN adapter that basically installs itself, such as the 3Com IQ External ISDN modem. With all of the confusing ISDN parameters to deal with, this can be a big-time help. Some adapter vendors such as Motorola, U.S. Robotics, and 3Com offer services to order an ISDN line for you and set you up with a local ISP.

Is ISDN worth installing in your business or home? This will depend on what you and your business need, and how much you're willing to pay for it. As an example, here's a simple business projection. Let's say that a business spends 80 hours a month connected to the Web on a single line. If you connect to your ISP via modem, you would expect to pay about $25 per computer per month for unlimited use. Assuming that you make ISDN connections only during business hours, the ISDN line will cost about $50 a month for the service, and around $80 at 64Kbps and $160 at 128Kbps for the per minute charges. The ISP service will also cost about $50 a month. Add this up, and this scenario costs about $285 per month (at the highest speed), and this is just a start for a basic connection.

You can share an ISDN line just as you can a modem connection. To do this, you'll need to purchase special software that can share the ISDN line with a network, such as Artisoft Modem Sharei or LanSource WINport. Also, you can purchase devices called *ISDN routers* that will accomplish much the same thing.

Other Access Technologies

Technologies such as *cable* and *Digital Subscriber Line* (*DSL*) can deliver the Internet at blazing speeds, and it's likely that at least one and maybe even both technologies will soon be available in your area. With download speeds that can be as fast as 10Mbps (that's an "M," folks), you'll find that the Web can deliver information in almost no time at all. While providers of both technologies offer services more on the level of 384Kbps to 1Mbps, I've had a taste of this promised land, and I've been blown away by what I've seen. If you want to share your cable or DSL connection across a network, you'll need to work with the company that provides you with this service.

Definition, Please

cable-based Internet access—Fast Internet access that comes through the same cable that provides a home with cable TV.

Digital Subscriber Line (DSL)—Technology that uses existing phone lines to carry voice and digital data.

Mbps—Megabits per second. (For example, 10Mbps equals 10 million bits per second.)

Cable-Based Internet Access

Cable-based Internet access relies on the same cable that brings those myriad television channels into your home. With cable access, you don't make Internet connections across a phone line or modem. Your computer houses a conventional network (Ethernet) card that connects to a special cable modem, which, in turn, connects to your television cable. For now, cable access is only available in select areas.

With cable, your Internet connection is always on. The benefits of this arrangement are as follows:

- You never have to dial in and connect (unless your cable provider offers a "hybrid" service only: cable download with modem upload).
- You don't tie up a phone line when connected to the Internet.
- You'll never run into those frustrating busy tones when you try to connect during peak times.

On the downside:

- You share your cable data pipe with your neighbors.
- During peak times, your performance will slow down; how much is still not known at this point.

To see if you have cable-based access, call your local cable provider (the same one who provides cable television) and ask whether cable access is available in your city or town. If the representative says yes, don't jump for joy yet. As it turns out, although parts of a city might have cable Internet access, others may not. In fact, there are cases in which one resident has cable Internet access, but the neighbor next door or across the street does not. In this case, the cable company will follow its schedule for installing the necessary junction boxes that support the service and you'll have to wait. In some areas, businesses will have to negotiate the cost of installing the cable connection. In such cases, some cable companies are willing to amortize the cost.

If you're lucky enough to have a home or business that's wired for the service, you'll make an appointment so technicians can come to your home or office to wire the cable and connect your PC to the cable modem and line (this typically costs $99 to $149, depending on your cable company). Most of the cable companies that I've spoken with are charging around $40 a month for performance that starts at 256Kbps, a bit more than what you would pay an ISP. Also, some cable companies are offering tiered services—the more you pay per month, the faster the performance.

DSL

DSL is technology that works across the same telephone lines that now carry your voice and dial-up Internet connections, and it's available through your local telephone company. Like cable-based Internet access, DSL gives you a dedicated Internet connection that is always on—you don't have to dial in. The other cool aspect is that you can be connected to the Internet and still talk across the very same telephone line—you don't need to have a second telephone line just for Web surfing.

On the downside, to subscribe to Asymmetric Digital Subscriber Line (ADSL)—a popular flavor of DSL that sends information faster than it receives it—your business or home must be within three miles of the telephone company's central office. According to the phone companies, about 60 to 70 percent of businesses and homes are probably within this distance and should therefore be eligible for the service.

Definition, Please

Asymmetric Digital Subscriber Line (ADSL)—A popular flavor of DSL that sends information faster than it receives it (thus, the *asymmetric* in the name).

The availability of DSL depends solely on your local telephone company. Most phone companies have announced that they are working on introducing these systems. So far, the costs I've seen for these services start at around $60 per month, which is a bit pricey.

T1 and T3

The fastest Internet connections are available from your local phone companies, and this speedy access will cost you dearly. It's not unusual for these services to start at over $1,000 a month.

Definition, Please

T1—A type of connection that can transfer data at speeds up to 1.544Mbps and support up to 24 simultaneous users.

T3—A type of connection that can transfer data at 44.184Mbps and handle up to 672 users.

As you would expect, a T3 line is far more expensive than a T1 line. If you have enough users to justify a T1 or T3 connection, you will want to work with the company that provides your line to see how to make it work with your network, which is a complicated process.

Hosting A Web Site

If you've heard enough about businesses making their fortunes by having their own Web sites and are ready to jump into the online fray, this section talks about how you can set up your own Web site. This topic is quite involved, and depending on what you want to do, you might want to seek a consultant to help you with this. Also, many ISPs offer services for helping you host a Web page. I'll discuss the basic steps that are involved so you know what you're getting into.

When you want to create your own Web site, you have two options:

- Set up your Web site through your ISP
- Set up your Web site on your own

These alternatives are described next.

Setting Up A Web Site Through An ISP

The easy way to create a Web site is to work through your local Internet Service Provider and have it host your Web site at its facility. The ISP uses space on its system to store your Web page and takes care of the Internet connections.

When you call your ISP, be prepared for a range of prices that will depend on the level of hosting services that an ISP provides and the amount of space that your Web page takes up. Most ISPs give you some space on their systems for a Web page, usually 2 to5MB, when you open an Internet account. If you need more space (and you probably will, especially if your Web page features images and video), you'll pay more for the additional space.

Setting Up A Web Site On Your Own

The other way to create a Web page is to set up your own with a server computer that has a direct connection to the Web: either via a T1 or T3 connection (you can also use an ISDN line). This server will have to run Windows NT Server, NetWare, or Unix. And on top of the operating system, you'll need to install Web server software, such as Netscape Enterprise Server or Microsoft Internet Information Server. Microsoft Internet Information Server is free—you can download it from Microsoft's sites, and it comes as part of Windows NT Server 4. Keep in mind that both are rather complicated to install and maintain. If you go this route, be prepared for a significant learning curve.

If you connect a Web server to your network, you'll also run into security issues. With your network now connected to the Internet, it's possible for a hacker to access your system and get into your data or wreak havoc with your network. To prevent this, you'll want to consider a *firewall* to protect your network from unauthorized access from the Internet. Some firewalls use a technique called packet filtering that closely examines data to ensure that it comes from a known or trusted location, as defined by the administrator. These firewalls are typically less expensive. Another type of firewall, known as a proxy server, creates a barrier called a *bastion host*. This approach is generally more effective because the bastion host is a physical barrier that places the firewall server between your network and the outside world.

Definition, Please

A *firewall* is a specialized server that checks all the data that enters your network.

Creating An Intranet

Although the word *intranet* looks as if someone misspelled *Internet*, it's a legitimate word meaning a private, company version of the Web that runs on a network in an office or home. Employees and other users can use their Web browsers to view business documents, work with company databases, and check schedules and calendars. And to get around, employees simply click on links, just as they do on Web pages. Another plus is that all workers—whether they are running Macs, Windows workstations, or Unix workstations—can refer to the same data.

Definition, Please

intranet—A private version of the Web that users on a network can access.

Many small businesses have networks that allow them to share printers and send email, but these systems don't always promote effective communications. A company's *local area network (LAN)* lets workers share databases and document files, for example, but files are typically stored in a labyrinth of network drives, directories, and folders. To locate a file, a worker has to know that it exists and where it resides. And once workers find the files they need, they must have the correct application to view and open it.

When it comes to communications, most companies rely on email. However, it's up to workers to create lists of recipients, and it's not unusual for them to forget someone who needs the information, or flood someone else's email inbox with unneeded messages and files. Many companies print and distribute hard-copy documents, but this method can't provide immediate information to workers who are out of the office.

One solution is to use groupware products such as Lotus Notes, which lets employees share databases, documents, and information. However, these systems are complicated to set up and maintain, very expensive, and must be run by technicians. It's easy to see why most small offices have not installed traditional groupware.

With a company intranet, workers post key documents and databases on pages where everyone with a computer can find and view them. All information, whether it's a text document, database, or presentation, displays as a Web page within a Web browser. And when the information changes, workers can quickly update and post their documents to the intranet, where they're immediately available to everyone. A single document posted to a company intranet replaces all the attached versions of a file that may be distributed via email (and which would take up space on company servers and hard drives).

Common documents that companies may post to an intranet include: employee and company phone directories; newsletters; employee manuals, bulletins, and procedures; job listings; information on health and 401K plans; training information; sales catalogs and price lists; product bulletins; inventory databases; and customer service order status and tracking. Also, project teams can post progress reports, meeting minutes, and project assignments.

Intranets provide an ideal way for users on the road to stay up to date. And companies that want to give intranet access to key partners, vendors, and clients can create what's called an *extranet*. This allows outside users to place orders and check their status.

Definition, Please

extranet—A type of intranet that lets authorized users on the outside access limited data.

To access intranet data, workers simply use their Web browsers in the same way they would on the Internet. However, those who publish to an intranet do have to learn how to post documents. The documents must be written in the Web's *Hypertext Markup Language* (*HTML*)—a simple language that defines the layout of a Web page. Fortunately, many tools to help users lay out and create HTML Web documents are available, including Microsoft's FrontPage, Adobe PageMill, and a host of others.

Also, major business applications, such as Microsoft Word, Corel WordPerfect, Microsoft Excel, and PowerPoint, all offer Web publishing features that translate documents into HTML.

Definition, Please

Hypertext Markup Language (HTML)—A format/language that defines how Web pages appear.

So if an intranet is so great, how does someone go about building and installing one? Typically, the job requires installing Internet server software, such as Microsoft's Small Business Server or Netscape Enterprise Server, along with an ODBC-compliant database, such as Microsoft SQL Server. However, these packages are beyond most novice users, and usually require information system personnel to install and maintain them. The more complex the final system, the higher the cost and the higher the technical knowledge needed to install and maintain it (you will probably have to bring in consultants if you don't have employees versed in information technologies). But there are easier alternatives that small businesses may want to consider.

To set up an intranet, you'll need:

- A network.
- A server that is:
  - Running either Windows NT Server or Unix
  - Connected to the network
  - Has Web server software installed (if you're setting up a small intranet for a few users, you can use Personal Web Server, which works with Windows 95)
- Browsers installed on each computer on the network to access the intranet.
- Web authoring software, such as Microsoft's FrontPage, FileMaker's Home Page, and others. You can also use the Web publishing features in programs such as Microsoft Office, Corel WordPerfect Office, and other programs to publish documents into a format that the intranet can use.

Fortunately, other intranet-style solutions exist. FileMaker Pro is first and foremost a database, but it comes with convenient Web-publishing features that let you publish a database file to a network so anyone with a browser can view, sort, query, and modify data. You can see the features of FileMaker Pro in Figure 16.1.

Another easy intranet-style solution is subscription-based collaboration products that work across the Web. This includes products that let companies set up departments and projects, and that offer security, document-sharing capabilities, and email. Such products include HotOffice (as shown in Figure 16.2), 3-2-1 Intranet, eRoom, and Netopia Virtual Office. To access this type of intranet, workers need a dial-up or direct Internet connection and a browser. For the small business, little setup and minimal administration are involved, and these Web-based services are great for companies that have workers spread over wide areas and in different offices.

Another intranet option is a Web server, such as Cobalt Microserver's Qube 2700WG (as shown in Figure 16.3), Microtest WebZerver, or Whistle Communications' InterJet 100. These devices, which come with hard drives to provide storage, network connections, and Web server software, cost between $1,200 and $4,000. Web servers are for nontechnical users who want to plug in a device, connect it to an existing

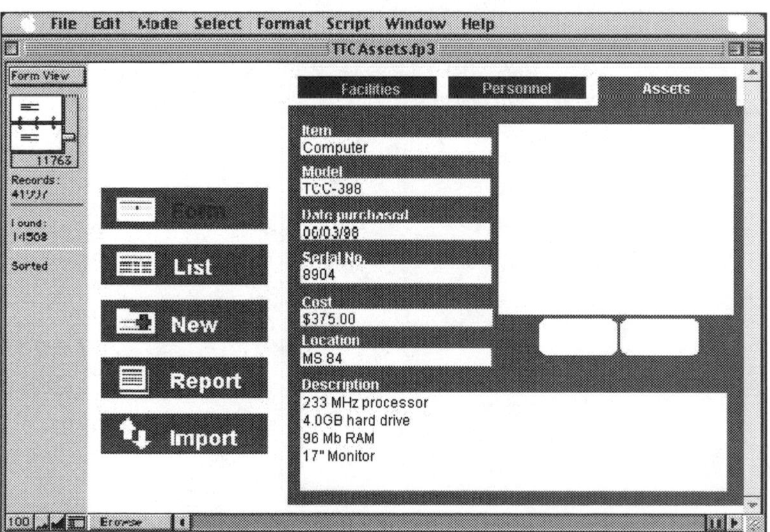

Figure 16.1 FileMaker Pro offers features for publishing a database to an intranet.

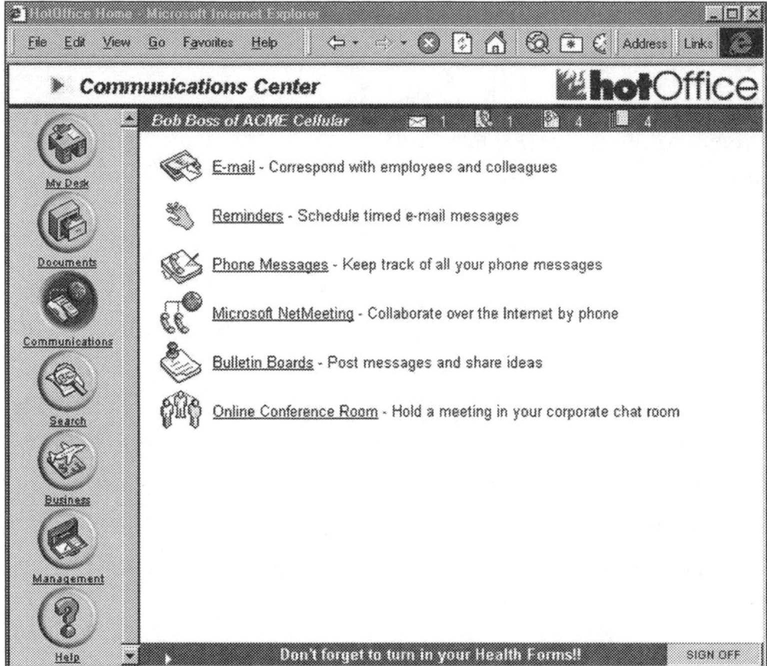

Figure 16.2 HotOffice offers intranet-style team features that you access across the Web.

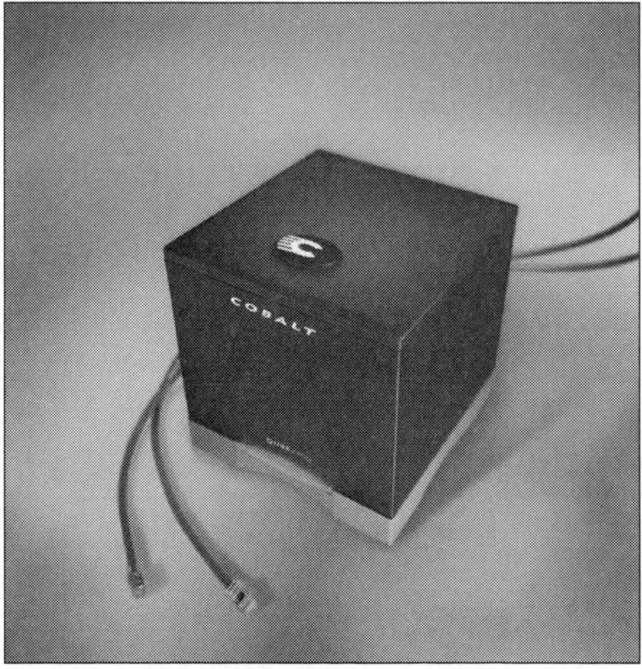

Figure 16.3 Cobalt Microserver's Qube offers hardware that you connect to your network to build intranet-style features.

network, and build a ready intranet that lets them share files. Although contrary to manufacturers' claims, the installation isn't as simple or easy as plugging and playing because you need to deal with networking and other issues, these devices are a definite step in the right direction.

At the high end, you might consider IntraNetics 97, a product that is much like the intranet systems for large businesses, but at $995 (for up to 25 users), it's priced to be attractive to smaller businesses. A product such as IntraNetics requires more technical expertise to install and maintain than the other options discussed here, but it is a high-powered alternative.

Intranets have proven their worth in large corporations, where they have improved communications and made information available to all employees. New intranet solutions are reasonably priced and far easier to use than their predecessors, and they can give a company the boost in communications that it's been wanting.

Moving On

In this chapter, I talked about ways to connect a network to the Internet, what it takes to create a Web page and Internet presence, and basics on intranets. In the next chapter, I'll talk about Dial-Up Networking—accessing your network across a phone line.

17

Dial-Up Networking

Sometimes, you absolutely, positively have to be in two places at the same time. It's the Superman syndrome—simultaneously fighting the bad guy and carrying on as Clark Kent. Often, when we're away from the office, we need to access data that's on the office network. If this is your situation, a computer and modem are, quite literally, the next best thing to being there. From a hotel room or another office, you can access your network and use it as if you were sitting in the office. In this chapter, we'll talk about different ways of dealing with this situation, as well as provide instructions on using Windows 95/98 Dial-Up Networking.

Windows Dial-Up Networking

Windows Dial-Up Networking comes with Windows 95 and Windows 98. Windows Dial-Up Server, which comes with Windows 98 (and can be used in Windows 95 after installing Plus!, Microsoft's add-on), is an integral part of Windows Dial-Up Networking that lets you use a modem-equipped computer to connect to another computer across a phone line. When you're connected, you can use the resources on the other computer (the host) and the network that it's connected to—using Network Neighborhood to browse the host network and open folders and files. In essence, you can use the same techniques that you would use on a network to access folders and directories, but you do this across a telephone line that's connected to your remote computer.

Definition, Please

host—The computer that answers the incoming call and lets a remote computer (the remote or client) connect to it.

remote or *client*—The computer that connects to the host and uses its resources.

If you would like to use Windows Dial-Up Networking, read the next section for steps to configure your server at the office, as well your remote computer, and make the connection.

Configuring A Server So Others Can Connect To It

When you configure a computer as a Dial-Up Server (host), you set it so others can connect to it and share the files on its local and network drives. And just as you set folders and files on a host to be shared across a network, you'll need to set folders and files on a local computer to be shared. For the following installations, I'm assuming that you already have a modem installed and connected to your server.

Definition, Please

local drives—The drives (typically hard drives) that are on the host system.

network drives—The network drives that a host system can access.

To use Dial-Up Networking and Dial-Up Server, both programs must first be installed on your system. To check whether these programs are installed, double-click on My Computer and look for a Dial-Up Networking folder. If these programs are installed, you should see icons for both in the folder.

To install Dial-Up Server (skip this step if it's already installed on your system):

1. Click on Start|Settings.
2. Select Control Panel.
3. Double-click on Add/Remove Programs.
4. Click on the Windows Setup tab.

5. Select Communications and click on the Details button.
6. Select Dial-Up Server and click on OK. Follow the on-screen instructions.

To configure a computer so others can dial in to it, try the following:

1. Choose Start|Programs. (You can also double-click on My Computer and then double-click on the Dial-Up Networking folder.)
2. Select Programs|Accessories|Dial-Up Networking.
3. In the Dial-Up Networking window, as shown in Figure 17.1, choose Connections and then Dial-Up Server.
4. In the Dial-Up Server window, as shown in Figure 17.2, click on Allow Caller Access. This allows others to call and connect to the computer.
5. Click on the Change Password button, enter a password in the New Password box, and then retype the password in the Confirm New Password box. When you set a password, this requires that anyone who accesses this computer via a phone line will need to know the password to connect with and use the computer. It's important that you do assign a password; otherwise, anyone who knows the phone

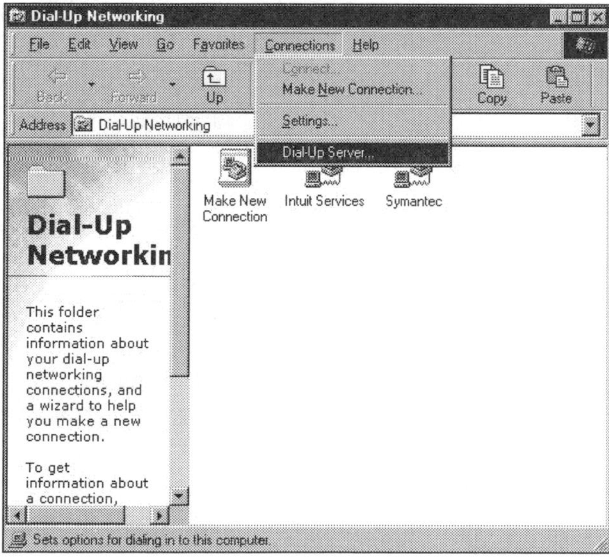

Figure 17.1 The Dial-Up Networking window.

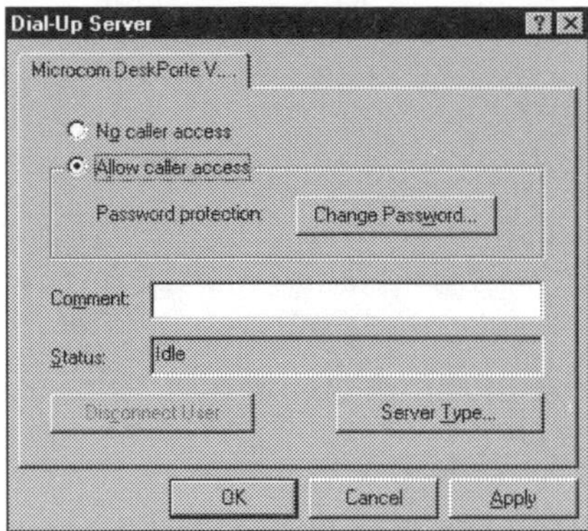

Figure 17.2 The Dial-Up Server window.

number for the PC will be able to access it, as well as the network that it's connected to.

6. If you like, you can add a comment by filling in the Comment line. This comment will appear to anyone who connects to the computer.
7. At this point, the PC is set up so that others can dial in and connect with it. Now you need to configure any disk drives and printers that remote computers will want to access. For more on how to do this, please refer to the instructions in Chapter 10. A Dial-Up Server icon should appear in your Windows Taskbar. This indicates that the server is ready to answer the phone and establish a dial-up connection.

Configuring A PC So It Can Connect To A Server

Before you can connect a PC to a server via a phone line, you have to set up the connection on the PC.

To use Dial-Up Networking, it must first be installed on your system. To check this, double-click on My Computer and look for a Dial-Up Networking folder. If you see a folder with the name Dial-Up Networking, it's installed.

To install Dial-Up Networking (skip this if it's already installed on your system):

1. Click on Start|Settings.
2. Select Control Panel.

3. Double-click on Add/Remove Programs.
4. Click on the Windows Setup tab.
5. Select Communications and click on the Details button.
6. Select Dial-Up Networking and click on OK. Follow the on-screen instructions.

To configure a computer so it can dial up and connect to a server (this process assumes that you have already installed a modem):

1. Choose Start|Programs. (You can also double-click on My Computer and then double-click on the Dial-Up Networking folder.)
2. Select Accessories|Communications|Dial-Up Networking.
3. Double-click on the Make New Connection icon in the Dial-Up Networking folder.
4. The Dial-Up Networking Wizard, as shown in Figure 17.3, will ask you to create a descriptive name for your connection and define the modem that you wish to use (if your system has more than one modem).
5. In the second section, shown in Figure 17.4, provide the wizard with dialing information that includes the phone number of the server computer.
6. Click on Finish at the end of the process.

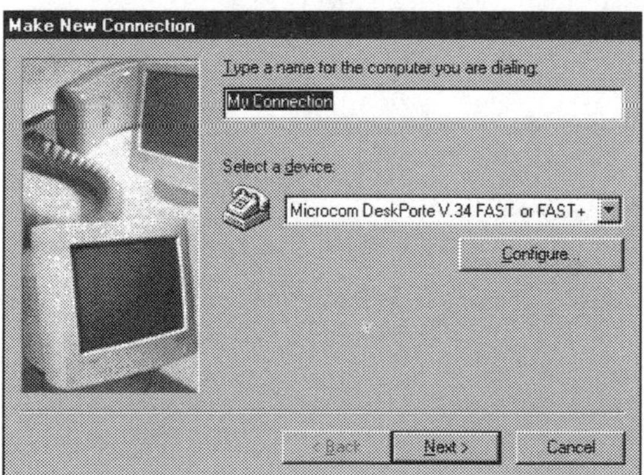

Figure 17.3 The Dial-Up Networking Wizard asks for the name of your connection and your modem.

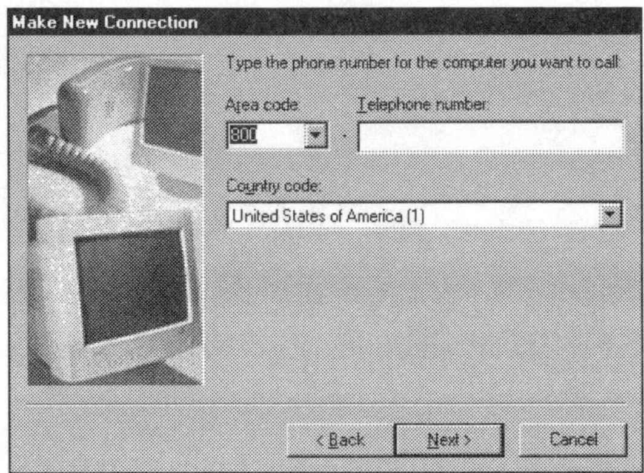

Figure 17.4 The second section of the Dial-Up Networking Wizard asks for dialing information for the server computer.

Connecting To A Server Using Windows Dial-Up

To connect a computer to a server using Windows Dial-Up, try the following:

1. Double-click on My Computer and then double-click on the Dial-Up Networking folder.
2. Double-click on the Dial-Up connection that you configured in the prior section. You'll see the dialog box that appears in Figure 17.5. Click on Connect.
3. When the computer connects (this can take a minute or so), you'll be asked to log in by providing a name and password.

When you've successfully connected to the server, a Connected To dialog box verifies that your system has made a connection and tells you how long

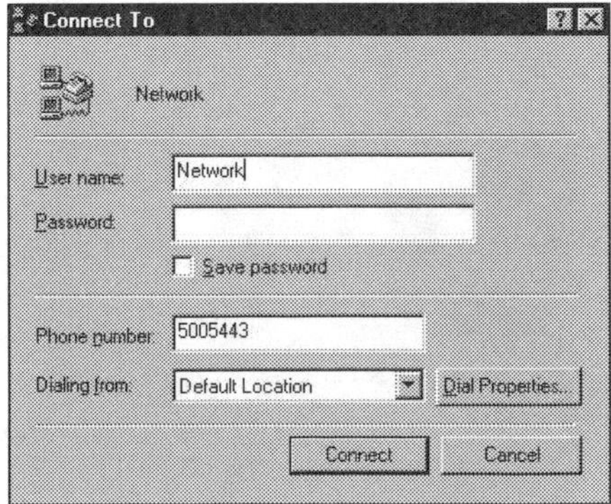

Figure 17.5 The Connect To dialog box.

you've been connected. At this point, you can use Network Neighborhood through either My Computer or Windows Explorer to use the resources on the host network and print to the network printers. You're in.

Remote Access

Remote access software, such as Compaq's Carbon Copy and Symantec's pcANYWHERE (as shown in Figure 17.6) offer a different solution for accessing a network from another location. These programs let you set up an office computer as a host and then dial in from a modem-equipped computer to connect with the office system. After establishing a link, you can remotely control the office PC just as if you were sitting in front of it—every keyboard entry and mouse movement controls the host computer at the office, and the host's screen appears on your computer. Also, you can transfer files back and forth between office and home computers.

Across a 33.6Kbps modem connection, remote access software offers decent remote-control performance. You will be able to adequately control a PC, transfer and synchronize files, and log onto the network to run applications and read email. The office (host) computer actually runs the applications and does all the processing. The software only transmits

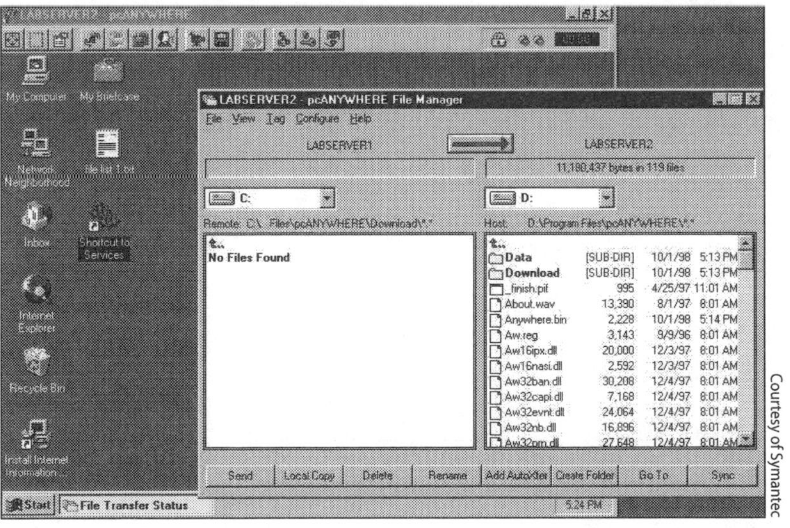

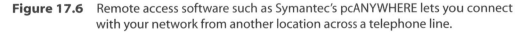

Figure 17.6 Remote access software such as Symantec's pcANYWHERE lets you connect with your network from another location across a telephone line.

commands from the remote computer to the office one and relays back changes to the display.

Because office computers must be set to receive calls from the outside, remote-access programs offer built-in security that includes user and password identification, and the ability to lock the host keyboards and make the host screens go blank, which keeps data safe from other office workers. Also, the software can perform callbacks, so that it connects only with those working at specific locations.

On the downside, it's not practical to have lots of workers leaving their systems and modems on to receive incoming calls. Also, because these connections usually happen over phone lines, the expense of long-distance calls can add up. Of course, you can make remote connections in other ways, such as through the Internet, which I'll talk about later in "The Internet" section of this chapter.

For the most part, remote access software offers a solution for those who occasionally need to access the office network to perform work on the network or on office computers, and transfer data files back and forth. To use remote access software, you will need modem-equipped computers that connect to direct-dial telephone lines.

Windows NT Remote Access Service

A more conventional dial-in approach may make use of the *Remote Access Service* (*RAS*), which is a part of Windows NT. Using its features, you can dial in to the office NT server from a remote computer and connect and work on the network, just as if you logged in from an office workstation. RAS receives the incoming call and lets you log on to the system so you can do your work. To remote users, the Network Neighborhood and all its mapped hard drives and printers appear as they do in the office, and you can pretty much work as you would during a normal office day.

The advantages of RAS are as follows:

- RAS can reduce all the incoming calls to a single network connection.
- RAS can set up a single system as your RAS server.
- The security of the RAS server is that of Windows NT.

A disadvantage with RAS is that it lets you access only the shared files and applications on the network. If you want to work from the hard drive of your office PC and access its files, you can't. To help with this, remote access software such as pcANYWHERE lets you connect to the network via RAS and then link to your own PC (which is running as a host on the network) to remotely run applications and transfer files.

Instead of dedicating a computer to handle RAS, you can purchase a device called a *remote-access server* from vendors such as Cisco and Shiva. These self-contained devices handle the processing, networking, communications, and security so that remote users can call in and connect with the network. Remote servers generally make it easier to set up and manage RAS on your network, and they can accept incoming calls from multiple telephone lines, support different network protocols, and report on usage and statistics.

You can purchase remote servers with internal modems; this lessens the potential for compatibility problems between the server and modems. You can also purchase remote servers that let you connect your existing external modems; these can accept ISDN adapters as well.

The performance that you get via RAS will depend on the speed of the dial-up connection. Remote connections across a conventional 33.6Kbps modem and telephone line will be rather slow. Because of this, RAS by itself is most useful for transferring files and not for running network applications. However, you can use an add-on package (such as Traveling Software's Remote Net-Accelerator) and technologies (such as ISDN and ADSL) that can make faster connections to speed up RAS performance.

Remote Net-Accelerator is a Dial-Up Networking enhancement program that speeds the performance of remote-access connections into Windows NT. Remote Net-Accelerator uses a system of compression, buffering, and caching to more efficiently transmit and receive data. In use, it transfers and opens remote files in about one-third to one-half of the time of a normal (un-accelerated) session, and its caching capabilities can open files in about one-fifth of the time when called up again during the same session.

Integrated Services Digital Network (ISDN) is a digital telephone line that communicates at speeds up to 128Kbps. An ISDN digital line consists of two *bearer* channels, each of which carries up to 64Kbps of data or voice information. Telecommuters can use these as two distinct lines—for example, to download files on one line while talking or faxing on the other. A process called *Bandwidth on Demand Internet Working Group (BONDING)* lets telecommuters use both channels simultaneously to send data at up to 128Kbps (the Internet Service Provider has to support this). Another technology, *Asymmetric Digital Subscriber Line* (*ADSL*), provides fast communications over copper telephone lines at speeds of 1.5Mbps to 8Mbps. Keep in mind that ADSL is available only in limited areas. For more on ISDN and ADSL, refer to Chapter 16.

The Internet

Direct telephone lines aren't the only means to connect with the office network—you can use the Internet. An advantage with Internet-based remote access is that you can call a local number to connect with your ISP, and then make the link to the office network across the Internet. Instead of costly long-distance calls, you can make local calls.

But to use Internet-based remote access, your company must have a permanent connection to the Internet, with a T1 or other direct link. And with access to the office network through the Internet, you'll need to consider your network's security. You'll definitely want to consider a *firewall*—a specialized server that prevents unauthorized entry into your network. One other potential disadvantage is that the speed of your connection across the Internet varies with the traffic at your ISP. During busy periods, you may not be able to even connect with your ISP.

All of the major remote-access programs can make connections and perform remote-control sessions across the Internet. As with dial-up solutions, the performance depends on the speed of the connection. In this case, it's the speed of the link with the ISP. Connections via 33.6Kbps modems may provide adequate remote control and decent file transfer capabilities, and, these can be improved with faster ISDN, ADSL, or cable-based connections to the ISP.

A special network connection uses something called the *Point-to-Point Tunneling Protocol* (*PPTP*) to let remote users link with office networks through the Internet. This connection creates a *virtual private network* (*VPN*) that essentially extends an office local area network (LAN) across dial-up Internet connections. From the workers' perspective, they have direct connections to the office network that let them work as if they were sitting at an office-based workstation. The VPN removes the need for long-distance calls, and its performance is as fast as the remote user's connection to the ISP. To set up a VPN, you'll have to work with your ISP.

Definition, Please

virtual private network (VPN)—A means to connect to the office network via an Internet connection.

Besides offering traditional cable television, cable companies now offer cable-based VPNs, as well as business Internet access. With impressive download transfer speeds that can, according to the cable companies, approach 10Mbps (shared), you can log onto office networks and copy files, access databases, receive email, and run applications almost as quickly as you could while sitting at a workstation in the office. Cable-based VPN services vary in price and performance with each cable company, and for now, these services are not available everywhere. For more on cable availability, refer to Chapter 16.

Working Outside The Home Or Office

Only *you* know what's best for your network. The type of access you and your users need, the amount and type of data they use and transfer, and the frequency of their network access will determine the access that best supports your network.

After deciding how users will access the office network from their homes, you can consider the technology that will give them the performance that they need. Users who only occasionally access the office and mainly transfer files back and forth can probably live with slower modem connections, and the telephone costs won't be too high. Users that live farther away can use Internet-based connections that will save money on long-distance calls, but this approach means that you have to tighten security. It's largely a matter of give and take.

Moving On

This chapter covered how to use Windows Dial-Up to access a network from locations outside your home or office, and other methods for accessing your network remotely. In the next chapter, I'll discuss network troubleshooting techniques.

18

Troubleshooting The Network

When someone in an office says, "The network is down," the common retort is likely, "So what else is new?" I hope that you won't have to consult this chapter, but if you're having trouble with your network, here it is. This chapter presents strategies for troubleshooting networks and lists symptoms, possible problems, and suggestions.

Problems With One Computer

If the problem is with a single computer on the network, here are some things you can try to check it:

- Is the computer actually on? Some computers, particularly those that come in a type of case known as an ATX case, have two power switches. So if you've been pushing the button on the front of the case, another on the back may be off. It's not uncommon to use this switch to turn off a PC when it freezes up and can't be turned off.
- Is the PC plugged into a power strip? If so, is the power strip on? Is the power strip itself getting power? Sometimes, an electrical outlet may stop working. To test this, you can get a lamp to test the outlet to make sure that it's offering power.
- Is the monitor on? Sometimes, a computer may be on, but its monitor is not. You can check to make sure that a monitor is on—most have little light-emitting diodes (LEDs) that light up when they are powered. Also, check to make sure that the monitor is receiving information from the PC by checking its cable connection. If you're not sure

about a monitor, hook up another monitor to the PC to verify that the video output is working. Another thing to check on a monitor is whether the contrast and brightness settings have been adjusted in such a way that you can't see the screen. Your kid may have been playing with the monitor and left it in such a state.

- Sometimes, a computer can't boot because it can't find a keyboard. For these reasons, be sure to check the keyboard connection, as well as all connections to the PC.

Network Problems

If you are having network problems, try the following:

- Try and perform the same network task that is giving you problems on a different computer. If the same problem occurs when you are working on another system, you can conclude that the problem is with the network, not an individual PC.
- Try logging in as yourself on someone else's PC. If a certain network task doesn't work with your ID, but does work with someone else's, you can conclude that you have a configuration problem with your ID and password.
- Sometimes shutting down and then powering up a computer can solve a network problem. To do this, be sure to use the following procedure to restart a PC:

  1. Close all of your open applications.
  2. Click on Start.
  3. Select Shut Down.
  4. Select Restart.

- In some cases, you may have to power a PC all the way down and then turn it back on. Use the following procedure to shut down a PC:

  1. Close all of your open applications.
  2. Click on Start.
  3. Select Shut Down.
  4. Select Shut Down The Computer.

Network Connections

If you think that the problem is with the network, verify that all of the network connections—including network cabling and the hub—are secure, and that the hub is plugged in.

Checking Network Cables And Connections

Here are some things to consider when checking network cables and connections:

- Make sure that all cable connections are secure. You should check the cables themselves to make sure that they have no major kinks, frays, or worn-out spots. If you can, swap cables to be sure that the problem has to do with your network or connections, and not with the cable itself. Sometimes shutting off the PCs and disconnecting, then reconnecting, the network cables can fix a problem.
- If you are using a hub, you should see a light on the hub next to a computer's cable connection that indicates that the hub recognizes your computer on the network. If the light is continuous, the cable is probably fine.
- Some network interface cards display a small light near where the network cable plugs in. If the light is continuous, the cable connection is probably fine. However, if it's blinking, there may be something wrong. For more information, check the documentation that comes with your network card.
- Check to make sure that network cabling is not running near any device that emits electromagnetic energy, including fluorescent lamps, microwave ovens, and other devices.

Checking Error Messages

Do any error messages display? Sometimes, these can provide important clues.

Checking Network Hardware And Cards

Verify that your network hardware—in particular, your network interface cards—is correctly installed, and that Windows is recognizing it.

To do this:

1. Click on Start.

2. Select Settings|Control Panel, then double-click on the System icon.
3. Click on the Device Manager tab, then double-click on the Network Adapters icon. Underneath, you should see an icon that represents your network card. If no listing for your network card displays, Windows 95/98 is not recognizing it. And if the Device Manager lists your network interface card, but a yellow circle with an exclamation point next to it displays, your new card is conflicting with another peripheral or not working properly. If this is the case, you can perform certain tasks to troubleshoot the problem:
   - Check your network interface card installation to be sure that the board is properly seated in its socket. (Be sure to shut off your PC and disconnect power before removing the cover to check it.)
   - Make sure that the card is installed in the correct type of expansion slot (ISA, PCI, VESA, etc.).
   - Some other card in your system may be using the same address spacing. Consult the documentation for your various other cards to see if conflicts exist.
   - Consult with the motherboard's manufacturer to ensure that the bus is indeed a true PCI or VESA and ask if they know of any problems with certain network cards. You can also check with the network card manufacturer for known problems or conflicts with certain systems.
   - Refer to the documentation that came with your network card for any troubleshooting suggestions and potential problems that are too specific to cover here.
   - Try moving the network card to a different slot.
   - Call tech support for the network card for further help.

Checking Conflicts With Another Computer Peripheral

Your network card may not be working correctly because it is conflicting with another computer peripheral. Try the following:

- To resolve a conflict in Windows 95, click on Start|Help|Troubleshooting and select If You Have A Hardware Conflict, then follow the on-screen instructions to resolve the conflict.

- To resolve a conflict in Windows 98, click on Start|Help|Troubleshooting|Windows 98 Troubleshooters|Hardware Conflicts, then follow the on-screen instructions to resolve the conflict. If you're not sure whether you have installed your network card correctly, click on Start|Help|Troubleshooting|Windows 98 Troubleshooters and select I Am Unable To Install A Network Adapter.

General System Troubleshooting

When something goes wrong with your system, your first inclination might be to open up the case immediately and start poking around—get under the hood, so to speak. But most of the time, you can trace problems to something that you just did, which has nothing to do with the computer's hardware. Some computer problems that I've seen are system conflicts—unexplained phenomena that seem to belong in the Twilight Zone.

When something goes wrong with a computer, it can be hard to determine exactly which component is faulty. Sometimes the culprit is something that appears to be unrelated to the apparent problem. I'll talk about strategies you can use to identify such problems in the following sections of this chapter.

When something stops working, take a minute to think:

- Did you recently add a new component?
- Did you recently install a new software package?
- Did you recently change any settings in your system or operating system?

If the answer to any of these questions is yes, chances are good that you just introduced a new system conflict or something isn't configured correctly. Also, be sure to check all of your PC's plugs and connectors. It's not unusual for someone to accidentally unplug a monitor connection, power cord, mouse, phone, printer, or anything else in the general vicinity. I can't tell you how many times I've unsuccessfully tried to print something and found that I had dislodged the printer cable by accident.

Some things you can do to troubleshoot the system include:

- Re-creating the problem is a key strategy. Once you can make the problem surface consistently, you can begin to see what components relate to it; then, you can home in on it and solve it. Try to retrace everything you did before the glitch appeared and see if it shows up again. If you can identify what software or hardware may be involved in the process, you'll have a valuable clue as to what's going on.
- Look at the LEDs on your modem, hard drive, or CD-ROM drive to see if they're trying to access the system when the lockup occurs. If so, they might be involved.
- Software can cause internal conflicts. Newly installed software may be looking for hardware that doesn't exist or may be configured incorrectly. Try to identify the software that is causing the problem, then work on its configuration. Software problems usually recur in the same place while you're performing the same task.
- One thing that's easy to do is reinstall the software package in question. It may configure itself correctly and solve the problem. If that doesn't work, you can uninstall the program completely to see if your computer now runs smoothly. If, after you remove the software, your computer runs smoothly, you can begin checking configurations of your hardware components as they relate to the problem software.
- Incorrect complementary metal-oxide semiconductor (CMOS) configurations can also cause problems, and these don't always immediately surface. When something goes wrong, check your system's CMOS to make sure that all configurations are correct and that they agree with those listed by each component's manufacturer.
- If a board isn't working, you may have an internal conflict. Two or more devices are fighting over the same computing resources, with the result that one of the devices isn't working. In this case, Windows 95 or 98 can help you troubleshoot the problem. Access Help in Windows 95 as follows:

  1. Click on Start|Help|Troubleshooting.
  2. In the list of troubleshooting topics, select If You Have A Hardware Conflict. Follow the on-screen suggestions.

To resolve a conflict in Windows 98:

1. Click on Start|Help|Troubleshooting|Windows 98 Troubleshooters|Hardware Conflicts.
2. Follow the on-screen instructions to resolve the conflict.

- If you've checked everything from the outside and the problem persists, it's time to open your computer and check the internal cables, board installations, and chips. Make sure all boards and connectors are seated where they should be and all cables are connected tightly (look for loose and dangling cables). Also, it's not unusual for cables to stop working because they've been nicked or pinched by boards, the case, or other parts. If so, a new cable will fix the problem. It's probably a good idea to replace any cable that has a nick in it; one with even a serious crimp can be suspect. Check that all expansion cards are seated properly in their slots and that anything connected to them is secure.
- If you have just installed a new component, take it out and see if the system works. Also, you may have installed a board improperly, so it wasn't making a good connection (sometimes a properly installed board shifts position when you put in the retaining screw). A new component can conflict with existing ones, in which case your system should work immediately when you remove the culprit component. Then you can check the part's documentation to see how to configure it so that it will address system resources differently.

If you've tried all of these general troubleshooting suggestions and are still having a problem, you will need to do more specific diagnostic checks to try to determine which system component is the culprit. When you figure out which component is causing the problem, you're more than halfway to the solution.

Isolating A Faulty Component

After you check for and resolve system conflicts, most of the troubleshooting you can do will involve looking for faulty components. When your computer won't run and you have no way of guessing which component is causing a conflict, it's best to remove components gradually from your system, one by one, until the problem clears up. Here are some suggestions for solving component problems:

- Set your computer on a workbench and boot it. When the problem occurs, turn off your computer, remove a nonessential expansion board—the sound card, for example—and reboot. If everything works correctly, then the problem or conflict is probably with the sound card. You can continue this process of systematic elimination until the computer operates properly. This method has worked well for me.
- However, an even better way to locate suspect components is to use two similar computers and swap components between them. If you do have two systems, simply remove a component from the system that isn't working and place it in the system that is working correctly. When the working computer stops functioning or the newly installed component doesn't do what it's supposed to do, you've found the culprit. Now, simply replace it.
- Don't forget about cables. When a printer, mouse, monitor, or hard drive fails, often the culprit isn't the component itself, but rather the cable that connects it. Fortunately, a cable is a fairly low-cost item to buy and replace. (Sometimes cables come undone within a system. Just reconnect them.)
- Finally, if a component isn't working, don't hesitate to call the manufacturer for help. You can also visit a company's site on the Web, or on an online service such as CompuServe or America Online for tech support.

More Specific Troubleshooting

This section provides troubleshooting tips for specific problems you may be having. If you don't find your particular problem described here, the suggestions provided for a similar problem may prove to be useful.

If Your Hard Drive Is Failing

Try these suggestions for hard drive failure problems:

- If you have hard drive problems, your primary task is to retrieve and save your data. If you have a recent backup, great. If you don't, try booting from a floppy, then access your hard drive and copy your data to floppies if you can. If you can succeed up to this point, you can troubleshoot without the risk of losing data. Once you have your data backed up, you're free to work with your drive.

- If you can boot from a floppy and access your hard drive, chances are that your hard drive is in working order, but something has gone wrong with its configuration. If you see a message that says "No ROM Basic—System Halted," run FDISK (see the following instructions) and be sure that the hard drive that is used to boot the system is set as the active drive.

Caution

Be careful when working with FDISK. If you give the utility the wrong command, it can wipe out your disk's partition and all your data. FDISK is a helpful, but potentially dangerous, tool.

- Before you do anything with your drive, check your CMOS setup. Your drive may be configured incorrectly. Check the parameters listed in your hard drive's documentation to see if they match.
- Another thing you can do before you actually touch the drive is run any software disk utilities, such as Norton Utilities, that can evaluate and fix your hard drive.

Running ScanDisk (Windows 95 Or 98)

If you are running Windows 95 or 98, you can run ScanDisk by doing the following:

1. Click on Start|Programs|Accessories (this is the default; your system may be different) |System Tools|ScanDisk.
2. Within ScanDisk, highlight the hard drive in question, check Thorough and Automatically Fix Errors, then click on the Start button. ScanDisk evaluates your hard drive and repairs any problems that it finds.

Running ScanDisk And FDISK (Without Windows)

If you can't run Windows, you can activate ScanDisk and FDISK by doing the following:

1. After booting your computer from a floppy, you should see a blank screen and the A:\> prompt.

2. Type the following commands and press the Enter button after each line.

```
CD\Windows\Command
Dir *.exe/p
```

3. You'll see a list of files with ".EXE" in the extension (SCANDISK.EXE, FDISK.EXE, and so on).
4. To run ScanDisk, type "Scandisk" and then press Enter.
5. To run FDISK, type "Fdisk" and then press Enter.

If your hard drive isn't working after you run the software utilities, open up your computer and check the cables and connections to make sure everything is in order.

If these steps fail to yield results, you can move to more drastic measures:

- Although there are ways to reconstruct the drive step by step, I recommend using a disk utility such as Norton Disk Doctor to do this, because many of the steps are very involved. You also can use the FDISK command to see if it acknowledges that the hard drive exists, then repartition and reformat your hard drive (you can follow the instructions in Chapter 22). Remember that when you do this, you will lose all the data and programs on your hard drive. Make sure that everything is backed up.

Caution

When you use FDISK to repartition your drive, you will lose all the data and programs on your drive.

- If you just can't access the hard drive, you probably have a serious crash at hand. If the drive is still covered under warranty (some companies cover them for up to three years), you can contact the company to get a replacement. Otherwise, you may have to buy a new one.
- A hard drive often will give some warning before it crashes. You may notice that the drive is making funny noises or taking a lot longer than usual to access data. If you see your drive acting up in any way, run, don't walk, to your floppy disk drawer or tape drive and back up all your data.

Caution

When you copy data from a suspect hard drive that appears to be failing, don't copy the data onto your normal backup disks or media. If the drive is acting up, it might write corrupted data on top of your older backups, and then you'll lose everything.

By the way, specialized companies are available that can retrieve data from crashed drives, but this service is very expensive. In fact, it's really only for large companies that can afford such rates. Your best insurance for the data on a drive is to routinely back it up.

If You Can't Read A Floppy

Sometimes when you insert a floppy disk to be read by your computer, you'll hear an incessant grinding noise, which means that the drive just can't read the disk. Sometimes taking the floppy out and then putting it back in will work (it has to do with the alignment of the disk in the drive). Here are some other things you can try:

- If there's a problem with your floppy drive, your system may tell you when you boot up that you have a bad floppy drive. In this case, either the controller card or the floppy drive has failed. To test them, you can swap components between machines, as described previously. Before you do that, you might open up your computer and check that all of the power connections and data cables are in place.
- Although floppy drives do get out of alignment now and then, it's more likely that the disk that you're trying to read has failed. The first thing I would try is to see if another computer can read the disk, preferably the computer that originally formatted the disk. If the other computer can read the disk, you can at least get to your data and copy it to a disk that's been formatted on your computer.
- To evaluate and possibly repair a bad floppy disk, you can run a utility such as Norton Disk Doctor, if you have it, or, if you're running Windows 95/98, you can use DiskScan. To run DiskScan, do the following:

  1. Make sure the questionable floppy is in the drive.
  2. Click on Start|Programs|Accessories (this is the default; your system may be different) |System Tools|ScanDisk.

3. Within ScanDisk, highlight your floppy drive, check Thorough and Automatically Fix Errors, then click on the Start button. ScanDisk evaluates your floppy disk and repairs any problems that it finds.

- If your floppy drive is out of alignment, you can usually tell, because other machines will have a hard time reading a disk formatted with a misaligned drive. As with a hard drive, it's a good idea to try and salvage any important data that you can from the floppy, using a utility if necessary, and check your floppy drive. If it looks as if your floppy drive is not functioning properly, you can have it repaired, but it's less expensive to buy a new floppy drive and install it yourself.

If Your System Locks Up

Periodic lockups are difficult to trace. A computer that's hard to boot when it's cold may indicate a hardware problem. Although many lockups can be attributed to software conflicts, you can use the process of elimination to troubleshoot the hardware. Remember that if it's software, you might be able to re-create the problem.

If you get a "Parity Error" message, you'll have to use the process of elimination to see which component is causing the problem. This message indicates that something has gone awry in memory, but it doesn't tell which component is faulty.

If Screens Don't Look Right

Try the following to correct screen problems:

- Check your video card installation, CMOS settings, and board settings in Windows.
- Recheck your video card installation to be sure that the board is properly seated in its socket.
- Check your system setup to make sure that you haven't set the software for a different video card or monitor.
- See that the monitor cable is fastened securely to the output port of the video card.
- Another card in your system may be using the same addressing spacing. If this is the case, you'll have to consult the documentation for

your various cards to see if conflicts are present. One simple step that sometimes works is to move the video card to a different slot. Another possibility is that driver remnants from your old video card may be interfering with the new one. You'll want to remove these.

Checking A Video Card

To check that your video card is working properly, you can try the following:

1. Choose Start|Settings|Control Panel.
2. Double-click on the System icon.
3. Click on the Device Manager tab, and then expand the Display Adapters listing. Under this heading, you should see the name of your video card, along with an icon. If the icon looks like a small monitor, according to Windows, everything is fine with your display adapter. However, if you see a small yellow balloon with an exclamation point in it next to the listing of your display adapter, Windows is telling you that a problem is present with the installation of your video card. To fix this, refer to the following instructions. If you see no listing for your video card under Display Adapters, then your board isn't installed. You'll need to reinstall the drivers for your video card.

Troubleshooting Video Problems

If you see a yellow balloon with an exclamation point next to the listing of your display card, it may be conflicting with another hardware device. To fix this, you can have Windows 95 help you troubleshoot the problem by trying the following:

1. Choose Start|Help|Troubleshooting.
2. In the list of troubleshooting topics, select If You Have A Hardware Conflict. Follow the on-screen suggestions.

Access Help in Windows 98 by performing the following:

1. Click on Start|Help|Troubleshooting.
2. In the list of troubleshooting topics, select Windows 98 Troubleshooters, then select Hardware Conflict. Follow the on-screen suggestions.

Other things you can try include:

- You can consult with the motherboard's manufacturer to learn if there are any known problems with certain video cards. You also can call the video card manufacturer to check on known problems or conflicts with certain systems.
- If your screen is flickering, the picture is scrambled, or the display is small, you may have to make adjustments to your monitor's horizontal and vertical frequencies. Be sure that you don't set your card to a frequency that exceeds that of your monitor. You can also try adjusting the settings for your display card—you may have it set at a resolution and/or color depth that your monitor can't support. To fix this, you can try the following:
    1. Click on Start|Settings|Control Panel.
    2. Double-click on the Display icon.
    3. Click on the Settings tab.
    4. Reduce the color palette so your display card works with fewer colors (a lower color depth) and reduce the display area to show a lower-resolution screen.
- Refer to the documentation that came with your video card for any troubleshooting suggestions and potential problems that are too specific to cover here.
- If your screen comes up blank, check your video and monitor first for power and connections. If you can, try installing the video card in another system to see if it works; if it doesn't work, it has probably gone bad.

If You're Having CD-ROM Problems

If your CD-ROM drive can't read a CD, check your configurations. You can look at Windows Explorer to see if it recognizes that your drive exists. If not, try these suggestions:

- If your system doesn't recognize that you have a CD-ROM drive installed, check to see if anything has changed in your software configurations. Consult the documentation for your CD-ROM drive to verify the correct configuration.

- Examine all cables to ensure that they are securely attached, and check that they are free from crimps and nicks. If you have a suspect cable, replace it.
- If your CD-ROM drive connects to a separate board, be sure that your controller board is seated properly.
- Be sure that the port is active (you'll have to check the board's documentation), and check to see that you don't have two ports on at the same time that may be conflicting with each other. This can happen, for example, if you install a new sound board with an active port but also have a proprietary port on another card installed to control your CD-ROM.

Checking Your CD-ROM Drive

To check that your CD-ROM drive is working properly within Windows, try the following:

1. Click on Start|Settings|Control Panel.
2. Double-click on the System icon.
3. Click on the Device Manager tab, then double-click on CDROM. You should see the name of your CD-ROM drive along with an icon. If the icon looks like a tiny CD and drive, everything is fine with your drive, according to Windows 95. However, if you see a small yellow balloon with an exclamation point in it next to the listing of your CD-ROM drive, Windows is telling you that a problem with its installation is present. To fix this, you should reinstall the drivers for your CD-ROM drive.

If You're Having Printing Problems

If you're having general problems with a shared printer, try the following:

- Make sure the shared printer is powered up and online.
- Make sure that the network computers are on.
- Double-check all of those network connections that include hubs and cables. If you are using a hub, you should see a light on the hub next to a computer's cable connection that indicates that the hub recognizes your computer on the network.

- Check the printer cables.
- Do any error messages display? These can provide important clues.

Checking A Computer For File Sharing

If you're trying to share a file to be printed, be sure that the computer that stores the files is set to share them. To do so:

1. Click on Start|Settings|Control Panel, and then double-click on the Network icon.
2. On the Configuration tab, click on the File And Print Sharing button, and verify that the box that's labeled I Want To Be Able To Give Others Access To My Files is checked. Also, you can double-click on My Computer and view the drives. A hand underneath a drive icon indicates that the drive is a shared drive.
3. Verify that no restrictions are set on accessing the drive.

Checking For Printer Sharing

If you're trying to share a printer, be sure that the printer is set to be shared. To do this:

1. Double-click on My Computer. Double-click on the Printers folder.
2. Right-click on the name of the printer that should be shared across the network, and select Properties.
3. Click on the Sharing tab to display the Sharing portion of the printer's Properties dialog box. Verify that the printer is set to be shared. Also, you can double-click on My Computer, open the Printers folder, and view the printers. A hand will appear underneath the printer when it's set to be shared.
4. Verify that no restrictions are set on accessing the printer.

What To Do If Nothing Is Printing

If your printer isn't printing:

- First, check that the printer has paper in the tray from which you are printing.
- Be sure that your printer has toner or enough ink left in its cartridges to print. Most newer printers indicate when they are low on toner or inks.

- If a printer has two paper trays, be sure that your software is configured to print from the correct one. See that your software is set properly to output to your printer. It's easy to accidentally change this, particularly if you regularly use more than one printer.
- Check that the printer is set to Online, so it's ready to print. For more information, consult the documentation that came with your printer. If it doesn't help, reset the printer and try again. Shut the printer off and then back on, run the printer self-test (if it has one), and try again.
- If nothing seems to be out of place with the printer or its connections, you might test whether it will print from another PC.
- Two other suspect areas are the printer cable and the parallel port. Try swapping cables and see if that clears up the problem. If you recently extended your parallel cable, this could be a problem, because the PC isn't able to send the data far enough. You might check with the cable's manufacturer to see how far you can extend a printer connection.
- You can also check to see if you're having a problem with your cable or parallel port.

Checking Your Windows Printer Installation

To check that your printer is properly installed in Windows, do the following:

1. Click on Start|Settings|Control Panel.
2. Double-click on the Printers icon.
3. If you see an icon for your printer, this means that Windows is recognizing it and everything appears to be fine. But if the icon appears somewhat transparent, this means that Windows can't work with it. Recheck the connections and follow the directions in the next step.
4. If your printer doesn't appear at all, it means that it's not installed. In this case, double-click on the Add Printer icon from within the Printers folder in My Computer, and follow the on-screen instructions to add your printer.

Checking Your Printer's Parallel Port

If Windows 95 is looking for your printer and can't find it, something may be wrong with your parallel port (the computer's port that normally connects with a printer). To check that your parallel port is working properly within Windows, you can try the following:

1. Click on Start|Settings|Control Panel.
2. Double-click on the System icon.
3. Click on the Device Manager tab, and then double-click on the Ports (COM & LPT) listing. Under this heading, you should see a listing of your computer's LPT port along with an icon. If the icon looks like a tiny cable and connector, everything is fine with your parallel port, according to Windows. However, if you see a small yellow balloon with an exclamation point in it next to the listing of your parallel port, Windows 95 is telling you that a problem with its installation is present. To fix this, refer to the instructions in the next section.

Fixing A System Conflict With Your Parallel Port

In Windows 95, to fix a system conflict that may involve your parallel port:

1. Click on Start|Help|Troubleshooting.
2. In the list of troubleshooting topics, select If You Have A Hardware Conflict. Follow the on-screen suggestions.

In Windows 98, perform the following steps:

1. Choose Start|Help|Troubleshooting.
2. In the list of troubleshooting topics, select Windows 98 Troubleshooters, and then select Hardware Conflict. Follow the on-screen suggestions.

If you see no listing for your video card under Ports (COM & LPT), then your port isn't installed. You'll need to reinstall the drivers for your computer's parallel port. See the next section.

Reinstalling Parallel Port Drivers

To reinstall your parallel port drivers in Windows:

1. Click on Start|Settings|Control Panel.
2. Double-click on the Add New Hardware icon.
3. Follow the on-screen instructions and ask Windows to search for your hardware. You'll probably need to have your Windows installation CD handy so the program can copy drivers from it.

Lack Of Communication—Modem Problems

If you use your software to dial a number and nothing happens (with an external modem, you should hear a dial tone and then the number dialing), something is probably wrong with your modem or communication settings. In this case, you'll want to recheck your modem installation within your software. Make sure that you have the correct port and baud rate set. Also, if you selected your modem from a list during the configuration, select another modem from the same manufacturer. If your problem is a driver, this might work.

If your modem isn't specifically listed in the program's installation, you may have to check and set parity, data bits, stop bits, and local echo on or off, according to the documentation. Just to make sure that the problem isn't a particular software program, you might try your modem with another piece of software. For example, if you're having problems with a fax program, you can set up and run America Online or a communications package. If the modem works, the problem is the software.

Checking And Troubleshooting A Modem In Windows

To check that your modem is working properly within Windows, you can try the following:

1. Click on Start|Settings|Control Panel.
2. Double-click on the System icon.
3. Click on the Device Manager tab, and then double-click on Modems. Under this heading, you should see a listing of your modem along with an icon. If the icon looks like a tiny telephone, everything is fine with your modem, according to Windows 95. However, if you see a small yellow balloon with an exclamation point in it next to the listing of your modem, Windows is telling you that a problem with its installation is present.

To fix the problem if you are running Windows 95:

1. Click on Start|Help|Troubleshooting.
2. In the list of troubleshooting topics, select If You Have A Hardware Conflict. Follow the on-screen suggestions.

You can access similar Help in Windows 98 by performing the following steps:

1. Click on Start|Help|Troubleshooting.
2. In the list of troubleshooting topics, select Windows 98 Troubleshooters, and then select Hardware Conflict. Follow the on-screen suggestions.

Reinstalling Modem Drivers

If you see no listing for your modem under Modems, then your modem isn't installed. You'll need to reinstall its drivers. To do this in Windows:

1. Click on Start|Settings|Control Panel.
2. Double-click on the Add New Hardware icon.
3. Follow the on-screen instructions and ask Windows to search for your hardware. You'll probably need to have your Windows installation CD handy so the program can copy drivers from it.

Keyboard Problems

If your system stops recognizing your keyboard, more than likely there's a problem with your keyboard. Try these suggestions to solve the problem:

- Try the keyboard on another system to see if it works there. If it doesn't, it's probably time to buy a new keyboard, a relatively inexpensive prospect.
- If your system doesn't recognize your keyboard, it should tell you as it boots up. I've found that I can sometimes unplug the keyboard and then plug it back in to fix the problem (usually temporarily).

Mouse Traps

If your mouse should suddenly stop working, chances are good that you've changed something in your system that is now conflicting with your mouse or that something has gone wrong with the mouse cable. If this continues even after you reboot your computer a few times, here are some suggestions:

- First, check your mouse's connections. Is its connector securely plugged into its port?

- Go into your system and check to see if your mouse settings are correct. Windows usually offers a mouse utility in the Control Panel (this varies with the type of mouse you have). You can refer to it to see if the system is recognizing your mouse. When your system doesn't see a mouse, it will usually tell you on bootup. You probably have a system conflict and will have to evaluate your system and change the configuration of your system's devices.

Checking And Troubleshooting A Mouse Within Windows (95 Or 98)

To check that your mouse is working properly within Windows 95, you can try the following:

1. Click on Start|Settings|Control Panel.
2. Double-click on the System icon.
3. Click on the Device Manager tab, and then double-click on the Mouse listing. You should see a listing of your mouse along with an icon. If the icon looks like a tiny mouse, according to Windows, everything is fine with your mouse. However, if you see a small yellow balloon with an exclamation point in it next to the listing of your mouse, Windows is telling you that a problem with its installation is present.

To fix the problem, you can try the following:

1. Click on Start|Help|Troubleshooting.
2. In the list of troubleshooting topics, select If You Have A Hardware Conflict. Follow the on-screen suggestions.

You can access similar Help in Windows 98 by performing the following steps:

1. Click on Start|Help|Troubleshooting.
2. In the list of troubleshooting topics, select Windows 98 Troubleshooters, and then select Hardware Conflict. Follow the on-screen suggestions.

Reinstalling Mouse Drivers

If you see no listing for your mouse, then it's not installed; you'll need to install the drivers for it. To do this in Windows:

1. Click on Start|Settings|Control Panel.
2. Double-click on the Add New Hardware icon.
3. Follow the on-screen instructions and ask Windows to search for your hardware. You'll probably need to have your Windows installation CD handy so the program can copy drivers from it.

Access Help in Windows 98 by performing the following steps:

1. Click on Start|Help|Troubleshooting.
2. In the list of troubleshooting topics, select Windows 98 Troubleshooters, and then select Hardware Conflict. Follow the on-screen suggestions.

Here are some other strategies:

- To ensure that your mouse is functioning properly, you can install it on another PC to see if it works. If it does, then the problem lies in your system's configuration; if it doesn't, it's probably time to take a close look at that mouse and possibly buy a new one.
- If your mouse's pointer is not responding to your movements, it may be dirty. To remedy this, you can usually remove the mouse ball and clean it and the rollers on the inside of the mouse. For more information, consult the documentation that came with your mouse.

Moving On

In this chapter, I talked about general strategies you can use to troubleshoot your system and network if you run into problems. Using these suggestions, you should have a reasonable chance of identifying problems and fixing them. In the next chapter, I'll talk about ways that you can improve the performance of your network.

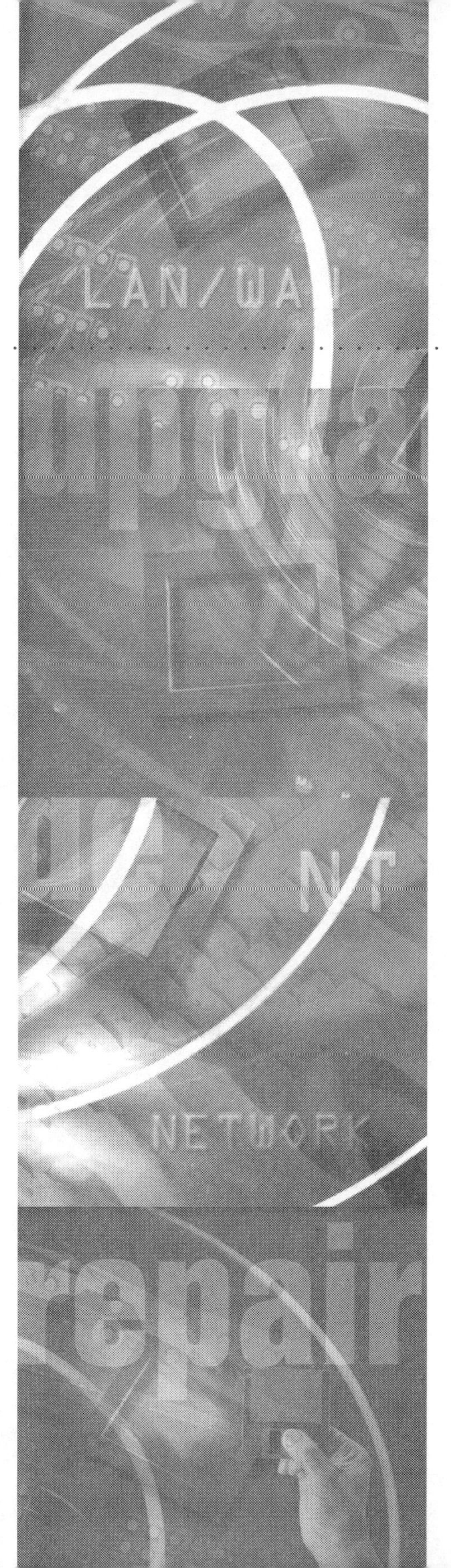

Part 4

Upgrading Your Network

19

Improving Your Network

Whereas the chapters that follow this one talk about ways to improve your network's performance by either upgrading components in a system or purchasing entire new systems, this chapter discusses things you might consider doing that aren't as much work. If you're the type who likes to fill your car with premium gas instead of buying a new engine, you may find something here that can add to the performance of your network.

Getting Peak Performance From The Server

If your server is slow—it takes forever to retrieve and open files or print documents—the first thing to check is whether your server is running at its peak. Here are things that you can try, whether you have a peer-to-peer or server-based network.

- Be sure that no active screensavers are on your system. Although screensavers do display those cool flying toasters and 3D pipes, the fun visuals take their share of processing power. So if you're running a screensaver on a server, the system won't be running at its best. To improve performance, you can turn a screensaver off by performing the following:

  1. Click on Start|Settings|Control Panel.
  2. Double-click on the Display icon, then click on the Screensaver tab.
  3. Under Screensaver, select None, then click on OK.

- Schedule your anti-virus software to scan a system's hard drives at a time when you and others in your office aren't working, such as early in the morning or late at night. Virus checkers work by scanning the hard drives of a system and looking for the signatures of any viruses that may be present, which takes processing power.
- If you often send large numbers of faxes at a time, schedule them to be sent late at night. You will not only free the resource from having to perform double-duty (computing and sending faxes at the same time), you can also take advantage of the lower phone rates that are available at night and keep the telephone line free during the day.
- Run large print jobs—those 800+ mail merges, for instance—late at night or during lunch hours, thus keeping the print queues free for other print jobs.

Checking The Cables

Sometimes a network that's performing poorly has wiring that has deteriorated over time. To test for bad wiring, replace a cable to see if performance improves. In particular, look for cables that have kinks in them or may have been squashed. In these cases, it's a good idea to replace the cable.

Also, if a network cable is running near sources of electromagnetic interference—flourescent lights, for example—the interference can lower a network's performance.

Another common problem can occur if you run a network cable too far. Doing so can cause some degradation in the signal, which will be translated into slow network performance. This problem probably won't show up in small offices, but if you're routing cable to the opposite end of a large building, you may want to consider getting a *repeater*—a device that can boost the signal.

Swapping Computers' Functions

You can often switch network computers to obtain improved network performance. For systems that act as servers, you usually want the fastest and most powerful machines. On the other hand, you don't necessarily need a fast system if you dedicate a computer solely to a specific task and no one is using it as a workstation.

Here's how this works. On a peer-to-peer network, in theory, every computer is a resource to every other computer, and often a computer that is being used to share a key resource (for example, the printer) is a computer that someone in the office is using as a main work computer. If someone is conducting database searches while the computer is sharing the printer, this slows down the printing performance for everyone else on the network. And if everyone in the office is constantly waiting for documents to print, you'll want the fastest computer that you have for this job.

On the other hand, if you have a slow system on your network that no one wants to use anymore, such as an old 486-based computer, you can connect this system to the printer and use it exclusively for managing printouts. Because the computer is dedicated to a single task, it doesn't have to be a speed demon. By simply swapping computers for different purposes, you can increase the performance of your network and remove bottlenecks.

Upgrading Components

Even though most bottlenecks on a small network are probably not due to the network connection, you can see that network performance increases by replacing the components with higher-performance network hardware. The easiest way to do this is to replace your hub and network interface cards with faster 100Mbps Ethernet hardware, which sends information at roughly 10 times the speed of a conventional 10Mbps Ethernet. As you would expect, the 100Mbps hardware is more expensive than 10Mbps hardware; however, if you need the performance increase, you may want to consider this option.

So you can continue to use your existing investment of 10Mbps network hardware, here are some considerations:

- You can purchase 10/100Mbps network interface cards that will work at 10Mbps when connected to a 10Mbps hub and at 100Mbps when connected to a 100Mbps hub. Install the 100Mbps hardware to the crucial servers and keep the 10Mbps hardware with the workstations.

- You can purchase 100Mbps hubs that accept both 10Mbps and 100Mbps connections. This way, you don't have to replace all of the network cards in all of the systems in your network. Just replace those that need the peformance upgrade.

If you find that the suggestions here don't give your network the performance that it needs, it's probably time to upgrade your existing systems or purchase new ones.

Moving On

In this chapter, I talked about performance enhancements for your network that you can consider before you upgrade your computers or purchase new ones. In the next chapter, I'll talk about hardware upgrades that you can perform to improve the speed of the servers and workstations on your network.

20

Ways To Upgrade Your Server And Workstations

If your computer systems are too slow, you know the symptoms: Applications take forever to load; database searches take an eternity to find, sort, and display data; computations are slow because your network is constantly running out of space. Although you can purchase brand-new systems, you can save money (the shoestring angle, once again) by upgrading your computers instead.

Definition, Please

Upgrading means that you replace key components in a system to increase its speed and give it more storage capacity.

By buying select components and adding them to your workstations or server, you can get much of the benefit of newer and faster PCs. And it costs far less to replace a few components than to buy an entire new system, even though the industry continually introduces better computers at lower prices.

If you're thinking about upgrading, you probably have a reason. If you answer yes to any of the following questions, it's probably time to upgrade:

- Does it seem to take forever for your applications to load?
- Are your applications unable to quickly handle your data? For example, are you unable to quickly scroll from one part of a document to another part?

- Do database searches take an eternity?
- Does your computer often keep you waiting?
- Have you avoided purchasing new software or a new operating system because your computer can't run it?
- Are you constantly running out of storage space on your workstations or on your server?

Let's talk briefly about the major areas that you should consider upgrading: a system's memory, hard drives, motherboard, and central processing unit (CPU). In Chapters 21, 22, and 23, I'll show you how to perform the upgrades.

Memory

Memory plays a key role in a system's performance, and adding additional memory to a computer is one of the best performance-enhancing upgrades you can make. If you're working with lots of large applications with equally large data files, the more memory you can provide, the better.

In particular, if you need to use your system to *multitask*—that is, to switch between programs running simultaneously under Windows—you should have a lot of RAM on your system. When you run Windows programs, they usually load into RAM or memory. The more programs you use and the larger they are, the more RAM they take up. When Windows runs out of RAM, it starts using a *swap file* (which acts like an overflow buffer for applications and information) on your hard drive as if it were memory (this is called *virtual memory)*. Because a hard drive is a lot slower than memory, using your hard drive as memory slows down your system. Adding more RAM increases your system's performance.

Definition, Please

A *swap file* is a part of your hard drive that's set aside to accept overflow of programs and data from RAM or memory. When Windows uses your hard drive in this way, it's called virtual memory.

If you have a system that is being used as a server, you'll probably want lots of RAM for it—depending on how many stations it's supporting. Keep in mind that it's not unusual for servers to have 128MB or even 256MB of RAM. For more on making memory upgrades and the types of memory, refer to Chapter 21.

Tip—Cost

When comparing the cost of RAM, determine the cost per megabyte: Simply divide the price of the RAM chip by its size in megabytes. The lower the number, the better the deal.

Hard Drives

Like a desk or file drawer, your hard drive stores all the applications and data that you use on your computer. On a network, a system that's being used as a server may be used to store the applications and data for a number of people. And, like a desk or file drawer, a hard drive can never be too large.

A hard drive is different from random access memory (RAM) because it retains data even when the computer is shut off. When you work with your software or files, the hard drive loads these into memory, where the computer can use and process them.

Today, applications continue to get bigger, and hard drives continue to grow. Operating systems such as Windows 95 and 98, and many business applications—such as word processors and spreadsheets—require huge chunks of disk space.

Currently, the standard sizes for hard drives start at 6.4GB and go up from there. Over 6,000MB may sound like a nearly endless expanse, but it doesn't take a lot to fill it, particularly when it's on a network.

Today, *enhanced integrated drive electronics* (*EIDE*) remain popular and are on most Pentium systems; the newer Ultra DMA/33 drives are found on the latest systems. EIDE is similar to the earlier *integrated drive electronics* (*IDE*), but can handle larger drives, transfer data at a higher rate, and support tape and CD-ROM drives. Ultra DMA/33 is a high-speed data transfer feature that can transfer data at up to 33.3 MB per second; it uses the same standard 40-pin IDE interface cable that connects to most Pentium motherboards.

Ultra DMA/33 drives are backwardly compatible and will work with your existing EIDE controllers. If you purchase and upgrade to a new motherboard, the board's hard drive controller will undoubtedly support Ultra DMA/33 drives but will also be able to run your EIDE drives.

Another standard drive that is still popular is the kind that conforms to the *small computer system interface (SCSI)*. SCSI-2 is immensely popular for use on high-end servers. If you are using SCSI-2 with your PC, it does have advantages, but EIDE and Ultra DMA/33 drives are the clear favorites and cost less.

Definition, Please

SCSI, which stands for small computer system interface, is a popular standard for connecting peripherals, such as hard drives and CD-ROMs, to a computer.

If you already own SCSI drives, it may make sense to stay with SCSI (note that you should upgrade your SCSI adapter if you want to use components that support the newer SCSI-2 standard).

So far, I've talked only about storage and haven't discussed the *speed* of hard drives. The speed at which your computer operates depends on what kind of work you do. In general, programs that load and work mostly in RAM won't run much faster when you have a fast hard drive. However, databases and other applications that constantly access the hard drive can greatly benefit from a speedy drive.

The speed of your hard drive depends on three major factors: *data transfer rate*, *average access time*, and *average seek time*. When you're shopping for a drive, you can use these figures to get an idea of how fast it will perform.

Another factor that affects your hard drive's speed is how data is stored on the drive. Files are stored on the hard drive in units called *clusters*.

Definition, Please

The *data transfer rate* tells you how fast data can move from the hard drive to the CPU. It's one of the most important indicators of hard drive performance and is measured in megabytes per second (MBps). IDE drives can transfer data at around 11 to 16MBps, and SCSI-2 drives are supposed to reach somewhere around 40MBps.

Average access time is the time it takes for the heads (the devices that read and write information to the drive) to move to the different tracks on a disk. In general, look for drives that have an average access time of around 10 to 12 milliseconds (ms).

Average seek time is the time it takes for the read/write head to move between two adjacent tracks. This figure is not as important as the data transfer rate or the access time.

In practice, clusters can become separated and spread over disparate parts of the drive. When that happens, the hard drive has to read them from different parts of the drive, which slows it down. The optimum situation is for clusters to lie right next to each other so that the hard drive can simply read the clusters one after another, increasing the speed at which it reads information.

Definition, Please

A *cluster* is a unit of information stored on a hard drive. When a system stores a file, it doesn't find one place on the drive for the entire file; the operating system breaks up the file into clusters and stores each cluster in a different area of the drive. You can think of clusters as subsets of a file.

To achieve this state on your hard drive, you can use software that's called a *defragger* or *defragmenter*.

Definition, Please

A *defragger* or *defragmenter* is a special software program that rearranges a hard drive's clusters so a drive can operate as efficiently as possible. If you have a drive that has data spread all over the disk (a condition that occurs naturally over time), you will see some performance gains by using defragmentation software.

You might consider using a defragger periodically, especially if your computer seems a bit sluggish. Depending on how far the clusters are distributed across the drive, you can see some performance improvement. In my experience, however, I've never seen anything better than a 10 percent increase in speed. Thus, using a defragger is more of a system maintenance process than an upgrade. To defrag your hard drive, you can use the utilities that come in Windows 3.x, 95, and 98.

Buying A New Hard Drive

When buying your hard drive, you should compare the following:

- Size
- Data transfer rate
- Access time
- Average seek time
- Cost

Tip—Cost

When comparing the cost of hard drives, determine the cost per gigabyte. To do this, simply divide the price of the hard drive by its size in gigabytes. The lower the number, the better the deal.

The first step in buying a hard drive is to decide how much hard drive space you need. Most drives sold today come in a 3.5-inch size, but you should take a careful look at a computer's case, specifically at the *drive bay*—a cage that holds hard drives.

Hard drives are sold in kits or sold "bare." Unless you're already comfortable with installing drives, buy the kit, because it will be more complete and include related hardware and instructions. Before buying, be sure to check what type of documentation comes with the drive and verify that everything you need is in the kit. This way, you can tell ahead of time how difficult the installation will be.

In general, make sure that the kit comes with the *mounting components*, *adapters*, and *cables*. Nothing is more frustrating than buying a kit and then having to make several trips back to the computer store to buy related parts.

Definition, Please

The *mounting components* are the adapter rails, nuts, bolts, and other hardware that let you mount the drive in your PC. The *adapters* and *cables*, as their names imply, let you connect a hard drive to the power supply and the controller card.

Before you buy a kit, check to see whether it includes:

- Cables
- Adapters
- Instructions
- Mounting components

Please refer to Chapter 22 for instructions on installing a hard drive.

The CPU And Motherboard

The heart and soul of a PC is its *central processing unit* (*CPU*). The CPU is the brain of a computer system; it lies at the center of those vast substrates of silicon, transistors, and switches that make up the system. It routes information and processes instructions between the various functions of your computer.

The CPU has a significant impact on the ultimate speed of your computer. Although areas such as random access memory (RAM) and the overall speed of the hard drive also play crucial and interrelated roles, the CPU and its motherboard are the major factors. You can think of a computer as if it were a high-performance car. If a car has high-performance tires but a weak engine, it's not going to go anywhere very fast. On the other hand, a car might have a heavy horsepower engine, but cheap retread wheels will limit its pace to a crawl. In the same way, your computer contains many interrelated factors that influence its performance.

CPUs run at different speeds, which are measured in *megahertz* (*MHz*). The computer's actual speed is called *clockspeed*. You can think of clockspeed as the fellow on the galley in a movie like Ben-Hur, who beats a drum to keep the oarsmen rowing together. The faster he pounds the drum, the faster the oarsmen row. If the fast drum isn't enough, the mean-looking guy with the whip is called in.

Definition, Please

A *megahertz* (MHz) is one million cycles or occurrences in a second.

The original IBM PC ran at a then-impressive 4.77MHz. Today, Pentium II systems scream along at 450MHz, and the processors will undoubtedly continue to speed up. As you've already figured out, the faster the clockspeed, the more instructions a CPU can process in a given time. And if you want to change a system's CPU, chances are you'll probably have to change its motherboard.

Definition, Please

The *motherboard* is your computer's main board that holds the CPU, memory, and expansion cards.

For the most part, motherboards are built to be used with specific processors and certain types of memory or RAM; they offer different ways to accept expansion cards. This leads us to a major motherboard factor, the *bus*, which determines the kind of *expansion cards* you can install. Motherboards come with different bus styles that accommodate different expansion cards. We'll look at buses a little later in this chapter, as well as other motherboard factors.

Definition, Please

You can think of a *bus* as a data highway. The more lanes on this data highway, the more data can be transferred smoothly. The bus defines the internal data highways on the board; thus, it defines how much data can be relayed. It also defines the data path in an expansion card slot, which accepts expansion cards.

An *expansion card*, also called an *expansion board*, is a panel containing microchips that you can install in a motherboard's expansion slot to add features. Some of the functions provided by expansion cards are essential to the computer's operation—like a video card that sends video information to your monitor. Internal modems and sound boards are also expansion cards.

Why Replace Your CPU?

For the same reasons that you want to upgrade your computer, you should consider upgrading your CPU and motherboard. The newest processors let you run the latest applications, offer fast performance, and take advantage of the newest features in operating systems, such as *multitasking*—running several programs at the same time.

Tip—Cost

Not surprisingly, the faster or more powerful the CPU, the higher the price. Looking to the future, buying the fastest processor on the market can keep you up to date for some time. Even if you don't necessarily need the fastest processor now, in the long run it's probably worth the extra money.

Basic Motherboard/CPU Options

When you upgrade your CPU and/or motherboard, you have three basic choices:

- Replace the CPU with a performance-enhancing Overdrive or upgrade chip (some motherboards let you do this)
- Replace the existing chip with a faster one (some motherboards support this)
- Replace the entire motherboard with a new one that is based around a newer and faster CPU

Your computer's upgrade potential depends on whether it has fairly fast components and peripherals that will work well with a newer and faster motherboard and CPU. If you have fairly fast components—hard drive, CD-ROM, RAM, and video card—it makes sense to upgrade your motherboard and CPU instead of buying a new PC. On the other hand, if the components won't work well and will slow down a new, hot-rod PC, it makes sense to purchase a new system.

By the way, most Pentium motherboards and some 486 motherboards feature *zero insertion force* (*ZIF*) sockets that let you easily swap processors by lifting a lever to release the chip so you can easily pull it out. You then install the new chip and replace the lever. The hardest part is lining up the chips with the socket. Although swapping a processor is quite easy, changing a motherboard involves some real work.

The Chips

For most computing today, a Pentium-based system is an absolute minimum. If you are using a system for word processing and databases, going online, and for nongraphical type of work, a Pentium will probably do the job. In this category, you can also consider the AMD K5. Although the K5 generally gives slightly faster performance than a Pentium at the same clockspeed, AMD rates the K5 with a different scale (the PR scale). Thus, a K5-PR133 sounds as if it's running at 133MHz, but the chip is really running at 100MHz and offers performance comparable to a Pentium 133. For comparison purposes, you can pretty much rely on the numbers.

Intel's Pentium Pro came after the Pentium. This chip offers enhancements over a Pentium, but it only provides increased performance when running true 32-bit operating systems, such as Windows NT. If you're running Windows 95 or 98, you won't see much of an increase in performance between a Pentium and a Pentium Pro running at the same clockspeed. The Pentium Pro will probably continue to be a player in network servers, and it does a great job running Windows NT, but from an upgrade standpoint, it's basically a dead end. I recommend that you not consider a Pentium Pro for an upgrade.

A big leap forward is the Pentium with *multimedia extensions* (*MMX*). The MMX capabilities in this family of chips means that they can process multimedia, such as video or animation, more efficiently. Pentiums with MMX give you slightly better performance than non-MMX Pentium processors running at the same speed, but to see significant speed gains, the software must specifically support MMX. More and more titles, particularly ones that display lots of graphics, support MMX.

As I write this, Pentiums with MMX come in versions that run at 166, 200, and 233MHz. The Pentium with MMX fits into a connector on the motherboard known as the Socket 7, which also accepts and works with processors from AMD (the K-6 series) and Cyrix (the 6x86 series). The

Socket 7 is an open standard, so you'll find that a Pentium motherboard equipped with a Socket 7 (this is usually clearly stated in the ads and specifications) will accept a wide variety of Socket 7–compatible chips. (To check a motherboard's compatibility with AMD and Cyrix chips, you can visit the AMD and Cyrix Web sites, where the manufacturers provide a list of motherboards that they have tested and can recommend.)

If you're thinking about upgrading to an AMD or Cyrix chip, you should consider the type of software that you will be running. Although the AMD K6, with its faster integer speed and floating point, offers slightly better performance than its Intel counterpart when running at the same speed, if your software is optimized for the Pentium, you'll be better off with an Intel chip. To accommodate a Socket 7 motherboard for an AMD or Cyrix chip, you will need to adjust the settings on the board—usually with jumpers—for clockspeed, voltage, and bus speed. I'll explain how to deal with these in Chapter 23.

Currently, the fastest processor on the market is Intel's Pentium II, shown in Figure 20.1, running at 450MHz (the Pentium II is also available in versions that run at 233, 266, 300, 333, 350, and 400MHz).

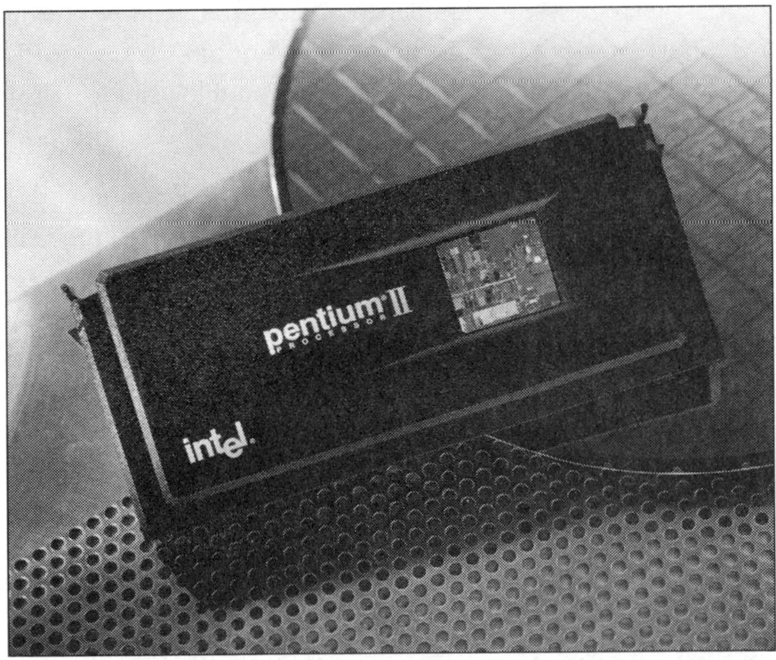

Figure 20.1 The Pentium II.

The latest 350 and above Pentium II processors support the faster 100MHz system bus, which improves on the performance of the 66MHz system bus and lets the CPU communicate more quickly with other computer components. All of the Pentium II processors (including the Celeron, a low-cost processor but slower performer than the Pentium II) connect with a Slot 1, Intel's proprietary motherboard connector.

If you use your system for 3D rendering, image-editing, multimedia development, or as a high-traffic server, the Pentium II should be your chip of choice. As always, I recommend that you take a good look at what you plan to do with your system and purchase your processor accordingly. Note that if you wish to upgrade from a Pentium or Pentium with MMX to a Pentium II, you will have to purchase a new motherboard.

If you own a Pentium-based PC that runs at 100MHz or slower—and if it has fairly large EIDE hard drives, 72-pin SIMM memory, a speedy CD-ROM drive (12X plus), and a PCI video card—you have a great candidate system for a motherboard upgrade. You can purchase a new motherboard and CPU and use your existing components.

Many Pentium motherboards can accept different speed Pentium chips. By simply changing some jumpers on the motherboard, you can insert and support a faster Pentium chip. Some Pentium motherboards come with a ZIF socket that lets you simply raise and lower a lever to release and then install a new chip.

Some Pentium motherboards can also accept the Pentium with MMX chip, but the motherboard has to be designed to do so. The Pentium with MMX chip requires a voltage of 2.8 volts, whereas the older Pentiums required 3.3 volts. Again, you'll have to adjust settings on your motherboard to alter the voltage. And if your motherboard won't accept a faster Pentium with MMX, you might consider installing an Intel, Evergreen, or Kingston upgrade chip. Keep in mind that older Pentium 60 motherboards are not compatible with upgrade chips because they use a different (incompatible) motherboard connector.

Intel's IntelDX2 and IntelDX4 upgrade chips can add Pentium-with-MMX performance to older, 75MHz and Pentium systems. Like the Intel solution, Evergreen's MxPro, based on the IDT WinChip C6 processor, improves the performance of 75MHz and higher Pentium systems to that of a faster MMX-enabled Pentium running at 180 or 200MHz. At less than $200 for the Evergreen chips, the cost of this upgrade is a bit less than buying a new motherboard and CPU, but the installation is a lot easier.

And for Pentiums running at 75MHz and higher, Kingston offers its TurboChip 200, based on a 200MHz AMD-K6 MMX, and the TurboChip 233, based on Intel's 233MHz Pentium with MMX. Both of these are available for just under $300, which I find rather pricey. You can easily buy a new motherboard and chip at this price.

I've personally used and tested the Evergreen solutions and found that the manufacturer's claims are real. Also, the installation is quite simple, but you do have to make certain adjustments to your motherboard. The Evergreen chips come with superb documentation and software that helps you through this process.

Again, when shopping for an Overdrive or upgrade chip, be sure to check that the upgrade chip will work with your motherboard; also consider such factors as clockspeed and voltage levels. In addition, it doesn't hurt to check with the board and chip manufacturers to make sure that the upgrade will work and that no known problems or incompatibilities exist.

If your system is based on a Pentium with MMX, your motherboard can probably accept faster Pentium with MMX chips. If so, you can swap the chip and adjust some motherboard settings so that the bus and clockspeed match that of your new chip. Most of the time, you can find instructions for making the settings in the documentation that comes with your motherboard, and most motherboards have a chart that's printed on the board itself that shows you these settings.

If your Pentium chip is already running at the motherboard's fastest speed (usually 200 to 233MHz), you won't be able to install a faster CPU. But if you currently own a system that runs off a Pentium with MMX, you undoubtedly have great components to move with your upgrade.

If you own a Pentium with MMX, you might gain new support for AGP graphics with a new motherboard. For the most part, AGP improves the performance of 3D applications by providing a way for graphics to work with a system's main memory, bypassing the CPU's bus. But other than enhancing the performance of 3D applications, the benefits of AGP, when compared to those of solid PCI-based video cards, are marginal. If you run mainly business applications, you won't gain much by paying extra for AGP. But if you are serious about games, you may very well want to move up to AGP.

Most Pentium II motherboards can accept faster Pentium II chips, but this will depend on something called the *chipset*.

Definition, Please

The *chipset* is a special chip on the motherboard that defines the motherboard's capabilities, including:

- What CPU it accepts
- What types of memory it accepts
- Its bus speed
- The number and types of expansion slots
- Whether it can support AGP, USB, and multiple processors

Once you purchase a motherboard, you can't replace the chipset until you buy a new motherboard.

Here are the basics on chipsets: If your system uses the Intel 440LX chipset, the fastest processor it can accept is a Pentium II at 333MHz. To support a Pentium II at 350MHz, 400MHz, or higher, you'll need to purchase a motherboard that has the newer 440BX chipset.

For a summary of motherboard and CPU upgrade options, refer to Table 20.1.

Table 20.1 CPU upgrade options.

Option	Available On	Result
Replace the CPU	Certain motherboards	Better performance
Add an Overdrive chip	Certain 486 and Pentium boards	Pentium performance
Replace the motherboard	Certain cases	Faster performance
Replace the chip with a faster one	Only on some motherboards	Better performance

You probably already know which chip you would like to upgrade to. However, here are some factors to consider. You will pay top dollar for the fastest chip and motherboard on the market, or you can save money by making a more modest upgrade—say, to a fast Pentium with MMX that is not the fastest available but can be purchased for a reasonable cost, or an entry-level Pentium II that runs at 266 or 300MHz. You can save money by buying a chip that's a step below the cutting edge, but still offers excellent performance.

As another upgrade option, AMD and Cyrix sell MMX-compatible chips of their own that cost less than Intel's offerings and are solid products. The K6 delivers slightly better performance than a Pentium MMX, but less than that of a Pentium II running at the same clock-speed. For further comparison, the Cyrix chips give you comparable performance at the same clockspeed, but the technology is limited to the slower clockspeeds. The AMD K6 and Cyrix 6x86MX perform almost as well as a Pentium with MMX, but usually don't perform as well when running MMX applications. If you need a high degree of 3D capabilities or MMX performance, I recommend you go with a true Intel Pentium with MMX.

The Chipsets

After deciding between a Pentium with MMX, or Pentium II, you should consider the chipset that a motherboard uses. Along with the CPU, the chipset defines the motherboard's capabilities (as discussed earlier in this chapter). And once your purchase a motherboard, you're stuck with its chipset until you buy another motherboard.

When buying a Pentium II motherboard, choose a Slot 1 motherboard with either the Intel 440BX AGPset or the older 440LX AGPset chipset. The latest 440BX AGPset offers support for the faster 100MHz system bus, and you'll want this if you plan to upgrade to the fastest 350 and above Pentium II chips.

The 440LX AGPset is the predecessor to the 440BX and supports all Pentium II speeds up to 333MHz, but can't support anything faster. As I write this, motherboards that feature the 440LX are still available, but the 440BX is rapidly flooding the market. Another chipset, the 440EX, supports only the Celeron, Intel's stripped-down Pentium II that runs at 266MHz. Because it lacks an internal cache, this chip's performance is slower than that of a Pentium II running at 233MHz, but it is Intel's low-cost solution.

Meanwhile, if you're shopping for a motherboard that will support a 75 to 200MHz Pentium and 166 and 200MHz Pentium with MMX chips, look for a Socket 7 motherboard that has Intel's 430TX chipset. Keep in mind that when it comes to chipsets, Intel isn't the only player in town. Other manufacturers such as Via and Silicon Integrated Systems Corporation (SiS) sell compatible chipsets that are found on competing motherboards.

If you're planning to use the memory from your existing system on your new motherboard, you have to consider several things. First, if your system dates back to before 1996, it probably uses standard DRAM. Since then, new types of RAM have become available, most notably *Extend Data Out RAM (EDO RAM)*, *parity RAM*, and *Synchronous DRAM (SDRAM)*.

When purchasing a new motherboard, make sure that it can accept and use your existing RAM. Some boards may handle one type of RAM, but not another. You should never mix different types of memory in your system, and always match the speed of your RAM (in nanoseconds) so the memory chips are consistent. (You can, in theory, mix different speeds of memory, but it's best not to.) Also, some motherboards, particularly with single inline memory modules (SIMMs), require that you install memory in pairs. You'll have to check with the motherboard documentation or manufacturer on this point.

If your current system uses old 30-pin SIMMs, you'll have to purchase new 72-pin SIMMs or 168-pin dual inline memory module (DIMM) RAM, because all boards now accept and work only with these. In fact, most Pentium II motherboards only accept RAM in the 168-pin DIMM format. Pentiums with MMX motherboards come in versions that accept 168-pin DIMMs, 72-pin SIMMs, or both. If a motherboard comes with sockets for DIMMs and SIMMs, you can't use both types at the same time. Another factor to consider is the voltage—DIMMs come in 3.3

and 5.0 versions. Check the specifications on the motherboard for more information.

Another consideration is that to support the faster 100MHz bus that works with the latest 350+ MHz Pentium II chips, you'll need PC100-compliant memory modules. If you are upgrading to a 350+ MHz Pentium II, you won't be able to use non-PC100 RAM.

Size Matters

Motherboards come in different sizes to fit different cases; this has nothing to do with the physical size of your system (mini-tower, full-tower, and so forth), but with the style. More than likely, your existing case is a Baby AT, which dates back to the old 286 days, or an ATX, which has recently gained in popularity. If you purchase a motherboard that is the wrong size for your case, it won't fit or work.

Although you can find Baby AT–sized Slot 1 motherboards for a Pentium II chip, most of these come in the ATX style. I find the ATX format easier to work with because screw holes in the motherboard line up better with those of the case—something that rarely happens with Baby AT motherboards and cases. Also, ATX-style cases and motherboards can take advantage of soft-power features that let you shut down your computer by using commands in the operating system. If you are looking for a Socket 7 motherboard for a Pentium with MMX, you'll find these in either Baby AT or ATX sizes.

If you own a newer Pentium with MMX, or a Pentium II system, you probably have an ATX case. If you own an older 486 or an early Pentium (60, 90, and 100MHz era), you probably have a Baby AT case. You can usually identify an ATX case by a cutout in the case that accepts a thin metal plate with punch-outs; the plate, in turn, accepts the various cables from external devices. Also, ATX cases usually have fans that blow air into the box, but the fans in Baby AT cases usually blow the air out of the back of the case.

If your PC comes from a major manufacturer, such as Hewlett-Packard or Packard Bell, you may have a case that's called a *slimline*, or other nonstandard case. Finding a motherboard to fit one of these cases is usually a hassle. In this situation, it's best to salvage the components—

drives, cards, and so forth—and buy a new case to go along with your motherboard and CPU.

Because cases are relatively low in price (ranging from $60 to $120), don't let an incompatible case hold back your upgrade. Given a choice, I prefer working with an ATX case, because the motherboard installation is usually easier, and I like having the soft-power shutoff features.

Another factor to consider in choosing a new motherboard is the number and type of expansion slots. Generally, the more slots the better; but you need to consider the boards that you will be bringing from your existing system so that you can be sure that your new computer can accept and use them. Count how many ISA and PCI boards you will be installing on your new system and make sure that the motherboard you purchase has the necessary number of appropriate slots.

These days, most motherboards come with 1 AGP, 2 ISAs, and 4 or 5 PCI slots—however, these do vary. And when you're considering slots, make sure that your boards will fit into the motherboard. You may have one of those old full-size ISA boards that looks as if it will fit into a slot, but won't because components on the motherboard are in the way. If your old system used a VESA or older local bus video card, you'll have to buy a new PCI or AGP video card for your new Pentium with MMX or Pentium II motherboard.

You will probably run across motherboards that can accept more than one Pentium processor. I've seen motherboards that accept two, four, or more processors, and—as you'd expect—this can give you better performance (after all, two chips have to be better than one). It may be tempting to purchase a motherboard that supports multiple processors so that you can simply insert additional processors at a later date for improved performance, but it's not that simple.

To use multiple processors, your operating system must be able to support them. Windows NT Workstation 4, for example, supports two Intel processors (AMD and Cyrix chips won't work), the Server edition supports four, and the Enterprise Edition supports up to eight.

In addition to your operating system, your applications have to support these multiple processors as well. The only applications that I've seen with this capability are high-end software, such as AutoCad and sophisticated 3D rendering programs. Unless you're running Windows NT and high-end applications, a multiple-processor motherboard won't give you any performance gains. However, if running more than one application at a time, you will see increased performance in each application—each will run on a new, available CPU. If you do go with a motherboard that supports multiple processors, keep in mind that you can't mix processors—they have to be all the same—and that the performance will increase, but won't actually multiply with the number of processors that you add.

Reputation And Other Factors

I recommend purchasing motherboards from major manufacturers with good reputations. Some of my favorites include Intel, Tyan, Gigabyte, A-Bit, Asus, and SuperMicro. Although you can find cheaper boards from other manufacturers, you run the risk of incompatibilities in these boards. Paying more for a reliable motherboard is money well spent.

Most of the manufacturers listed here don't sell directly. You'll have to purchase their boards through various mail-order companies, stores, and other vendors. When doing so, don't forget to take into account the reputation of your vendor, the support that the vendor offers after your purchase, and the return policy and warranty. For more details on such general buying tips, refer to Chapter 5. The support can be well worth any extra cost, because motherboards often come with rather difficult instructions to decrypt and understand.

Another important feature of your motherboard is the *basic input/output system* (*BIOS*), the internal instructions of a system that come with every board. This is a time when you can feel confident about buying your motherboard from any of the big names, such as AMI, Award, and Phoenix.

Definition, Please

The *basic input/output system (BIOS)* is internal, built-in software that controls hardware.

When purchasing a motherboard, don't forget to consider its *cache*, which helps to speed performance by providing a place to store needed information so it's readily available. The cache comes as part of the motherboard and is listed in the board's specifications. For most purposes, get an L2 cache of at least 256K—the bigger, the better.

Definition, Please

The *cache* is a system of memory that works closely with the processor to hold important data so it is immediately available. This speeds up the performance of your system.

How To Buy A Motherboard

To summarize the considerable amount of information in this chapter, you can refer to Table 20.2 for the basics on what you should consider before you buy a motherboard.

You can buy motherboards from a variety of places—your local computer store, mail-order outlets, and even warehouse stores. From the list in Table 20.2 you should have a fairly good idea of what you want to look for. When shopping, don't be afraid to ask questions. You're spending a good bit of money, and you have every right to know. For tips on shopping and finding the best prices, refer to Chapter 5. After you buy your motherboard and are ready to install it, refer to Chapter 23.

Table 20.2 Summary of what to look for in a motherboard.

Processor	**Pentium With MMX, Or Pentium II**
BIOS	AMI, Award, Phoenix
Bus	PCI/AGP
Cache	256K external
Chipset	430TX (Pentium with MMX), 440BX (Pentium II)
Input/output	Your choice
Number of slots	To accommodate your existing boards
Physical size	To fit your case (Baby AT, ATX)
Type of memory	Depends on your existing RAM
USB support	Yes

Moving On

In this chapter, we covered the basic considerations when adding memory, adding more storage with hard drives, and swapping a system's motherboard and processor to improve a system's performance. In the next chapter, you'll learn how to shop for and add memory to a system.

21

Upgrading Your System's Memory

Like the other major components in your PC, memory plays a key role. In the most basic sense, you can think of memory as a work area your computer uses to hold and process your data. In some ways, memory is like a desk. A desk usually has drawers to hold your tools (pencil, calculator, etc.) and a file drawer to store data and records. To work with your tools and data, you take them out of the drawers and put them on your desktop where they're handy. Of course, the more data or equipment that you have to use, the more room it will occupy in or on your desk. In the same way, memory—or, more specifically, *random access memory* (*RAM*—it's pronounced just like a male sheep)—can be used for storage or temporarily for immediate work.

RAM

Memory configurations, as well as memory technology, have changed and evolved over the years. Nowadays, memory comes on chips mounted on tiny boards. Adding RAM to your system is one of the best performance-enhancing upgrades you can make. If you're working with lots of large applications with equally large data files, the more memory you can provide, the better.

How To Measure RAM

To see how much RAM you have in a system, you can run any Microsoft application (Word, Excel, and so forth) and click on System Info under the Help|About menu. In Windows 95 or 98, you can select Start|Settings|

Control Panel, double-click on the System icon, and click on the Performance tab to view your PC's memory. In Windows NT, you can click on Start, the Windows NT diagnostics icon, and then click on the Memory page. With this information, you can then check your system's documentation or call the manufacturer of your system or motherboard and find out how much more RAM you can add and how much the motherboard can hold.

Speed And Type

The first major RAM consideration is speed. If you have a system with a blazingly fast processor yet with slow or insufficient RAM, you'll still have poor performance. Memory speed is rated in nanoseconds (ns); one nanosecond equals one-billionth of a second. Therefore, the lower the number, the faster the memory. Before 1990, memory could run as slow as 120 ns. Today, the most popular RAM comes in 60 ns and 70 ns configurations.

Memory also comes in different types. The most common type of memory used in older Pentiums and 486s is called *Dynamic RAM* (*DRAM*). Other popular types of memory go by the names *Extended Data Out RAM* (*EDO RAM*), which is in many Pentium systems beginning about 1996, and *Synchronous DRAM* (*SDRAM*), which is the most popular type of RAM for new systems right now. Each new type of RAM usually represents faster and more efficient performance. For example, the latest SDRAM is supposed to be about 25 percent faster than EDO RAM.

Other RAM factors are *parity* and *Error Correction Code (ECC)*—built-in methods of checking for errors in memory. If your current system is using these types of RAM, you'll need to make sure any additional RAM you purchase is of these types. Because of its high cost, parity is not a factor on the newest systems—it has largely fallen out of favor. You'll find parity and ECC RAM mostly on the high-end systems that are used as servers and other applications.

If you have one of the latest Pentium II systems that make use of the 100MHz system bus (Pentium IIs that run at 350MHz and above support the faster 100MHz bus), you'll need to purchase and install special PC100 RAM; otherwise, your system will have to be set to run at the lower 66MHz bus.

If you are adding memory to your system to complement what it already has, you should always match types. In other words, if your system currently has EDO memory, you'll need to purchase additional EDO RAM that is rated at the same speed as your existing memory.

Although it might be tempting to purchase the fastest RAM you can buy and add it to slower RAM, it's not a good idea to mix speeds. Also, computer systems are usually rated to work with memory of a certain speed. You can buy faster memory, but it won't help the performance of your system, and you will have spent extra money unnecessarily.

Physical Configuration

Besides speed and type, the other major consideration is the physical configuration of your RAM. If you're upgrading, the type of memory configuration you already have may or may not work with your upgraded system. Memory on *single inline memory modules* (*SIMMs*) remains popular, as shown in Figures 21.1 and 21.2. SIMMs come in 72-pin and 30-pin versions, with the 72-pin now being the most common and used

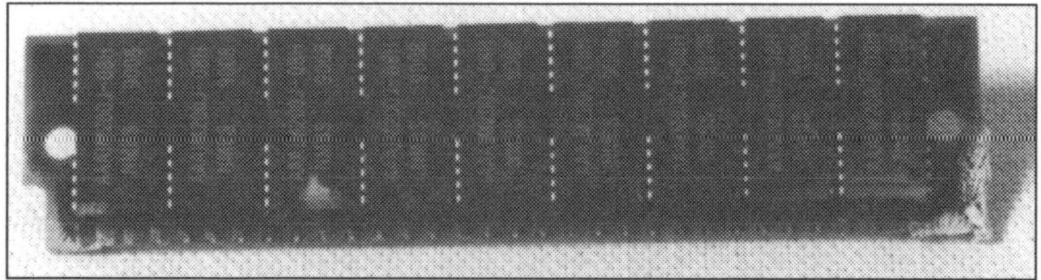

Figure 21.1 Memory in a 30-pin SIMM configuration.

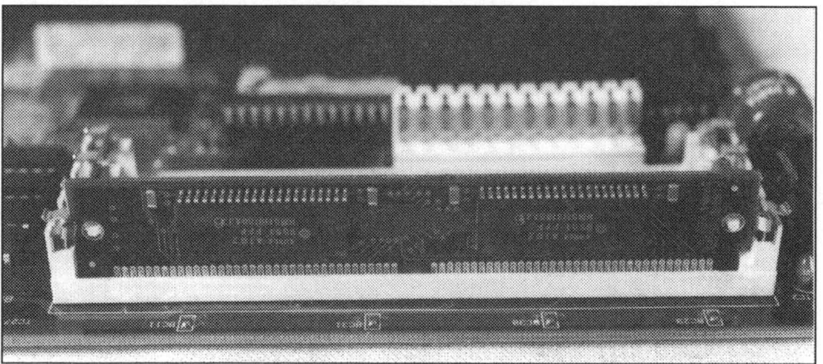

Figure 21.2 Memory in a 72-pin SIMM configuration in a memory slot. Notice the notch in the lower right-hand corner that prevents the memory from being installed incorrectly.

in most Pentiums and later 486 systems. Many older 486s used 30-pin SIMMs. It's important to note how many pins fit onto your motherboard to determine the type of SIMM it accepts.

Definition, Please

SIMM, which stands for single inline memory module, is a type of RAM. Although the 30-pin SIMM configuration used on older machines is outdated, many current systems use the 72-pin SIMM configuration.

Many of the latest motherboards accept memory in a configuration called *dual inline memory modules* (*DIMMs*), as shown in Figure 21.3. The 168-pin DIMMs look much like SIMMs, but install in a different type of socket. Again, you'll need to determine what type of RAM configuration your motherboard requires.

Definition, Please

DIMM, which stands for dual inline memory module, is a type of RAM accepted by many of the latest motherboards.

Because memory comes in different sizes, you need to check in the motherboard manual or with the manufacturer to confirm the type of RAM you will need. Some systems let you mix different size SIMMs or make you install them in specific groups—for example, two at a time (in "pairs"). Unlike SIMMs, you don't need to install DIMMs in pairs. If you are buying a new motherboard and want to reuse your existing RAM, be sure to purchase a motherboard that can accept it.

Figure 21.3 Memory in a 168-pin DIMM configuration.

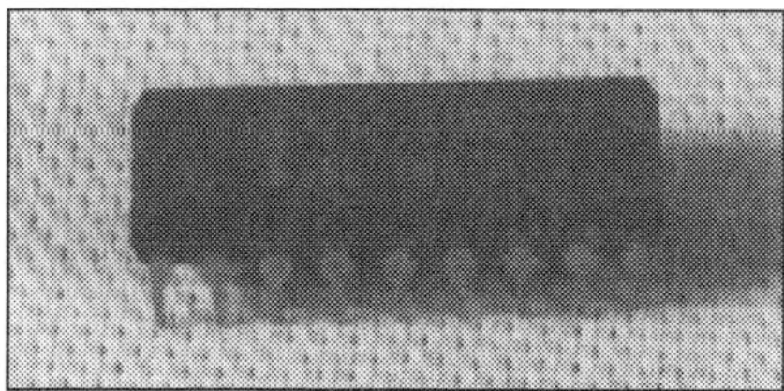

Figure 21.4 Memory in a DIP configuration.

Other memory that you may find, usually on older 386 or 486 computers, is in *dual inline packages* (*DIPs*), as shown in Figure 21.4. These aren't as common and are difficult to find these days. They're also harder to install and take up more chips.

All Pentiums and most 386 and 486 motherboards come with a place (a *socket*) for holding memory. If you install memory directly onto your motherboard, you'll get the fastest performance. Always use these sockets first, before resorting to expansion cards. Some older boards use proprietary expansion cards to hold additional memory. You'll have to check with the manufacturer of your motherboard, but some require that you add memory in pairs or only in certain configurations. You'll need to know this in advance to make your purchase.

Summary Of RAM Considerations

When shopping for memory, keep these questions in mind:

- How much memory do you need?
- How is it packaged (SIMM, DIMM, DIP)?
- How fast is the memory (70 ns, 60 ns, and so forth)?
- What type of memory is it (DRAM, EDO RAM, SDRAM)?

Many sources are available for buying memory. Most computer specialty stores sell memory. Be sure to check that the memory will work with your motherboard and system: Call the memory manufacturer if necessary. Another, potentially lower-priced, source is mail-order firms.

Tip—Cost

If you can't use your old memory in your upgrade, some firms, depending on the type of memory you have, will buy it from you. While you can't expect much money for old memory, regardless of what you originally paid for it, it can be a small down payment toward new RAM. Sometimes you'll save money by purchasing all new memory chips (particularly if you've had your computer's memory for years) rather than trying to salvage and use the older, existing ones in your PC.

Again, ask hard questions before you give up your credit card number. For more on shopping for computer parts, refer to Chapter 5.

Adding Memory

In this section, I'll show you how to add SIMMs and DIMMs. In some cases, before you can add memory, you must remove old memory, so that is covered here as well.

Adding A SIMM To Your Motherboard

Adding a SIMM is actually a fairly straightforward process. Some motherboards hold SIMM memory modules at an angle, but others hold them straight up. Regardless of the orientation of the socket, you install the SIMM in the same manner.

Caution

Always store the SIMM in an antistatic bag until you're ready to use it. Memory is one of the components most easily damaged with static electricity. Also, always try to hold the SIMM by the edges and not touch the connectors (the metal contacts along the bottom). If you aren't using a wrist strap, be sure to ground yourself before handling any SIMMs. To do this, simply touch the metal case of your PC before picking up the SIMM.

Back up all of the important data on your computer before installing new memory and take a minute to record information about your hard drive and system settings. Keep this information in a place where you can always refer to it later, if needed.

Shut off your PC and unplug it before you take the cover off. With the cover off, you're ready to begin.

Caution

Be sure to shut off your PC and unplug it.

Look at the motherboard in Figure 21.5 and the location of your memory sockets. Although the placement of these sockets varies from board to board, you'll be looking for the same type of sockets. For a close-up view of the SIMM memory sockets, refer to Figure 21.6.

Figure 21.5 Memory sockets on the motherboard.

Figure 21.6 A closer view of the memory sockets.

Removing Existing SIMMs

Follow this procedure to remove existing SIMMs:

1. First, you must release the latches that hold the SIMMs in their sockets. You'll find latches at the sides of the memory sockets, as shown in Figure 21.7. Gently press them toward the side to release a SIMM.

Tip

If your board already has memory chips installed, notice how they are placed before you remove them. This will help you correctly orient your new SIMMs and place them in the correct sockets.

2. Hold the SIMM and pull it forward to disengage it from the socket, as shown in Figure 21.8. You can now remove the SIMM.

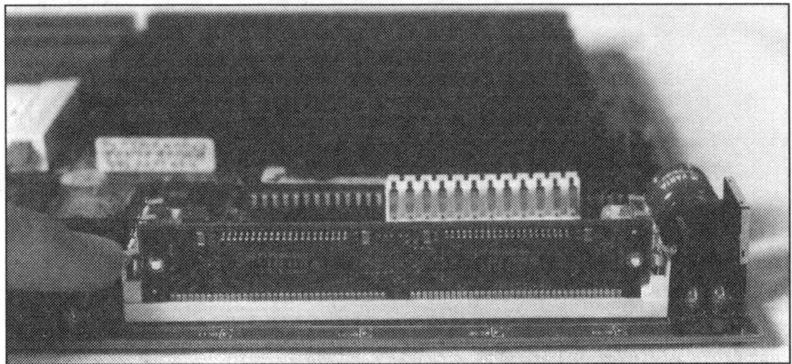

Figure 21.7 Latches hold SIMMs in their sockets.

Figure 21.8 After releasing the latches, gently pull the SIMM forward to disengage it from its socket.

3. Repeat the process with all of the sockets from which you want to remove old SIMMs.

Inserting A New SIMM

Follow this procedure to insert a new SIMM:

1. Holding the SIMM at a slight angle, position it so its contacts rest in the socket. Look for a notch that will help you align it correctly with the socket. This notch, shown in Figure 21.9, prevents you from installing the SIMM in the wrong direction.
2. Gently push the SIMM into the socket until it engages with the latches. You won't have to force it—the chip should engage easily, as shown in Figure 21.10.
3. Before you replace the case cover, connect the monitor to your PC, connect your keyboard and mouse, and reconnect power to the system. You should perform a quick test to ensure that everything is okay and that your system accepted the new memory.

Caution

Don't forget that you have a live machine. Under no circumstance should you probe your PC or touch any components while your system is running. Always shut off power before doing any work on your PC or

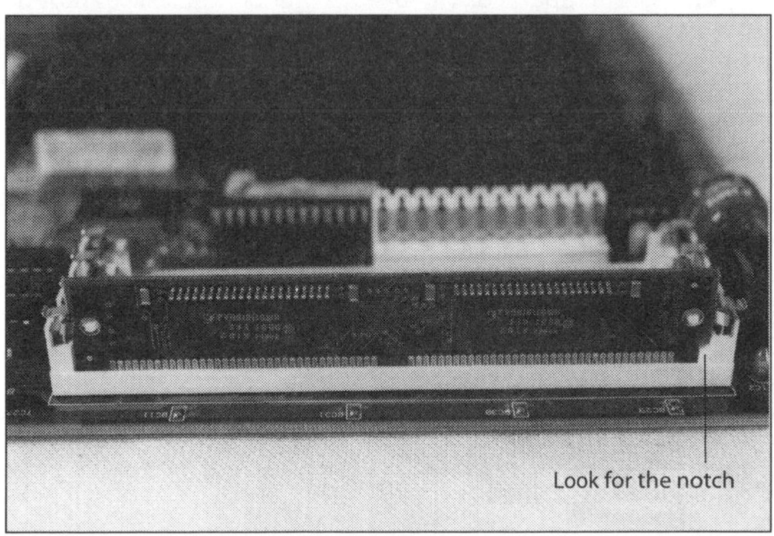

Figure 21.9 This notch prevents you from installing the SIMM in the wrong direction.

Figure 21.10 Gently push the memory module into the socket until it engages with the latches.

removing or adjusting any component. Not only could you get a dangerous shock, you could also damage or ruin system components.

4. Turn on your PC. You should see the usual initial screen that tells you that your computer is starting up and testing its memory. If this screen shows that more RAM is present in your system, so far, so good. This number won't necessarily reflect the exact amount of RAM in your system, but if the number is within 384K of the RAM you installed, it's okay.

   With some systems, the computer might kick you out into the CMOS setup screen because it detects more RAM than it was configured to have. At this point, the CMOS should list the correct amount of RAM. All you have to do is save the CMOS to configure your system properly.

5. If your system doesn't appear to be working correctly, please refer to the "RAM Troubleshooting" section later in this chapter. If everything appears to be normal, you can shut off your system, disconnect the power, reconnect all of the cables and connectors, and reinstall the case cover.

Adding A DIMM To Your Motherboard

Adding a DIMM is not difficult, but you should note the following precautions.

Caution

Always store the DIMM in an antistatic bag until you're ready to use it. Memory is one of the components most easily damaged by static electricity. Also, always try to hold the DIMM by the edges and not touch the connectors (the metal edges along the bottom). If you aren't using a wrist strap, be sure to ground yourself before handling any DIMMs. To do this, simply touch the metal case of your PC before picking up the DIMM.

Back up all of the important data on your computer before installing new memory and take a minute to record information about your hard drive and system settings. Keep this information in a place where you can always refer to it later, if needed.

Shut off your PC and unplug it. Open your PC's case. With the cover off, you're ready to begin.

Caution

Be sure to shut off your PC and unplug it.

Take a look at the motherboard in Figure 21.11 and the location of your DIMM memory sockets. Although the placement of these sockets varies from board to board, you'll be looking for the same type of sockets. (For a close-up view of DIMM-style memory, refer back to Figure 21.3.)

Removing Existing DIMMs

Follow these instructions to remove existing DIMMs:

1. First, you must release the latches that hold the DIMMs in their sockets. You'll find these latches at the sides of the memory sockets, as shown in Figure 21.12. Gently press both down toward the sides to release a DIMM.

Figure 21.11 DIMM memory sockets on the motherboard.

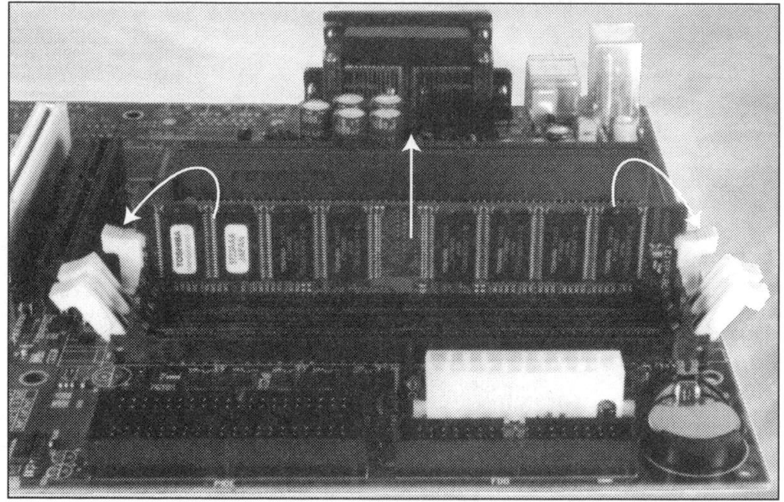

Figure 21.12 Latches hold DIMMs in their sockets.

If your board already has memory chips installed, notice how they are placed before you remove them. This will help you correctly orient your new DIMMs and place them in the correct sockets.

2. After unlatching the sockets, grab the top of the DIMM with your fingers and gently pull up, as shown in Figure 21.13.
3. Repeat the process with all of the sockets from which you want to remove old DIMMs.

Figure 21.13 After releasing the latches, gently pull the DIMM up to disengage it from its socket.

Inserting A New DIMM

Follow these instructions to insert a new DIMM:

1. A DIMM looks identical on either side, so you have to look at the contacts along the bottom edge, as shown in Figure 21.14. Note the

Figure 21.14 Look for groupings on the contacts that correspond to groupings in the socket. This helps you install the DIMM correctly.

grouping of the contacts and match them with the corresponding groupings in the DIMM socket. Gently position the new DIMM so the contacts rest in the socket. A DIMM will only install in one direction.

2. After aligning the DIMM's contacts with those of the socket, gently press down on the DIMM, letting the contacts engage with the socket. You won't have to force it—the chip should engage fairly easily. Once the DIMM is in its socket, pull the latches up on each side of the socket so they hold the DIMM in place, as shown in Figure 21.15.
3. Before you replace the case cover, connect the monitor to your PC, connect your keyboard and mouse, and reconnect power to the system. You should perform a quick test to ensure that everything is okay and that your system accepted the new memory.

Caution

Don't forget that you have a live machine. Under no circumstance should you probe your PC or touch any components while your system is running. Always shut off power before doing any work on your PC or removing or adjusting any component. Not only could you get a dangerous shock, you could also damage or ruin system components.

Figure 21.15 Pull the socket's latches up and over the DIMM to hold it in place.

4. Turn on your PC. You should see the usual initial screen that tells you that your computer is starting up and testing its memory. If this screen shows that more RAM is present in your system, so far, so good. This number won't necessarily reflect the exact amount of RAM in your system, but if the number is within 384K of the RAM you installed, it's okay.

   With some systems, the computer may kick you out into its CMOS setup screen because it detects more RAM than it was configured to have. At this point, the CMOS should list the correct amount of RAM. All you have to do is save the CMOS to configure your system properly.

5. If your system doesn't appear to be working correctly, please refer to the next section, "RAM Troubleshooting." If everything appears to be normal, you can shut off your system, disconnect the power, reconnect all of the cables and connectors, and reinstall the case cover.

RAM Troubleshooting

If your system doesn't boot properly, the following suggestions might help:

- Shut off your PC and unplug the power. Recheck your RAM installation. The SIMMs or DIMMs should be well seated in their sockets. Also, make sure that while you were working in your computer, you didn't inadvertently loosen other connectors or cables. Check for dangling or loose connectors and verify that all are seated properly.
- To check whether your new RAM is the cause, you can remove your new RAM and reinstall the old RAM (if you completely replaced your existing RAM). If you installed additional RAM, remove the added RAM to check if the old RAM works without the new RAM.
- If your old RAM works correctly, the problem is likely to be your new RAM installation. The RAM chips may not be the proper ones for your system, your system may not be configured correctly to recognize them, or the RAM chips may be faulty. Try reinstalling the new RAM chips again. If they don't work, review your system's documentation to check what type of RAM you can add. Also, you can double-check with your motherboard's manufacturer.

- Don't forget that if you're installing additional RAM, you must account for the existing RAM. If you're mixing RAM modules of different speeds, sometimes they will not configure correctly unless you go into your system's CMOS setup to change something called *wait states*. For this change, you'll have to check with the manufacturer's instructions. Also, double-check how you can add new RAM. In many cases, motherboards require that you install SIMMs in pairs (this normally doesn't apply to DIMMs).

If you check all of these things and still have a problem, you may have a bad memory module. You should return the memory to the manufacturer and exchange it for another set.

Moving On

In this chapter, we've discussed how you can easily add RAM to greatly enhance your system. You should immediately see the difference it makes in your system's performance. In the next chapter, I'll talk about how to add hard drives to the computers in your network.

22

Adding Hard Drives

In this chapter, I'll show you how to increase a system's storage capacity by adding a new hard drive. This will enable your system to have more disk space to store data and program files. If you need some tips on buying a hard drive, please refer to Chapter 20. Otherwise, with your new integrated drive electronics (EIDE or Ultra DMA) drive in hand, you'll have room to burn. Temporarily, at least.

Tip

Most PCs have 200 watts of power and can adequately power two hard drives. However, 200 watts is probably a minimum. Check your system's power supply before adding a new hard drive.

In principle, adding a new hard drive isn't difficult. The things that tend to cause problems are correctly configuring the hard drive, setting the jumpers, and then properly configuring the system.

Tip

If you're adding a second drive, you may need a *Y-cable* that splits the power from one power connector and cable and ends up with two connectors—one for each of two drives. You can purchase a Y-cable from any computer store. Also, you may require a *ribbon cable* that has two connectors. Although it isn't rocket science, it is trickier to route a two-connection ribbon cable around your system; this may require planning ahead.

Preliminary Considerations

The first step in installing your hard drive is to make sure that its settings are correct. Most of the time, your new hard drive will come with a booklet that describes any particular settings or jumpers and how to set them. The documentation also should mention other secondary issues. For example, the BIOS (basic input/output system) on an older system may not be able to support a drive larger than 528MB. If this is the case with your BIOS, some manufacturers, such as Seagate, include a disk utility that can fool the BIOS into thinking you have a smaller drive.

Probably the most important consideration to keep in mind is whether the drive that you're adding is the first or second drive in your PC. That's because you will have to configure the drive to be either a *master* or a *slave*, as described in the following paragraphs.

If the hard drive is the first one that you're adding to your system, it should be set as the master. Check your hard drive documentation, but most hard drives arrive already set as master drives so you shouldn't have to do anything. If your drive is not set as the master drive, your documentation should give you advice on how to do so.

If the hard drive is the second one in your system, set it as a slave drive. You should check your hard drive documentation for instructions. Keep in mind that when you add a second drive, you have to consider the settings on your master drive. Again, check the hard drive documentation.

Caution—Data

Be sure to back up all of your important data on your computer before installing a drive. Also, it's a good idea to record the information about the hard drive you are removing—the type, cylinders, and so forth. If you have the hard drive documentation, it will include this information. You'll also find this information in your computer's setup, which you usually can see by booting up your PC and then holding down a key to view a menu screen (computers vary; check your manual). Keep this information in a safe place. If you're replacing a drive, you can use your backups to reinstall your applications and data. I've found that when it comes to important data, it doesn't hurt to do two backups of your data, just in case one medium fails.

Shut off your PC and unplug it.

Caution—Safety

Before you open your PC, turn it off. I always unplug my PC as well, although some experts will tell you to leave it plugged in (just as long as it's turned off). When working on your system, don't probe screwdrivers in areas that you're not working on, particularly the power supply.

Opening The Computer Case

The first step to install a new hard drive is opening your computer. Follow these steps to open your computer case:

1. Disconnect all of the cables and connectors attached to your computer: power, printer cables, speakers, telephone line, keyboard, mouse, video connections, and so on.
2. Remove the screws, which you'll usually find along the back side of the computer case, as shown in Figure 22.1.

Caution

When removing screws from the back of the case, be sure to remove only those that appear to hold the case. If you go overboard and remove all the screws, you may hear internal components—the power supply, for example—drop loose and fall down inside your computer. Be conservative: Remove the obvious screws first and then see if the case cover budges.

3. Gently push the cover to see if it moves. If it does, slide it off the case. If it doesn't, you probably missed a screw. Check for any errant screws and then try to budge the cover again.

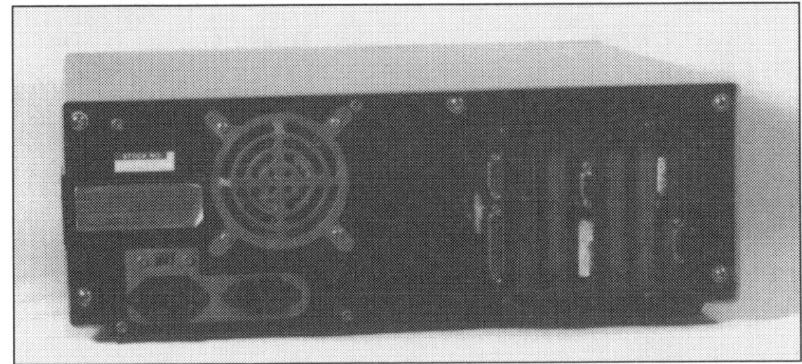

Figure 22.1 The screws that hold the case on are usually on the back of the computer.

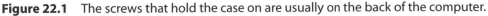

On a desktop machine, as shown in Figure 22.2, the cover usually is removed by sliding the chassis backward, away from the front of the computer. On a tower case, the cover can slide either forward or backward, as shown in Figure 22.3. Of course, your case may not fall into either of these categories. Some cases swivel, others lift off, and

Figure 22.2 A typical desktop case cover opens by sliding the chassis back from the front of the computer.

Figure 22.3 A typical tower case cover opens by sliding either forward or backward off the case.

still others don't even use screws—you simply depress a couple of buttons to open the case. Please refer to your system's documentation for more information on how to open the case.

4. With your PC's cover off, you're ready to begin working.

Caution

Be sure that your PC is shut off. Also, if you aren't using a wrist strap, ground yourself before handling any components: Simply touch the metal case of your PC.

Removing The Existing Hard Drive

Perform the following steps if you are replacing an existing hard drive with a new one. If you are adding a new hard drive and keeping your existing oncs, skip the following instructions and go to the next section, "Installing And Formatting The New Hard Drive."

To remove the existing drive:

1. Open your computer and inspect the existing hard drive; you'll find that both the floppy and hard drives are mounted in a metal cradle or cage, as shown in Figure 22.4.

Figure 22.4 The drives are mounted in a metal cage.

Figure 22.5 Removing the screws that hold the drives.

2. To remove the hard drive, use a screwdriver to carefully loosen the screws that hold the hard drive to the cage, as shown in Figure 22.5. Most drives attach to the cradle with four screws—two on each side. Once you loosen these, you'll find that you can move the drive a bit.
3. Remove the connectors and cables from the drive, noting where they attach and to which drive (if you'll be using the same controller card). Even better, you can use adhesive labels to identify connectors.
4. Remove the screws and pull the drive out of the cage. You now have an empty drive bay space for your new hard drive. It's time to go out with the old and bring in the new.

Tip

Be gentle when handling hard drives—they are fragile.

Installing And Formatting The New Hard Drive

Now we're ready to perform the actual installation. Follow these steps to install the new hard drive:

1. Hold your new drive in the drive bay. If you bought the hard drive with an installation kit (highly recommended), then all of the proper

rails and screws should be readily available, as shown in Figures 22.6 and 22.7. Just use the hardware to mount the new board, similar to the way the old hard drive was mounted. You should also find documentation with your installation kit that explains some of the variations for installation.

2. With the rails in place (if they're necessary), attach the data cable to the connector on the back of your hard drive, as shown in Figure 22.8. Take extra care to check the orientation of the connector—look for the side of the ribbon cable that has a single wire of a different color. The

Figure 22.6 You may need rails to fit your hard drive into your system's cradle.

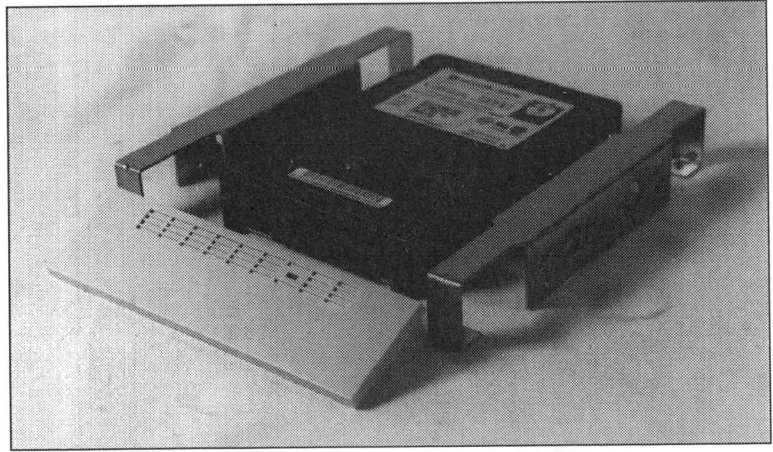

Figure 22.7 The type of rails that come in a hard drive kit.

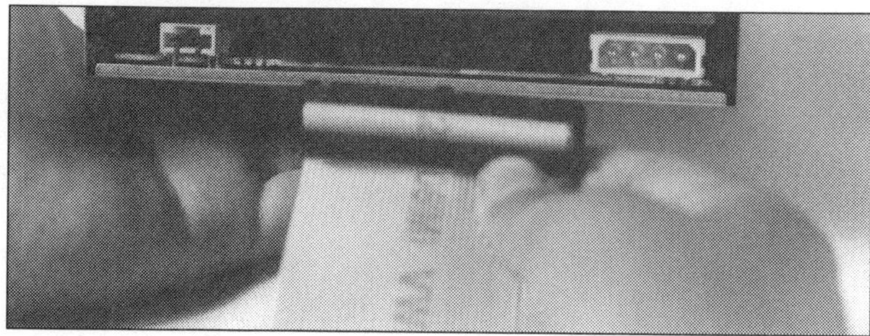

Figure 22.8 Attach the cable to your hard drive. Look for the colored wire on the cable that will attach to the first pin of a connector.

side of the connector nearest the colored wire needs to be aligned with pin 1 on the hard drive connector and pin 1 on the controller card—both of these usually have a diagram that shows you the connections.

3. Attach the power connector as shown in Figure 22.9. If you labeled the connectors, they will be easy to find. You can insert these cables in only one way.
4. Check all connections and screws to ensure that your installation is secure.
5. Before replacing the cover, reconnect your video card, keyboard, and mouse, then reconnect the power to your PC and check to see that the computer boots up.

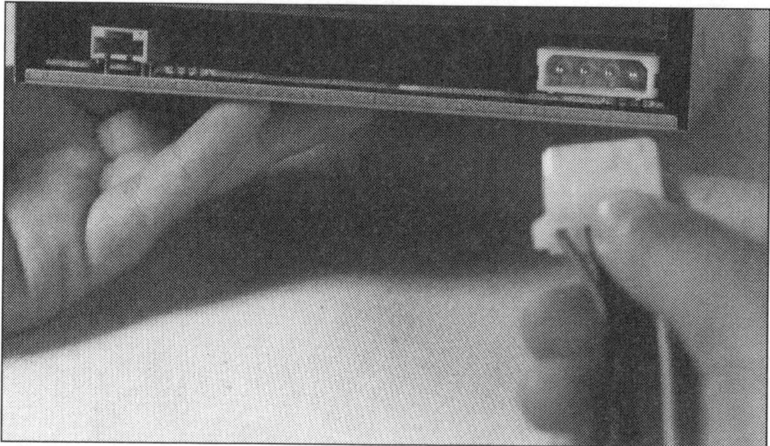

Figure 22.9 Install the power cable. (Please note that the previously installed data cable has been removed for picture clarity.)

Caution

Don't forget that you have a live machine. Under no circumstance should you probe your PC or touch any components when your system is running. *Always* shut off power before doing any work on your PC or removing or adjusting any component. Not only could you get a dangerous shock, you could also fry system components.

Also, it's very important to install your hard drive so that it can't move. It must be stationary in order to run properly.

6. If everything looks okay, put the cover back on. You're now ready to move on to the configuration of your hard drive.

7. At this point you've physically installed your new hard drive, but your system doesn't know it's there. So that your system and BIOS can recognize it, you might have to set your system's CMOS. Most newer motherboards will automatically detect your new drive and configure it when you turn on your system.

   If your system doesn't automatically detect a new hard drive, check your hard drive's documentation first, because some drives come with very specific instructions. You will have to access your system's CMOS by booting the computer and holding down a key (this key varies from system to system). With most installations you can work with an auto-detect mode in your system's CMOS and your computer will automatically identify and configure the hard drive. In other systems, you will have to manually enter the parameters for your new hard drive. Check your PC and hard drive documentation for instructions and for information about what settings (cylinders, heads, tracks, and so on) to enter for your drive. Access the CMOS screen and type in the hard drive settings.

8. Reboot your system (if you are adding a new main drive, use a bootable floppy disk that contains the basic DOS commands; see Chapter 6). Most new drives come from the factory already low-level *formatted*. What you will have to do now is create a disk *partition*.

9. To partition your drive, use a DOS utility called FDISK (fdisk.exe). Depending on how you want your system to recognize your drive, you can use FDISK as follows: FDISK displays a screen that lets you create a DOS partition or logical DOS drive. Look for the command that says "Create a DOS Partition or Logical Drive."

Definition, Please

Formatting refers to preparing your drive so that it's ready to be used. It's much like defining how it will use its space to store data.

When you *partition* a hard drive, you define how the drive will appear in your system. For example, if you have a 2GB drive, you can have your system recognize and use this drive as a 2GB space or drive or you can partition the drive into two 1GB drives.

When asked if you want to use the maximum size available for the partition, answer Y (yes) if you want to create one large disk or N (no) if you want to divide your new drive into smaller disks. You then specify the size of the disks in terms of number of megabytes or percentage of capacity. After that, set the main drive as the active partition by typing the command "Set Active Partition."

10. Reboot your system.
11. After partitioning your new drive, you must format it. For this, use the DOS utility called FORMAT (format.exe). If you've installed a main bootable C: hard drive, type: "format c:/s". For other drives, replace the letter c with the appropriate drive letter and remove the /s, which tells the computer to format a disk so that it can boot. For example, to format drive D:, type: "format d:".

    This procedure will also format the new disks you created when you partitioned the disk.

Caution

If you type the wrong drive letter while using the FORMAT utility, you can wipe out an entire disk. Be extra sure that you're typing in the number or letter of the drive that contains the disk that you want to format. Just to play it safe, try typing DIR on any drive before you format it. If you see data and directories, you may be formatting the wrong disk.

12. If your system boots up properly after the partition and format, you will now have a lot of new hard drive space. So far, so good. At this point, you can try to copy files to the hard drive. If successful, you're set.

13. Turn off your system, disconnect the power, put the cover back on, reconnect everything, and you're done. On the other hand, if things aren't working, please refer to the next section.

Troubleshooting

If, at any point in the previous procedure, your system won't read your drive, the following suggestions might help:

- If you're greeted with a message that says "Hard Disk Drive Controller Failure," double-check your connections and power. If these are in order, your problem is likely an incorrect system configuration or setting. Recheck your CMOS to see that you have the right settings and then go over the drive settings that you initially made.
- If you see a message that says "No ROM Basic—System Halted," rerun FDISK and be sure that the hard drive used to boot the system is set as the active drive.
- If your system boots up but doesn't seem to recognize the new drive, your master/slave settings may be incorrect. Check them.
- If your screen comes up blank, check your video and monitor first for power and connections.
- If, after experimenting, you can't make your drive work, call technical support for the drive manufacturer. They can help you troubleshoot your setup.

Moving On

After following the instructions in this chapter, you now have a newly installed hard drive. In the next chapter, I'll show you how to install a new CPU and swap a motherboard.

23

Swapping The CPU And/Or Motherboard

In this chapter, I'll show you how to upgrade the computers on your network by either swapping the CPU, or the motherboard and CPU. If any task resembles computer brain surgery, this is it. However, the resemblance only has to do with the part being operated on, not the difficulty. Although this is the most involved task you can do with your PC, it's manageable.

The first part of this chapter covers replacing the CPU on your motherboard—either by installing an upgrade chip or a faster processor. The second half of this chapter explains how to replace the motherboard itself. For background information on CPU and motherboard upgrades, refer to Chapter 20.

Upgrade And Overdrive Chips

You can upgrade some 486 and Pentium motherboards by adding an Intel Overdrive chip or Evergreen or Kingston upgrade chip; some Pentium motherboards will let you change some board settings and replace the Pentium CPU with a faster one. If you're installing a faster Pentium (not an upgrade or Overdrive chip), please jump to the "Upgrading The CPU On A Pentium Motherboard" section later in this chapter.

With Pentium class systems, the upgrade or Overdrive chips replace your current Pentium CPU. In 486 class systems, the upgrade chips either replace your current chip or fit into a special—and separate—Overdrive socket. You'll find that an upgrade chip usually comes with its own fan or radiator to cool the chip, so you can simply install the chip.

If you're not sure whether this is the correct upgrade path for you, read Chapter 2; it will help you decide whether a CPU upgrade will meet your computing needs. In any event, this type of fast and simple upgrade can boost your computer's horsepower significantly.

Check with your dealer or manufacturer to be certain your motherboard can accept an Overdrive or upgrade chip. I can't emphasize the importance of this enough. You might, for instance, see something on your motherboard that looks like an upgrade socket, but which is really for another chip. I've also seen boards that have a socket that looks as if it should accept the Overdrive chip—in fact, the Overdrive chip does physically fit in it—but it doesn't work. Finally, check on the type of Overdrive chip your motherboard can accept, because several different kinds are available. After you have verified which chip your motherboard can accept and have it in hand, the upgrade should go smoothly from there.

Another good place to check on compatibility issues is the Web site of the upgrade chip manufacturer (see Table 23.1).

Most motherboards, like the one shown in Figure 23.1, come with only one socket. In this case, you will have to remove the current CPU and replace it with the upgrade CPU.

Fortunately, most motherboards that accept an upgrade chip come with a zero insertion force (ZIF) socket. This type of socket has a mechanism that actually clamps down on the pins of the chip to hold it and releases to let it go. This makes it easy to remove one chip and install another. You can recognize a ZIF socket by the lever that's attached to it. You'll find ZIF sockets on Pentium motherboards and on many 486 boards. On the other hand, some 486 motherboards don't offer a ZIF socket. For these you'll have to use a chip puller (one usually comes with the

Table 23.1 Web sites of upgrade or Overdrive chip manufacturers.

Manufacturer	Web Site URL
Evergreen	**www.evertech.com**
Intel	**www.intel.com**
Kingston	**www.kingston.com**

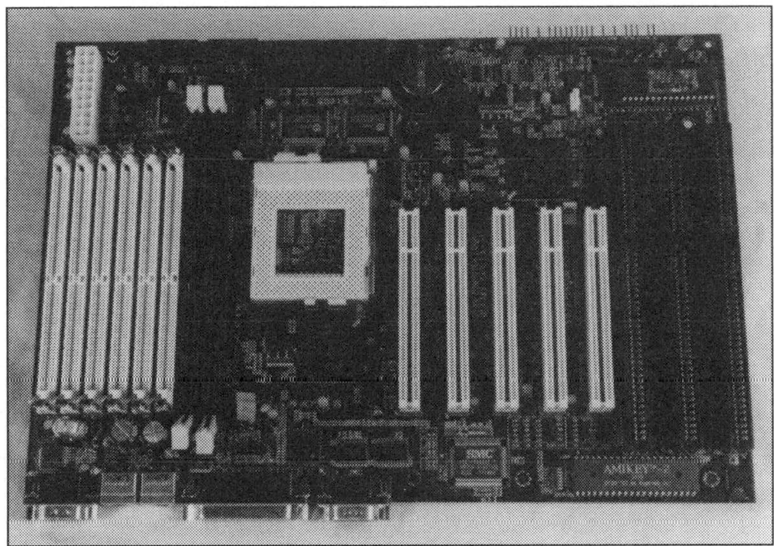

Figure 23.1 Most motherboards come with only a single socket for the CPU, Overdrive, or upgrade chip.

Overdrive chip) and install the replacement chip by lining it up and gently pushing it in.

Another type of 486 motherboard features an additional socket that holds the Overdrive chip in addition to the CPU already on the board. In this case, simply add a chip to the board, and the chip takes over the CPU's function.

Tip

Adding an upgrade chip makes for a fast and easy upgrade. If you don't run into any snags along the way, this very straightforward upgrade should take less than 45 minutes. From time and cost perspectives, it's a winner. Most of your work lies in verifying that your motherboard will accept this upgrade and buying the right part.

Caution—Data

Back up all of the important data on your computer before beginning any upgrade or repair and take a minute to record information about your hard drive and other system information listed in your *complementary metal-oxide semiconductor* (CMOS), as outlined in Chapter 22.

Opening The Computer Case

Follow these steps to open the computer case:

1. First, shut off your PC and unplug it.
2. Disconnect all of the cables and connectors attached to your computer—power, printer cables, speakers, telephone line, keyboard, mouse, video connections, and so on.
3. Now you're ready to remove the screws, which you'll usually find along the back side of the computer case, as shown in Figure 23.2.

Caution

When removing screws from the back of the case, be sure to remove only those that appear to hold the case. If you go overboard and remove all the screws, you may hear internal components—the power supply, for example—drop loose and fall down inside your computer. Be conservative. Remove the obvious screws first and then see if the case cover budges.

4. When you have removed the screws, gently push the cover to see if it moves. If it does, slide the cover off the case. If it doesn't, you probably missed a screw. Check for any errant screws and then try to budge the cover again.

   On a desktop machine (see Figure 23.3), the cover usually slides backward, away from the front of the computer. On a tower case (see Figure 23.4), the cover can slide either forward or backward. Of course, your case may not fall into any of these categories. Some cases swivel, others lift off, and still others don't even use screws—you

Figure 23.2 The screws that hold the case on are usually on the back of the computer.

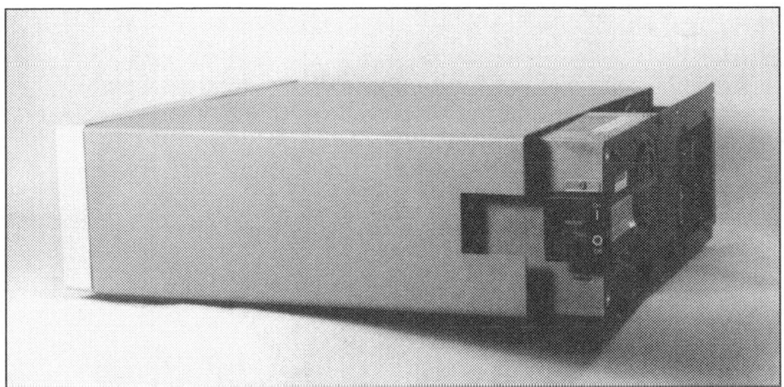

Figure 23.3 A typical desktop case cover opens by sliding the chassis back from the front of the computer.

Figure 23.4 A typical tower case cover opens by sliding either forward or backward off the case.

simply depress a couple of buttons to open the case. Please refer to your system's documentation for more information on how to open the case.

5. With your PC's cover off, you're ready to begin working.

Caution

Before making any changes to your motherboard and reaching into your computer, be sure that the power is disconnected and your system is off.

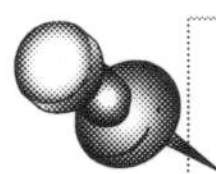

Upgrade chips come with their own installation instructions. Follow these more specific instructions when they differ from the more general directions in this chapter. For example, the first step in upgrading with an Evergreen chip is using a provided floppy disk to boot your system and check out whether your system will accept the upgrade chip and make system changes.

Switches And Speeds

When installing an upgrade chip, in most cases you'll have to adjust *switches* on your board so it's running at the correct speed to support your upgraded CPU. In some cases (and this is explained in the documentation that comes with the upgrade chips), you may not have to make any changes at all.

Definition, Please

A *switch* is a board device that lets you adjust settings.

The instructions that come with your upgraded CPU will feature a chart that tells you what speed your board should be set to in order to support the new chip. This speed is usually dependent on the type of motherboard you have and the upgrade chip you are installing.

To set the board's speed:

1. Check the documentation that comes with your motherboard to see how to configure the board settings. Most motherboards have diagrams right on them that show their configuration (see Figure 23.5). Even better, Evergreen upgrade chips come with software that tries to identify your motherboard; in many cases it also diagrams where on the board you make the settings and explains how to set them.

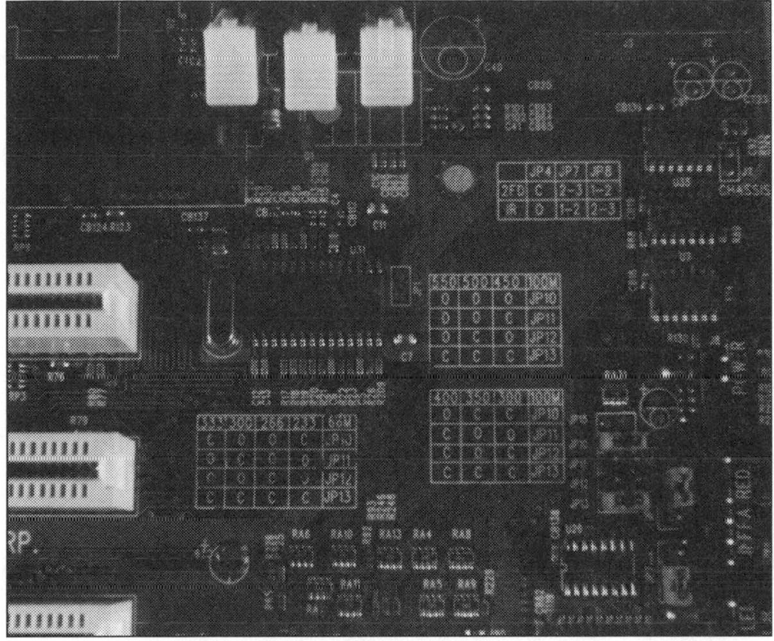

Figure 23.5 Many boards have diagrams that tell you how to set the speed of the board.

2. You make the settings with switches, like that shown in Figure 23.6, that you set "on" and "off." You can use tweezers or the tip of a screwdriver to make adjustments to the switches.

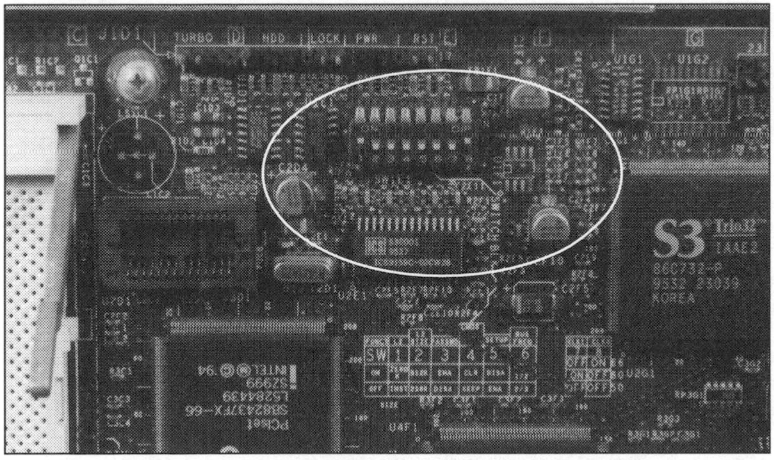

Figure 23.6 Many boards feature switches that you use to adjust the board settings to support your new upgrade chip.

3. Once you find the switches, you can usually make the adjustments in less than a minute, and then you're ready to add or replace your new CPU.

Replacing Your ZIF-Socketed Upgrade Chip

Follow these instructions if your motherboard has a ZIF socket:

1. Lift the lever on the ZIF socket to release the CPU chip, as shown in Figure 23.7. Gently remove the chip.
2. Insert the Overdrive chip into the socket. For alignment purposes, there's usually a notch in the corner, as shown in Figure 23.8. Align the notch on the chip with that of the socket, and then adjust the rest of the legs to fit into their corresponding sockets. You may need to move the chip around a bit, but it should fall into place the instant the legs are completely aligned. Once the chip drops down into the socket, it's correctly placed. Take a quick look to make sure that all pins are in contact.
3. With the chip in place, push down the handle that's attached to the ZIF socket to close it.

Figure 23.7 Lift the lever on the ZIF socket to release the CPU.

Figure 23.8 Look for the notch to align the chip with its socket.

Replacing Your Non-ZIF-Socketed Upgrade Chip

Follow these instructions if your motherboard does not have a ZIF socket:

1. Intel should provide a specialized tool—it looks like a small fork—that helps you remove your current CPU. Use it to pry the chip up carefully, one side at a time, until it is released.
2. With the socket free, you now can install the Overdrive chip. Carefully align it with the socket, as explained in the instructions that come with the chip, and gently push it in. It helps to apply pressure evenly across the chip.

Installing The Chip In A Socket Near Your CPU

You will need to follow these instructions when your motherboard offers a separate socket that's specifically designed for the upgrade chip:

1. Place the Overdrive chip on the open socket and line up its pins, as explained in the instructions that come with the chip.

2. Carefully push the chip down into the socket. It helps to apply pressure evenly across the chip.

Testing The System

Before you close up your computer, it's a good idea to test your system. Double-check your chip installation, plug your computer in, and see if it boots up normally.

Caution—Safety

Don't forget that when you test your computer with the cover off, you have a live machine. Under no circumstance should you probe your PC or touch any internal component when your system is running. Always shut off power and unplug your computer before doing any work on your PC or before removing or adjusting any component. Not only could you get a dangerous shock, you could also fry your components.

If everything looks normal and the machine is running faster, you have successfully replaced the chip. Congratulations! Replace the cover on your machine, reconnect the cables, and you're done. On the other hand, if your computer isn't booting correctly, read the next section.

Troubleshooting The Upgrade Chip Installation

If your computer doesn't work correctly after you replace your CPU with an Overdrive or upgrade chip, something that occurred during the installation has caused a problem. After all, the computer worked fine before you made the upgrade. Check the following:

- Double-check the chip installation. Make sure the chip is installed properly and seated securely in its socket. Also, verify that you didn't disconnect any other cables or components when you replaced the chip. After inspecting the connections, expansion boards, and chip, try booting again.
- Look at the board settings. Make sure that you set the switches correctly, according to the instructions provided with the chip. Usually, the settings that you make on your board will depend on the type of motherboard that you have. Be sure that you are reading the settings for your motherboard and upgrade chip.

- Sometimes when working on your PC, your CMOS can become erased. To check for this, reboot your computer and bring up the system configuration screen (the way you bring this up varies from system to system—check your PC's documentation). In this case, you'll need to reenter the system information that you wrote down before you began the upgrade.

If you're absolutely sure that your connections look right and the computer still won't boot, see if the chip's manual has any other suggestions. Call the manufacturer of the upgrade chip for troubleshooting assistance. As a last resort, you can reinstall your old CPU chip and see if the computer runs (be sure to return your board to its original settings). If it does, there's probably something wrong with the new chip. However, if your old chip doesn't run anything, you've inadvertently changed something in your system. Check those connections again.

Upgrading The CPU On A Pentium Motherboard

With many Pentium motherboards, you can change board settings and swap a faster Pentium chip in the board's socket. This process is more involved than performing the processor upgrade mentioned previously—you have to adjust more settings on the board, and to do this, you may have to remove your motherboard from its case—no small task. In any event, it's a fairly fast upgrade that can boost your computer's horsepower significantly.

First, check your motherboard's documentation to see if it can accept a faster Pentium chip than the one that you are currently running. You should see a list of processors and speeds that your board supports. If your documentation doesn't list these, check with your dealer or manufacturer to be certain your motherboard can accept a faster chip. I can't emphasize the importance of this enough.

When you buy a new Pentium processor, it may not come with a fan. When you purchase the processor from a dealer, be sure to ask if you should also buy a fan or heat sink to use with the chip.

After you've purchased your new CPU, here's how to install it.

Caution—Data

Back up all of the important data on your computer before beginning any upgrade or repair and take the time to record information about your hard drive and other system information listed in your CMOS, as outlined in Chapter 22.

Caution—Safety

Before making any changes to your motherboard and reaching into your computer, be sure that the power is disconnected and your system is off.

Follow these steps to upgrade the CPU on a Pentium motherboard:

1. Shut off your PC and unplug it.
2. Following the directions and cautionary notes in the "Opening The Computer Case" section earlier in this chapter, open your PC's case. With the cover off, you're ready to begin.
3. So your board can accommodate a different speed Pentium chip, you'll need to make adjustments to various jumpers and switches on the board. Refer to charts that are in your motherboard documentation; find the chart in the documentation and then look up the chip that you are installing. You will see a series of settings.

Definition, Please

A *jumper* is a board device that lets you adjust settings.

Most boards use jumpers, as shown in Figure 23.9. This jumper is "on" because the jumper covers both pins (wires). To turn the jumper "off," you would remove the jumper and leave the pins unconnected, as shown Figure 23.10.

Still other jumpers may ask you to cover certain number pins. For example, the chart may tell you to cover "3&4." In this case, the jumper probably offers four or more pins, and you must use the jumper to cover (join) only the third and fourth pins. To help you find the order of the

Figure 23.9 A jumper that is on.

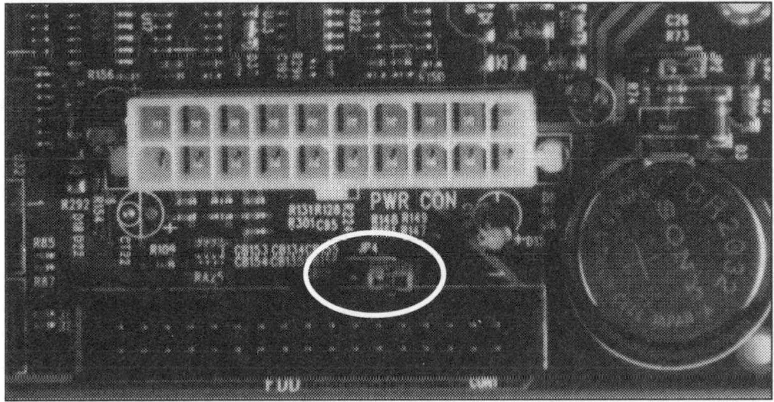

Figure 23.10 A jumper that is off.

pins, most boards will show you the location of the first pin with a "1," as shown in Figure 23.11.

Replacing Your ZIF-Socketed CPU

Follow these instructions if your motherboard has a ZIF socket:

1. Lift the lever on the ZIF socket to release the CPU chip, as shown in Figure 23.12. Gently remove the chip.
2. Insert the new chip into the socket. For alignment purposes, there's usually a notch in the corner, as shown in Figure 23.13. Align the notch on the chip with that of the socket, and then adjust the rest of the legs to fit into their corresponding sockets. You may need to move the chip around a bit, but it should fall into place the instant the legs are completely aligned. Once the chip drops down into the

Figure 23.11 A jumper with numbers.

Figure 23.12 Lift the lever on the ZIF socket to release the CPU.

socket, it's correctly placed. Take a quick look to make sure that all pins are in contact.

3. With the chip in place, push down the handle that's attached to the ZIF socket to close it.

Figure 23.13 Look for the notch to align the chip with its socket.

Testing The System

Before you close up your computer, it's a good idea to test your system. Double-check your chip installation, plug your computer in, and see if it boots up normally.

Caution—Safety

Don't forget that when you test your computer with the cover off, you have a live machine. Under no circumstance should you probe your PC or touch any internal component when your system is running. Always shut off power and unplug your computer before doing any work on your PC or before removing or adjusting any component. Not only could you get a dangerous shock, you could also fry your components.

If everything looks normal and the machine is running faster, you have successfully replaced the chip. Congratulations! At this point, you can replace the cover on your machine, reconnect the cables, and you're done. On the other hand, if your computer isn't booting correctly, read the next section.

Troubleshooting The Chip Installation

If your computer doesn't work correctly after you replace your CPU with another one, something that occurred during the installation has caused a problem. After all, the computer worked fine before you made the upgrade. Check the following:

- Double-check the chip installation. Make sure the chip is installed properly and seated securely in its socket. Also verify that you didn't disconnect any other cables or components when you replaced the chip. After inspecting the connections, expansion boards, and chip, try booting again.
- Look at the board settings. Make sure that you set the switches and jumpers correctly, according to the instructions provided with the motherboard.
- Sometimes when working on your PC, your system information can become erased. To check for this, reboot your computer and bring up the system configuration screen (the way you bring this up varies from system to system—check your PC's documentation). In this case, you'll need to reenter the CMOS information that you wrote down before you began the upgrade.

If you're absolutely sure that your connections look right and the computer still won't boot, see if the motherboard's manual has any other suggestions. Call the manufacturer of the motherboard for troubleshooting assistance. As a last resort, you can reinstall your old CPU chip and see if the computer runs (be sure to return your board to its original settings). If it does, there's probably something wrong with the new chip. However, if your old chip doesn't run anything, you've inadvertently changed something in your system. Check those connections again.

Replacing The Motherboard

Now we're talking major surgery. Replacing your motherboard is, quite frankly, the most involved task covered in this book. The task itself is fairly straightforward, but it takes time and careful, steady work. If things go perfectly, you should be able to complete it in less than three hours. However, things don't always go as they should, and you can get stuck trying to reinstall the cables. I'll do my best to help you avoid problems.

At this point, you're probably sitting there with your new motherboard in hand, ready to put it in. I hope that Chapter 20 helped you decide what type of motherboard you need and that you're now excited about the new possibilities of your upgraded machine. If you're still wondering what type of motherboard upgrade you want to make, review Chapter 20, which discusses your options.

Installing RAM For Your Motherboard

If you have random access memory (RAM) to install on your motherboard, it's best to do this before you actually install the board in the computer, because you'll have a much easier time getting at the sockets. (For more information on installing RAM, please refer to Chapter 21.) This tip also applies to any cache that you may want to add to the motherboard (most motherboards these days come with a built-in cache) and to CPUs.

Opening Your PC

Before you open your computer's case and begin, please take the time to read this entire chapter for an idea of the tasks involved and the overall scope of this project. Just in case, allocate a lot of time for this project. Don't try to squeeze this upgrade in between appointments, or you'll inevitably find yourself with your system completely dismantled and your biggest client breathing down your neck.

Caution—Data

Back up all of the important data on your computer before beginning any upgrade or repair, and take the time to record information about your hard drive and system settings in your PC's CMOS. To find out how to access the CMOS, check your system's documentation.

Shut off your PC and unplug it. Follow the directions and cautionary notes presented earlier in the "Opening The Computer Case" section of this chapter to open your PC's case. With the cover off, you're ready to begin.

Removing The Motherboard

If you are installing a new motherboard into a new case, please skip to the section "Installing The New Motherboard" later in this chapter.

To remove the motherboard:

1. First, you'll need to remove components so you can get at the motherboard. Before you begin removing expansion cards, be sure to disconnect all cables that connect to the power supply, the expansion cards, and the motherboard. It's a good idea to write down exactly where each connector goes and preferably label each of them.

2. You're now ready to remove the expansion cards. Unscrew and remove the screw that secures each board to its case's slot. Gently lift each board out, using a rocking motion if necessary.

Caution—Removing Expansion Cards

Always hold expansion cards by their edges and try not to touch the metal connectors that fit into the PC's slots. Your body can build up enough static electricity to fry an entire card or one of its components, rendering it useless.

Cable Tips

Some internal connectors and cables may be stretched to their maximum lengths in order to reach their boards. After you install your new motherboard, you'll probably have more success getting the cables to reach their boards if you replace each board in its original place first. On the other hand, you might need to switch the order of some boards to make it easier to route the cables. Do what is necessary. If you label your boards and slots (on the case) as you install them, it will be easier to reinstall them next time.

3. Disconnect all cables and connectors, including the power cables, between the motherboard and other components. As with the expansion cards, it helps to label the cable connectors so it's easy to figure out where they go when you reassemble your system. With a new motherboard installed, things can look different, though most components will go back in their original place in the case.

   When removing connectors that have flat ribbon cables (these look like a bunch of wires taped together in a flexible flat cable a couple of inches wide), look for the stripe on one side of the cable and note how it connects to the motherboard. You can use this as a reference when you connect it to a new motherboard. The stripe, as shown on the ribbon cables in Figure 23.14, represents the wire that connects to a connector's first pin.

You'll find that most power connectors are of the Molex variety, as shown in Figure 23.15. Although these can be stiff, you can work them off by carefully rocking the connector back and forth and

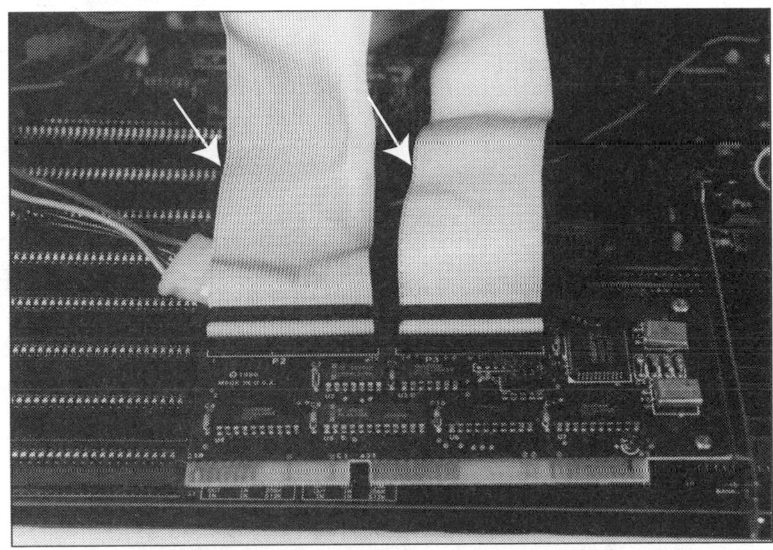

Figure 23.14 The stripe on one side of the ribbon cable is a distinguishable mark you can use as a reference.

Figure 23.15 A Molex power connector.

pulling gently. Record what component each power cable connects to; however, you won't have to note which direction to install a Molex connector, because they only mate in one direction. Also, you probably won't have to remove your power supply to take out the motherboard—at least, I've never had to do so.

Caution

When removing cables, pay particular attention to how the power cables—the ones that come from the power supply—are connected. If you reconnect these incorrectly, you can fry your new motherboard. Take notes or make a sketch.

4. Next, remove the hard drives and floppy drives, which are usually mounted with screws in a metal cradle or cage, as shown in Figure 23.16. To do so, carefully loosen the screws that hold them to the cage. Most systems use four screws. After you loosen these, you'll find that the drives can move a little. Remove the connectors and cables if you can, noting where and to which drive they attach. Then, remove

Figure 23.16 The drives are mounted in a metal cage.

the screws and pull the drive out of the front of the cage. Be gentle with drives, particularly the hard disk. For more information on removing drives, refer to Chapter 22.

Tip—Removing Components And Fasteners

An old auto repair trick that works for me is to place components in a circle as you pull them out. Then, when you put them back in, you reverse their order. If you also label each component, this approach is virtually foolproof.

After removing the cables and components, you should be at the motherboard itself, as shown in Figure 23.17.

Motherboards and cases come in two different types: Baby AT and ATX styles. Most Baby AT motherboards are attached to the case with screws and little plastic fasteners called *standoffs*. You can identify standoffs by their plastic heads, as shown in Figure 23.18. ATX-style motherboards, on the other hand, attach to their cases with screws. Keep in mind that Baby AT motherboards will only fit into Baby AT cases, and ATX motherboards will only fit into ATX cases.

Figure 23.17 After removing expansion boards, connectors, and system components, you should be right over the motherboard.

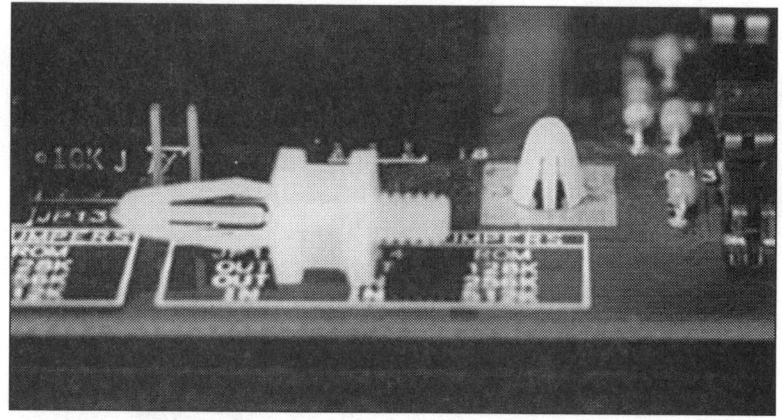

Figure 23.18 Plastic standoffs hold the motherboard in place.

Removing The Motherboard From A Baby AT-Style Case

To remove your Baby AT motherboard:

1. Remove the screws one by one.
2. With the screws gone, you should be able to slide the motherboard away from the power supply, and then lift the board out. If the board doesn't move, check to see if you missed any screws.

Removing The Motherboard From An ATX-Style Case

On many ATX cases, you'll find a panel that slides out and holds the motherboard, as shown in Figure 23.19.

To remove the ATX motherboard:

1. Remove the screws one by one.
2. With the screws gone, remove the PC's components (as explained in the "Removing The Motherboard" section earlier in this chapter).
3. Lift the board out. If the board doesn't budge, look to see if any remaining screws are still holding down the board.

Stay with me—we're more than halfway there.

Installing The New Motherboard

To put all the components now sitting on your workbench back together in your case (in the right place), begin by lining up your new motherboard at the bottom of the PC case.

Figure 23.19 Many ATX cases feature a panel that holds the motherboard; this panel can slide out.

Installing A Baby AT Motherboard Into Its Case

Follow these steps to install a Baby AT motherboard:

1. Look through the holes in your motherboard; you should see corresponding holes underneath in the PC case. Don't worry if you can't match all the holes. It's not unusual to have to skip some holes; Baby AT motherboards usually don't line up 100 percent with Baby AT cases. Decide if there are matchups for enough screws to safely and securely hold the board in the case or if you'll have to return the motherboard to the store and find another that will fit. Five or six matchups is usually a good number.
2. After verifying that the holes line up, hold the board in place and make sure that the slots on the motherboard line up with the slots on the case. Again, you can't do much if they don't, and you'll have to make a judgment call as to whether this motherboard is worth keeping or should be exchanged.
3. When the holes and slots line up reasonably well, you're in business. If you haven't added your new RAM chips or CPU, do so now, before you place the motherboard into the case. (Installing RAM is covered in

Chapter 21.) If you have to make any changes to board settings, as specified in your motherboard's installation instructions, make them now.

4. Hook the standoffs in their respective slots and slide your motherboard toward the power supply, reversing the process that you used to remove the old one. Standoffs sometimes get caught, so you have to persevere until they fall into place.
5. With the board seated, replace the screws.

Installing An ATX Motherboard Into Its Case

Follow these steps to install an ATX motherboard:

1. If you are working with a brand-new ATX case, it may have a panel that slides out and holds the motherboard. Pull out the panel first to make it easier to mount the board.
2. Install the metal standoffs (these usually come with the case in a little plastic bag). Line up your motherboard in its case and note the holes that line up with the case. Unlike Baby AT cases and motherboards, ATX cases and motherboards usually line up. Remove the motherboard and insert the metal standoffs by screwing them in, as shown in Figure 23.20.
3. If you have removed an ATX motherboard from an ATX case, you should have a series of metal standoffs on the bottom of the case that

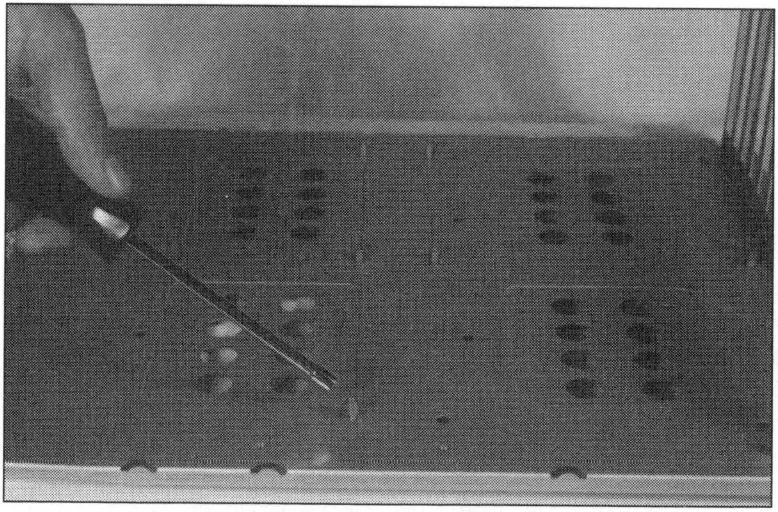

Figure 23.20 Insert the metal standoffs into your ATX case.

you can attach your motherboard to. You may have to move some of these to accommodate a new ATX motherboard. Line up your motherboard in its case and observe the holes with which it lines up; then, adjust the placement of the standoffs as needed.

4. Install the small metal connector panel, as shown in Figure 23.21, around the motherboard's external connectors (parallel, USB, and so forth).

   These panels usually come with the case. To install the panel, you may have to punch out holes to match the connectors on your motherboard. Many cases come with more than one panel, so you will need to choose the panel that best matches your motherboard. If you don't install this panel now, you won't be able to later. The plate basically lodges between the case and the motherboard.

5. If you haven't added your new RAM chips or CPU, do so now, before you place the motherboard into the case. (Installing RAM is covered in Chapter 21.) If you have to make any changes to board settings, as specified in your motherboard's installation instructions, make them now.

6. Lay your motherboard in place and screw in the screws so they connect to the standoffs, as shown in Figure 23.22.

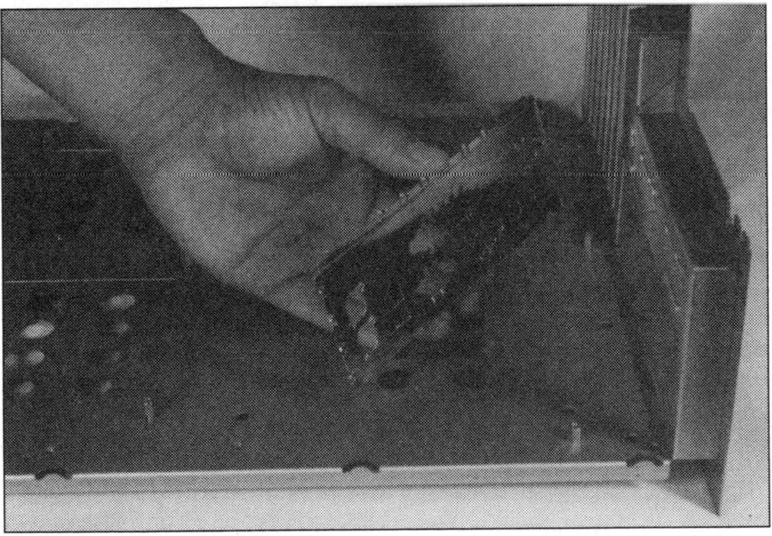

Figure 23.21 The thin metal panel that fits around the ATX motherboard's external connectors.

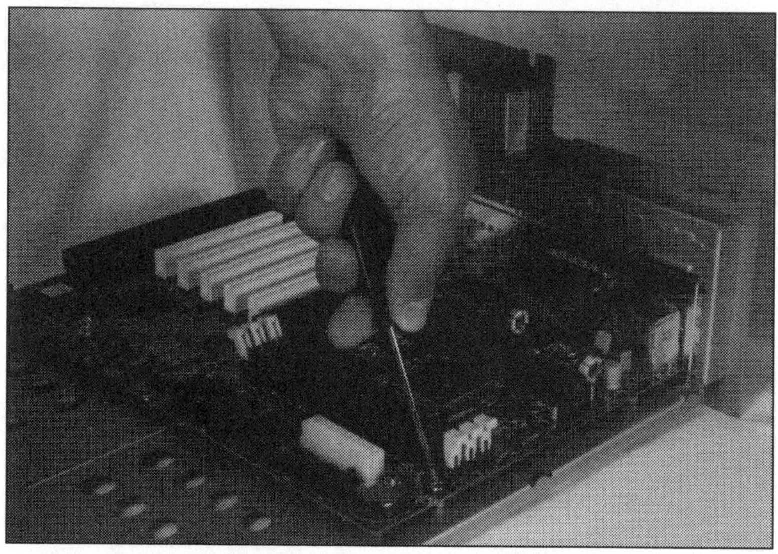

Figure 23.22 Install screws to hold the motherboard in place.

Testing And Finishing The Installation

After the motherboard is in place and before putting back the rest of the components and the expansion boards, it's a good idea to test the motherboard to make sure it works. Discovering a problem with your motherboard at this point will save a lot of troubleshooting later.

Caution—Safety

Before turning your computer on to test the new motherboard, be sure to recheck the power connection to the motherboard. It could be dangerous to turn the power on if the motherboard is not connected.

Also, don't forget that you have a live machine. Under no circumstance should you probe your PC or touch any components while your system is running. Always shut off power and unplug your computer before doing any work on your PC or before removing or adjusting any component. Not only could you get a dangerous shock, you could also fry your components.

To test the motherboard:

1. Reconnect power to the board. With a Baby AT case, refer to your diagrams. With an ATX case, you can simply connect the power cable, as shown in Figure 23.23.

Figure 23.23 The ATX Power Connection.

2. After connecting power, install the video card and connect the keyboard and monitor. With ATX cases that support *soft power* (the ability to shut off power when given a command from the motherboard), connect a cable from the case's switch (usually labeled) to a contact on your motherboard (also labeled). Figure 23.24 shows the various motherboard connectors for various PC lights and switches that you'll need to connect. If the labels on the motherboard aren't clear, refer to the documentation that came with your motherboard.
3. When you turn on the power, the computer should display a picture and text that shows the amount of memory in your system and other

Figure 23.24 Look for the contacts to make connections to your case.

configurations. (By the way, it's okay at this point if your computer gives you error messages; that's natural, since you haven't configured the system yet.) If you get the picture and text, you can assume that everything thus far is fine. Switch off and disconnect power and continue reassembling your computer.

4. Next, reinstall the components and their connectors. Here's where the notes and labels that you wrote during disassembly will come in handy. (You did write them down, didn't you?) Now you just reverse the process. Don't forget to reconnect those wires that drive such things as the lights on the front of the case. If the labels on the motherboard aren't clear, you'll need to check with the documentation that came with your motherboard for more information. With the components and most connectors in place, you now can reinstall the expansion boards.
5. At the end, be sure to check to see if you have any extra parts left over—usually not a good sign, depending on what the parts are. Double-check your installations and cabling; make sure everything looks secure and connected.
6. Now, before you slide the cover back on, check once again that the PC is working. Reconnect the video monitor, mouse, and keyboard and fire up your machine.

Caution—Safety

Recheck the power connection to the motherboard. It could be dangerous to turn the power on if the motherboard is not connected properly. Also, don't forget that once again you have a live machine.

7. If you get a picture again, so far, so good. Now, to make everything run, configure the system via your PC's setup or configuration screen—also known as the CMOS. (The name—short for complementary metal-oxide semiconductor—comes from the semiconductor technology used in microcomputers.) Once you enter the parameters for your hard drives and other information, you'll be ready to roll. For more on drive settings, refer to Chapter 22. Most newer motherboards will be able to automatically detect your hard drive and configure it.

8. As you boot up your computer, listen and look for the usual order of sounds and events (your computer will sound slightly different with the cover off). If nothing happens or the system hangs up, shut everything off and try again. If it continues to hang up, unplug the system and recheck all of your installations and cable connections. If things still are not working, refer to the troubleshooting guide in the next section. If your system seems to be running normally—presumably a lot faster because of your new upgrade—you're set. You can turn off your machine, pull out all of the power cables and peripheral connectors, reinstall the cover, reconnect everything, and you're ready to roll. Congratulations on a job well done!

Troubleshooting The Motherboard Installation

The following suggestions may help troubleshoot your motherboard installation:

- If your system doesn't power up, you may have forgotten to reattach the power cable to your system. Also, with an ATX case, you may need to connect the case's switch to a connection on the motherboard.
- If your system stops during bootup:
  - Examine the messages displayed as the computer boots to see if the system identifies any problems. Try booting with your boot disk and then getting into your system to examine it for problems. If you can't access the hard drive, the culprit may be your setup, which you'll probably have to reset. In this case, reconfigure your PC settings and double-check the connections to your hard drive. You should check your system documentation for more information.
  - If this doesn't work, another strategy is to remove all of the expansion boards and then reinstall them one by one, testing the system at each stage. If a board is the problem, you'll be able to identify it.
  - If you're absolutely sure that your connections look right and the computer still won't boot, see if the motherboard's manual has any other suggestions. Call the manufacturer of the motherboard for assistance.

Moving On

Following the instructions in this chapter, you've replaced a CPU on a motherboard or installed a new motherboard. Now that your system has a faster, more powerful CPU, I'll discuss how to purchase a new workstation or server in the next chapter.

24

Buying New Workstations And Servers

In previous chapters, we discussed at length the hardware upgrades that you can perform on servers and workstations to increase their speed and improve network performance. However, sometimes the best solution is to purchase a new workstation or server for your network. One common reason to do so is if you would have to replace a lot of components in an existing system to make it work well on your network, and it would cost less to simply buy a newer and faster computer. Another scenario is if you have no extra system that may be turned into a server. For these situations, you can follow the suggestions in this chapter to help you with the process.

Purchasing A New Workstation Or Server

Before you buy a new workstation or server, you should evaluate what it is you want to accomplish. More than likely, you're considering such a purchase because some tasks that you perform on your network take too long. And instead of a hardware upgrade for your server or workstation, you can resolve these issues by purchasing new systems.

When making this decision, keep in mind the following questions:

- Are applications taking a long time to load?
- Are applications sluggish when handling data?
- Do database searches take an eternity?
- Does your computer often keep you waiting?

- Have you avoided purchasing new software or a new operating system because your computer or network can't run it?
- Are you constantly running out of storage space on your workstations or on your server?

With these points in mind, here are some of the factors you should consider when buying new computers.

Memory

Memory plays a key role in a system's performance, and you'll want to purchase a server with lots of memory. In particular, if your network has to handle large files and several users at a time, the more memory that your system has, the better. Keep in mind that it's not unusual for servers to have 128MB or 256MB of RAM. For details on the benefits of additional memory, refer to the "Memory" section in Chapter 20.

Hard Drive

The hard drive space on your server determines its capacity. You'll need to purchase a server with a hard drive that will let users adequately access the applications stored on it, and meet your data file storage needs. For more details on hard drives, refer to the "Hard Drives" section in Chapter 20.

CPU

The heart of any computer is the *central processing unit* (*CPU*). The faster the CPU, the better the performance. As I write this, the 450MHz Pentium II is the fastest Pentium II on the market, and you can buy various multiple-processor configurations and a very fast Pentium Xeon that is meant for servers. For more information, refer to "The CPU And Motherboard" section in Chapter 20.

Tips For Purchasing New Systems

If you do purchase computers for your network, here are some tips that the pros use when they go on a buying spree.

Stick With A Trusted Vendor

Whenever possible, try to find a system vendor that you like and stay with that vendor. Although this isn't always possible, you'll often find that systems from the same manufacturer will work better with each other in a network.

You'll find other advantages when you work with the same trusted vendor. When you get used to the idiosyncrasies of a PC from a single vendor, you'll often find that systems from the same manufacturer will display similar tendencies. Also, if your systems come from the same company, you'll only have to deal with the tech support of a single company when you need to troubleshoot your network and computers. Finally, if you purchase several PCs from the same vendor, you may be able to negotiate a quantity discount that will save you some money.

Check Compatibility With Windows NT

If there's a chance that you will someday upgrade your network to run Windows NT (or the next NT incarnation, Windows 2000), you may want to check that the system you buy is compatible with it. Although most systems should be compatible, this is something that you may want to consider. You can find the list of compatible NT hardware on Microsoft's Web site (**www.microsoft.com**).

Investigate Pre-Installation Of Components

If you can afford it, have the vendor pre-install the operating system and the office applications. This also goes for the peripherals, the CD-ROM drives, and other add-ons. This will save you time when the system arrives.

Review Documentation, Warranty, And Return Policy

Make sure that the vendor includes all of the documentation. This can prove to be invaluable when you need to troubleshoot the system.

Also, thoroughly review and understand the vendor's warranty on the system, as well as the return policy. For more on buying hardware, refer to Chapter 5.

Consider Network-Specific Features

You can purchase network-specific features in a new system, but these will increase the price. Most small networks won't need these features; however, if they sound like they will be useful for your network, or you think that your network will grow to need these add-ons, you may want to consider them:

- *Desktop Management Interface* (*DMI 2.0*) *support*—This feature helps you track the hardware and software in a PC.
- *Lockdown settings*—This feature prevents users from changing the system settings on their computers.
- *Remote flash BIOS upgrade*—This feature lets you update the system BIOS when you need to.
- *Wakeup-on-LAN*—This feature lets you manage a PC when it's been turned off. You can send a message to a PC across the network, have it wake itself up, then configure it, add software, or whatever you have to do.

When you understand what you want to do with your new workstation or servers and have a vision for your network, you're ready to purchase those systems.

Moving On

In this chapter, we briefly discussed situations that may indicate that you want to purchase a new workstation or server, as well as issues to consider when purchasing a new system. In the next chapter, we'll talk about installing a CD-ROM drive.

25

Buying And Installing A CD-ROM Drive

When you have a network, you can effectively share a CD-ROM drive that is installed on one PC with other computers. So, when you have programs to install, you can use the CD on another PC, and even run programs by *mapping* the CD-ROM drive (for more on mapping a drive, refer to the instructions in Chapter 10). In this chapter, you'll learn everything you need to know about CD-ROM drives and how to install them.

Definition, Please

In function, a *CD-ROM drive* on your computer is similar to the one in your stereo system. Both rely on the same technology—a moving laser head that reads the grooves in a CD's surface. The difference is that a computer's CD-ROM holds data for programs and an audio CD holds data to play music. Also, like an audio CD drive, a computer CD-ROM drive usually can't write or save data to a CD-ROM.

With its impressive storage capacity of about 650 megabytes (MB), a CD-ROM can hold a lot more data than a floppy can. In fact, one CD-ROM is equivalent to more than 400 3.5-inch disks, each of which holds only 1.44MB of data. Also, specialized computer CD-ROM drives are available (called *CD-R* and *CD-RW* drives—we'll talk about these later) that can *write* or record data. Recordable and re-writeable CD drives are largely for users with special applications—usually developers, presenters, and those who want to store large amounts of information, and they can work well as your network backup tool.

You'll find that in addition to entertainment programs, many business applications and even operating systems like Windows 98 now come on CD-ROM. The games and educational titles usually read data directly from the CD-ROM as you run the programs; other titles simply use a CD-ROM, instead of disks, to store and conveniently install the programs.

Also, many organizations use CD-ROMs to distribute reams of timely information. It's not unusual to find monthly CD-ROMs with the latest information on bugs in an operating system, legal mumbo jumbo, case studies, and even software demos that come with magazines. You'll also find collections of clip art, pictures, videos, and even sound effects distributed on CD-ROM, all of which you can use in your own presentations, multimedia productions, and publications.

From our perspective as users, installing a program from a CD-ROM is convenient. Imagine a program that comes on 30 floppy disks (like some of the business suites that include a word processor, spreadsheet, and database in one package) and requires you to insert all those disks, one by one, into your floppy drive—a royal pain. With a CD-ROM installation, all you have to do is insert the disk, answer some questions, and walk away. The program does the rest of the work for you.

CD-ROM Factors

When you buy a CD-ROM drive, the most talked-about factor is the *data transfer rate.* As you'll see, this is an important factor, but it's not necessarily the entire story.

Data Transfer Rate

Years ago, when the first CD-ROM drives came onto the market, they could transfer data at a rate of 150 kilobytes per second (Kbps). This means that every second, the heads on the CD-ROM drive could read 150K of information. These original pioneering drives became known as *single-speed* CD-ROM drives.

As usual in the computer industry, faster drives were soon on the horizon. The next revolution came in the *double-speed*, or *2X* drive, which could transfer data at 300Kbps. From here, it's easy to see how the ratings work:

3X is three times 150Kbps, the speed of the original single drive, or 450Kbps, and so on. For the most part, a 2X drive is faster than a single speed, a 3X faster than a double, and so on. Examples of typical drive speeds are 12X, 16X, 24X, 35X, and faster.

Although the 2X and subsequent multiple drives are indeed faster, other factors, such as seek and access time, also play a role. Usually, you don't find these parameters clearly spelled out. *Transfer rate* tells you how much data a drive can read in a second; *access time* tells you how long it will take a drive to find the information. A drive with the following characteristics will give you decent performance:

- *Data transfer rate*—1800Kbps (12X) or faster
- *Access time*—200ms or less

Multisession Capability

Another consideration is what's called *multisession* capability, although with current drives this is almost a given. For the most part, you will want to purchase a drive with multisession capability just in case you later need it, particularly to support Kodak PhotoCD.

Definition, Please

Multisession is a technology that can burn new data onto a CD-ROM at different times, instead of all at once. This technology was developed to support the Kodak Photo CD, with which you can develop film and place the photos electronically on CD-ROM, so you can immediately use them on your computer.

Because a CD-ROM can hold some 100 electronic photos, the developers of this technology recognized that even the most avid shutterbugs won't always need to develop 100 photos at a time. They developed multisession technology so that users can have more developed pictures added to a CD-ROM whenever they wish. This way, you can receive your first batch of pictures on a CD-ROM, then let the developer add more photos at a later date.

EIDE Or SCSI

Another factor in your CD-ROM purchasing decision is whether to buy an Enhanced Integrated Drive Electronics (EIDE) or a Small Computer System Interface (SCSI) CD-ROM drive.

In the old days, all CD-ROM drives were connected to a PC via SCSI or through proprietary interfaces. In fact, most of the proprietary ports were actually variations on SCSI. If you have SCSI hard drives, you already have a way to connect a SCSI CD-ROM drive. Also, if a computer has an older sound card, chances are that the card provides a port to connect a SCSI CD-ROM drive. To find out if your sound card has such a port, you'll have to check its documentation.

Today, the most popular way to connect a CD-ROM drive to your PC is through something called the *advanced technology attachment packet interface* (*ATAPI*) standard. Using an ATAPI drive, you can connect your CD-ROM drive directly to your EIDE controller. Keep in mind that once you purchase either a SCSI or ATAPI CD-ROM drive, it will work only with that standard.

Multimedia Upgrade Kits

You can buy a CD-ROM drive by itself or as part of a multimedia upgrade kit. You'll find such kits available from a variety of hardware manufacturers, such as Creative Labs and Diamond Multimedia.

Definition, Please

Multimedia upgrade kits are packages that contain everything you need to upgrade your computer to handle multimedia. These kits include a CD-ROM drive, sound board, all connections, and some applications.

Multimedia kits are usually decent deals, and because the sound card and CD-ROM come together, you can be fairly confident that they will work together.

Tip—Cost

It makes lots of sense to purchase a multimedia kit if you are planning to upgrade a network computer to run the latest multimedia. However, if you aren't planning to add a sound board or if you already have a decent one, a multimedia upgrade kit may not be the best buy.

Internal And External Drives

CD-ROM drives come in both internal and external versions. It's usually more convenient to own an internal version, as shown in Figure 25.1, because it doesn't require extra desk space and costs less. On the other hand, if you're planning to use a CD-ROM drive with several computers, then the more expensive external version makes more sense.

Another variation in CD-ROM drives is that some require you to first load a CD into a holder, called a *caddy*, before inserting the disk into the drive. Most of the older drives require caddies. It's more convenient to have a CD-ROM drive that doesn't need a caddy. This way, you can load a CD disk the same way you load an audio disk into a stereo player. Otherwise, you have to locate a caddy before you can use the CD-ROM drive, and if your computer desk looks anything like mine, this is a definite disadvantage.

Figure 25.1 An internal CD-ROM drive, designed to mount into your PC, is the most popular style.

A summary of CD-ROM buying considerations follows:

- Speed (12X to 40X)
- Access time (200ms or faster)
- SCSI versus EIDE
- Internal versus external
- Buying a multimedia upgrade kit

Recordable And Rewriteable CDs

Recordable CD drives are specialized drives that let you *burn*, or record, your own CDs by copying files from a hard drive. You can also copy audio CDs or commercial CD-ROMs (watch out for copyright issues). Once you burn a CD, you can read it with just about any computer equipped with a CD-ROM drive or play it in your stereo's CD player (if you burn an audio CD). Most of the drives on the market are *CD-R* (*compact disc-recordable*) drives that write to a blank CD that accepts data a single time only and which cannot be erased or reused.

CDs once delivered only multimedia, but they are now popular for backing up hard drives and transferring large files. Lots of companies and individuals use CDs to distribute multimedia presentations created in programs such as Microsoft PowerPoint or Lotus Freelance, as well as online catalogs and demo disks. Recordable CD drives are popular with software companies that want to burn preliminary versions of software for beta testing. Until recently, the software that let you burn a CD was difficult to use. However, the latest programs offer step-by-step wizards that walk you through the process of copying files to a CD or making copies of audio or data CDs.

A new generation of *CD-RW* (*compact disc-rewriteable*) drives lets you reuse and rewrite information to a special CD, almost as you would to a floppy disk. According to the manufacturers, you can overwrite a re-writeable CD 1,000 times. These rewriteable drives offer cool capabilities at a price that is slightly more than that of a CD-R drive.

A rewriteable CD looks much like a regular CD, but it costs significantly more (it's actually a different media). More important, almost any PC with a CD-ROM drive can read a CD-R disk, but only a CD-RW drive or the newest CD-ROM drives can read a rewriteable CD. When you're trying to distribute data, rewriteable CDs somewhat defeat the universal-use aspect of writing to a conventional CD-R. But with ease of use comparable to copying files to a floppy, a rewriteable CD makes an ideal backup medium. Both recordable and rewriteable CD drives come in external and internal versions. The external versions connect to either a conventional SCSI interface or your PC's parallel port. Recordable and rewriteable CD drives can also work as your main CD-ROM drive to install and run programs. However, for now, recordable and rewriteable drives max out as 6X CD-ROM readers and typically read slower than stock CD-ROM drives with the same rated read capabilities.

DVD

One other consideration for your CD drive is *DVD*, the newest CD standard. DVD stands for either *digital video disk* or *digital versatile disk*—it depends on whom you ask. CD-ROM media holds a respectable 650MB of data, but DVD can hold 4.7GB (yes, that's gigabytes) of data, or about seven times the amount that a conventional CD holds, and some versions hold up to 17GB. DVD will eventually supplant today's CD as the medium of choice. But for now, DVD drives are expensive (they start at around $400 and can cost as much as $800), and computer software for these drives is scarce.

A single-layer DVD disk holds 4.7GB of information, but if both layers in the disk are used, the disk holds up to 9.4GB of data. Finally, manufacturers can actually glue two DVD disks together to make the disk dual-sided, which makes the capacity soar to 17GB.

With its ability to hold significantly more data, DVD is ideal for distributing future multimedia titles that contain reams of video, sound, and graphics (think of all the multi-CD game titles on the market). Also, DVD can hold two hours of high-quality, full-motion video to show movies on home players.

DVD-Video disks were the first type of DVD that was made available. This technology uses MPEG-2 compression and Dolby AC-3 encoding to store and play high-quality video and sound. The result is that DVD can store full-length motion pictures that have twice the quality of those on a VCR tape.

The computer version of DVD is *DVD-ROM*, which uses the same data format as the DVD players you use with your TV (called *DVD-Video*) so you can play the same DVD-Video disks (movies) on your PC that you can on your television. More importantly, you won't lose your investment of CD-ROMs, because DVD is backwardly compatible so it can read CD-ROM disks (it has the performance of a 10X CD-ROM drive).

DVD-ROM will be a rewriteable DVD format. Although this sounds quite promising, the industry is still not settled on the final format, and the technology is in flux. Still another consumer flavor is *DVD-Video Disk* (also known as *Digital Video Express* and *DIVX*). These disks will work something like pay-per-view television. You will be able to purchase a disk for $5 and watch it only for a set time—for example, 48 hours. After that, you'll need to pull out your credit card to watch it more, or you can simply throw it out. This technology is rather controversial, but it has the backing of some influential players, such as Pioneer and JVC, along with the major movie studios.

You can install a DVD-ROM drive in your PC to read data, but to view movies, you will need an *MPEG-2 decoding board* (a board that handles the compression and video). Most upgrade kits bundle an MPEG-2 board with the DVD drive. Definitely consider this new technology in your CD upgrade decision and research which format will work best for you. Also, don't forget to look at the system requirements necessary to support a DVD drive. You'll need at least a 133MHz Pentium system.

CD-ROM Drive Installation

Before installing that CD-ROM drive, you have to consider what type of drive it is and what type of port or board you'll need to connect with it and support it. As mentioned in the earlier sections, CD-ROM drives come in three major kinds: those that need a SCSI, those that operate with a proprietary board, and those that require an ATAPI port.

If you buy a multimedia kit with a sound card and CD-ROM drive, you can be fairly sure that the port on the sound card connects with and supports the CD-ROM drive. Some CD-ROM drives—although this is becoming rare—connect only with their own proprietary boards, and some sound cards offer a port for them. ATAPI CD-ROM drives connect with standard EIDE controllers. Just to make things interesting, some sound boards feature this connection, too.

Opening The Computer Case

To begin the drive installation:

1. Disconnect all of the cables and connectors attached to your computer: power, printer cables, speakers, telephone line, keyboard, mouse, video connections, and so on. Then you're ready to remove the screws, which you'll usually find along the back side of the computer case, as shown in Figure 25.2.

Caution

When removing screws from the back of the case, be sure to remove only those that appear to hold the case. If you go overboard and remove all the screws, you may hear internal components—the power supply, for example—drop loose and fall down inside your computer. Be conservative. Remove the obvious screws first and then see if the case cover budges.

2. When you have removed the screws, gently push the cover to see if it moves. If it does, slide the cover off the case. If it doesn't, you probably missed a screw. Check for any errant screws and then try to budge the cover again. On a desktop machine, as shown in Figure 25.3, the cover usually slides backward, away from the front of the computer. On a tower case, the cover can slide either forward or backward, as shown in Figure 25.4. Of course, your case may not fall

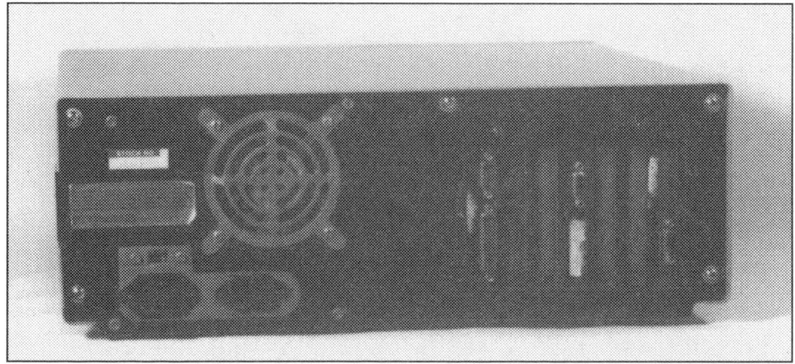

Figure 25.2 The screws that hold the case on are usually on the back of the computer.

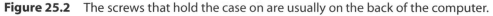

Figure 25.3 A typical desktop case cover opens by sliding the chassis back from the front of the computer.

Figure 25.4 A typical tower case cover opens by sliding either forward or backward off the case.

into any of these categories. Some cases swivel, while others lift off, and still others don't even use screws, you simply depress a couple of buttons to open the case. Please refer to your system's documentation for more on how to open the case.

With your PC's cover off, you're ready to begin working.

Installing The CD-ROM Drive

Now it's time to actually install the drive. Follow these steps:

1. Examine your system's drive bays to determine whether you need to physically rearrange your existing hard and floppy drives to accommodate your new CD-ROM drive. Also, consider how cables will have to run inside your computer so that your CD-ROM drive will connect easily with the board that supports it.

2. Connect the power, four-wire audio, and data cables, as in Figures 25.5 and 25.6. If you are installing an ATAPI-style CD-ROM drive, you will connect a cable from your IDE controller on your system's motherboard to your drive, or from your sound card (if it has an ATAPI connector).

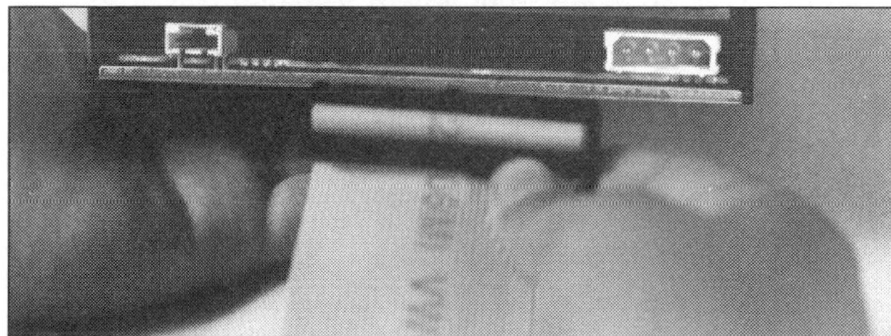

Figure 25.5 Install the data cable into your CD-ROM drive.

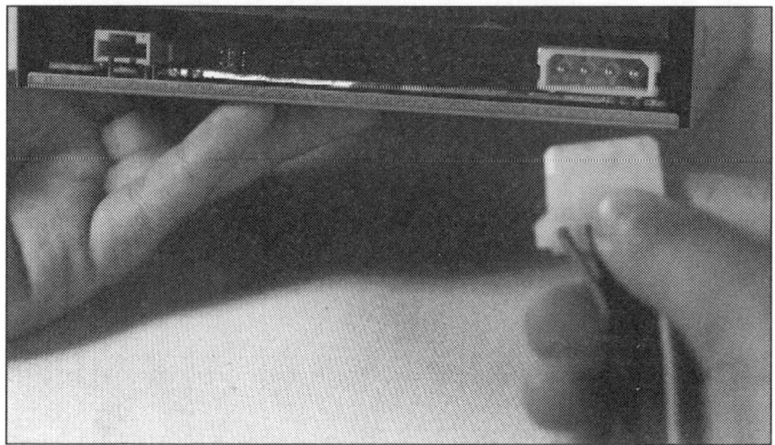

Figure 25.6 Install the power cable into your CD-ROM drive.

If you are connecting your CD-ROM drive to your system's motherboard, it's best to connect it to the secondary EIDE controller port (this is the second EIDE connector). On most newer motherboards, there's a primary and secondary EIDE connector, and it's best to connect your hard drives to the primary and your CD-ROM drive to the secondary. In the case of connecting your CD-ROM drive to the motherboard's secondary port, you would configure the CD-ROM drive as a "master." If you connect the CD-ROM drive so it "piggybacks" off of the same connection as your hard drive (you'll need a ribbon cable with two connectors on it), you'll have to configure your CD-ROM drive as a "slave." Connecting your CD-ROM drive to the secondary EIDE controller is not only easier (most CD-ROM drives come configured as "masters" by default), you should get better performance from both your CD-ROM and hard drives.

Refer to the instructions that came with your CD-ROM drive. Keep in mind that the red wire on the ribbon cable is pin 1, and you will have to match this with the connector on both the motherboard or sound board and on your CD drive. The power cable, on the other hand, only connects in a single direction. You may find that it's easier to install these cables before you install your CD-ROM drive in its bay.

3. Slide the CD-ROM drive into the bay that you have selected for it. Attach the screws to secure the drive in its bay.
4. Reconnect your monitor, mouse, power, and other cables. At this point, you'll have to install the CD-ROM drivers.

Installing The CD-ROM Drivers

You'll use the disks that came with your CD-ROM drive to install the CD-ROM drivers and a file called MSCDEX, which is essential for making your CD-ROM drive work with Windows.

To install the drivers:

1. Power up your system.

Caution—Safety

Don't forget that you have a live machine. Under no circumstance should you probe your PC or touch any components while your system is running. Always shut off power and unplug your computer before doing any work on your PC or before removing or adjusting any component. Not only could you get a dangerous shock, you could also fry your components.

2. Insert the driver disk into your floppy drive.

You will next use Explorer or My Computer, as in the following directions.

To use Windows Explorer:

1. Right-click your mouse on the Start button.
2. Select Explore.
3. Select the A: drive by double-clicking on it (assuming A: is the floppy drive holding the disk). Note that if your setup is different, your drive letter may be different.
4. Look for the Setup file or whatever file the manual tells you to execute in order to install the drivers. Double-click on this file to start the program, then follow the on-screen directions.

To use My Computer:

1. Double-click on the My Computer icon on the desktop.
2. Double-click on the A: folder. Note that if your setup is different, your drive may be different.
3. Look for the Setup file or whatever file the manual tells you to execute in order to install the drivers. Double-click on this file to start the program, then follow the on-screen directions.

Powering Up The System

If you got through the software installation, you should be in pretty good shape. At this point, you can reconnect power and turn on your computer to see if everything is running properly. Be sure to read some CD-ROMs, preferably ones with some sound and video, that will put the new drive through its paces. If everything appears to be in order and working, replace the system's cover. Before you move your PC back to its normal location, be sure to remove any CD-ROM disks you may have used.

If something isn't working, check out the next section, "Troubleshooting."

Troubleshooting

If your CD-ROM drive can't read a CD, check your configurations. You can use Explorer 3.1 to see if it recognizes that your drive exists. If not, try the following suggestions:

- If your system doesn't recognize that you have a CD-ROM drive installed, check the software configurations and recheck your installation. (Be sure to disconnect power again before removing the cover of your PC.) You may have missed a cable. Make sure that all cables are attached securely. Also, check that your sound board, or controller board (if you have one), is properly seated.
- Check with your manual to see what suggestions it offers for the particular configuration of your CD-ROM drive.
- Another possible problem is that you may have the wrong drivers or an incorrect version of these drivers. For this problem, you should contact the company to see what its latest drivers are. You can check the manufacturer's Web page to find out more information and download the latest drivers.
- Check your CD-ROM's controller card (if it has one). Be sure that the port is active (you'll have to check the board's documentation), and be sure that you don't have two ports on at the same time that may be conflicting with each other. This can happen, for example, if you install a sound board with an active port, but also have a proprietary port installed to control your CD-ROM.
- One other possibility is that your computer requires you to set up your CD-ROM drive in its complementary metal-oxide semiconductor (CMOS). For more on how to do this, check your system's documentation.
- When you've exhausted these possibilities, call the CD-ROM manufacturer for technical support.

Moving On

In this chapter, I've shown you how to install a CD-ROM drive. In the next chapter, you'll learn how to install a modem.

26

Installing A Modem

If you've bought a new modem so you can surf the Internet, use email, send faxes, or use your computer as an answering machine, this chapter will tell you how to install it and get it working with your system and software. I'll cover how to install both external and internal modems; simply go to the appropriate section of this chapter for installation instructions. If you're still not sure which type of modem to buy or whether you have chosen one that is right for your system and needs, refer to Chapters 15 and 16 for more information.

Installing An External Modem

Like a monitor, an external modem is one of the few upgrades that you can install without opening your computer's case.

For the most part, the installation involves plugging in your modem, as follows:

1. Shut off your PC and connect a serial cable between the port on your computer (COM1 or COM2) and the similar port on your modem. It's important that you remember which port your modem is connected to. Your modem may come with this serial cable or you may have to buy it separately. The serial port on the back of your PC will have either 9 or 25 pins, as shown in Figures 26.1 and 26.2.

   Depending on the serial port you have and want to use (you may have a mouse attached to one, usually the first 9-pin port, called *COM1*),

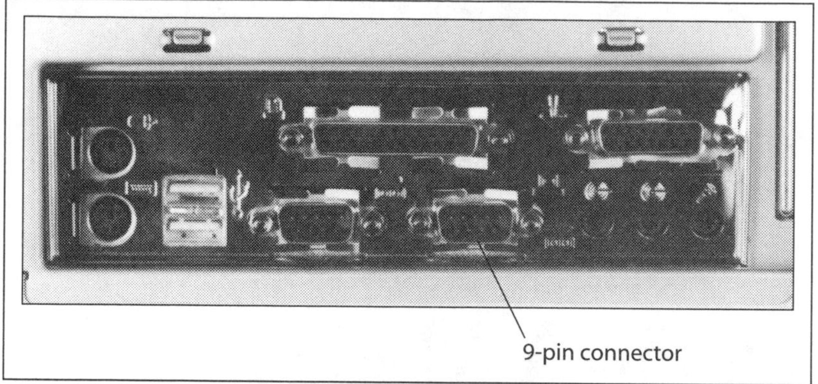

Figure 26.1 A 9-pin serial port.

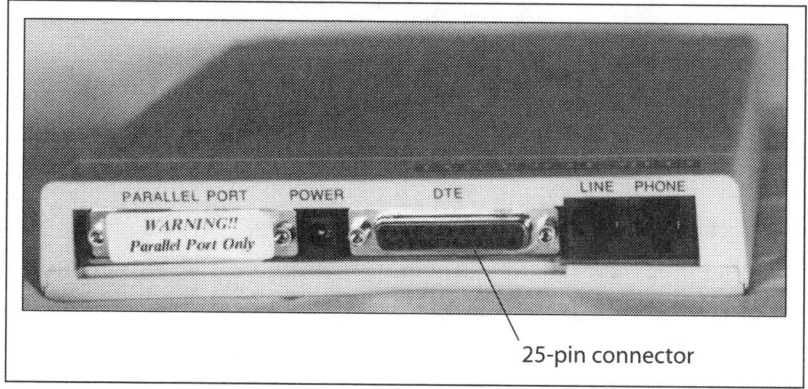

Figure 26.2 A 25-pin serial port.

you also may have to buy an adapter that connects the different connector sizes. You can buy one of these at any computer parts store.

2. Hook up the modem to power. The external modem will come with its own power adapter.
3. Connect the modem to the telephone line by plugging one end of a phone cord into one of the telephone ports on your modem (usually labeled “line”) and the other end into the telephone wall jack. If you would also like to use a telephone with this jack, you can connect the telephone’s cord to the other port on your modem (usually labeled “phone”).
4. Turn on your modem and boot up your computer.

Installing A Plug And Play External Modem

If you are installing a Plug and Play modem, note that when your system boots, it automatically detects your new modem and asks for your *driver* disk. Simply follow the on-screen instructions. After that, you can reboot your computer; your modem will be configured already and available for use by applications.

Definition, Please

A *driver* is a set of software that tells the operating system how to work with the new hardware.

If Windows 95/98 doesn't detect your new modem, click on Start|Settings|Control Panel and double-click on Add New Hardware. When the dialog box appears, have Windows search your system for your new modem and then follow the on-screen instructions to install the driver. If this doesn't work, you can also manually install the driver by selecting the option; however, you should probably check your installation first to make sure that your modem is correctly installed.

Installing A Non–Plug And Play Modem

If you are installing a non–Plug and Play modem, install the driver according to the instructions provided by the manufacturer. This will usually involve running a setup program on a floppy disk, which is described in the following sections.

Installing A Non–Plug And Play External Modem Using Windows 95/98 Explorer

To install an external modem using Windows 95 Explorer:

1. Right-click on the Start button of the Taskbar.
2. Select Explore to open the Windows Explorer.
3. Select the A: drive by double-clicking on it (assuming A: is the floppy drive holding the disk). Note that your setup may be different; thus, your drive may be different.

4. Look for a setup or install file (or whatever file the modem's manual tells you to execute to install the driver). Double-click on this file to start the program; then, follow the on-screen directions.

Installing A Non–Plug And Play External Modem Using My Computer

To install an external modem using My Computer:

1. Double-click on the My Computer icon on the desktop.
2. Double-click on the A: drive (assuming A: is the floppy drive holding the disk). Note that your setup may be different; thus, your drive may be different.
3. Look for a setup or install file (or whatever file the modem's manual tells you to execute to install the modem driver). Double-click on this file to start the program, then follow the on-screen directions.

Installing An Internal Modem

An internal modem is an expansion board that you install. The physical installation of the board usually is not difficult, but the setup can be a nuisance. If you purchase a modem that supports Plug and Play in Windows 95/98, this greatly simplifies installation.

It's a good idea to check the modem's documentation to see if you need to set any jumpers (although newer modems don't usually require this). If you need to, do so now. By configuring the jumpers, you're essentially evaluating your system to see what ports you already are using and what port your new modem will have to use. Because you can install your modem at COM4 as a general rule, that's a good place to try first. If your system is already configured with four COM ports, you'll have to disable one to use it with the modem. To do so, you'll probably have to adjust some switches on your motherboard or reconfigure your system's complementary metal-oxide semiconductor (CMOS) setup. For more on this, check your system's documentation.

Caution—Data

Before you open your PC and begin any installation, take a minute to record the information on your hard drive—the type, cylinders, and so forth. You'll find this information in your computer's setup, which you usually can see by booting up your PC and then holding down a key to view a menu screen (computers vary; check your manual). Write this information down and keep it. If you have the hard drive documentation, it will include this information.

Caution—Safety

Before you open your PC, turn it off. I always unplug my PC as well, although some experts will tell you it's okay to leave it plugged in (just as long as it's turned off). When working on your system, don't probe screwdrivers in areas that you're not working on, particularly the power supply.

Remove the PC cover. You'll find that most cases are designed so you can remove some screws and slide the top cover off, but other covers fit in different ways.

Opening The Computer Case

To open the computer case:

1. Turn off your PC and unplug it.
2. Disconnect all of the cables and connectors attached to your computer—power, printer cables, speakers, telephone line, keyboard, mouse, video connections, and so on.
3. Now you're ready to remove the screws, which you'll usually find along the back side of the computer case, as shown in Figure 26.3.

Caution

When removing screws from the back of the case, be sure to remove only those that appear to hold the case. If you go overboard and remove all the screws, you may hear internal components—the power supply, for example—drop loose and fall down inside your computer. Be conservative. Remove the obvious screws first and then see if the case cover budges.

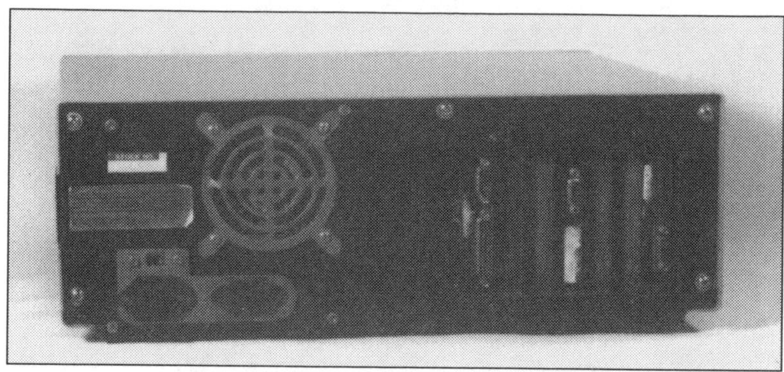

Figure 26.3 The screws that hold the case on are usually on the back of the computer.

4. When you have removed the screws, gently push the cover to see if it moves. If it does, slide the cover off the case. If it doesn't, you probably missed a screw. Check for any errant screws and then try to budge the cover again.

   On a desktop machine, as shown in Figure 26.4, the cover usually slides backward, away from the front of the computer. On a tower case, the cover can slide either forward or backward, as shown in Figure 26.5. Of course, your case may not fall into any of these categories. Some cases swivel, others lift off, and still others don't even use screws—you simply depress a couple of buttons to open the case. Please refer to your system's documentation for more instructions.

With your PC's cover off, you're ready to begin working.

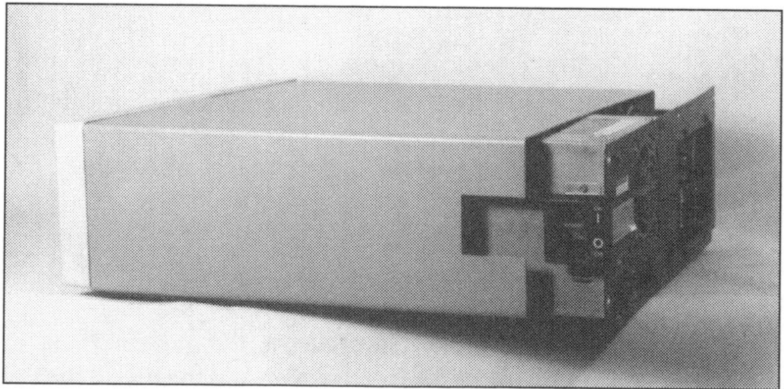

Figure 26.4 A typical desktop case cover opens by sliding the chassis back from the front of the computer.

Figure 26.5 A typical tower case cover opens by sliding either forward or backward off the case.

Caution

Be sure that your PC is shut off. Also, if you aren't using a wrist strap, be sure to ground yourself before handling any components. To do this, simply touch the metal case of your PC.

Installing The Modem

1. Find an appropriate slot, unscrew the retaining screw, and remove the slot cover to prepare a slot for the internal modem, as shown in Figure 26.6.
2. Slide the new internal modem into the slot and use a rocking, pushing motion to seat the board into the socket, as shown in Figure 26.7. Make sure that the board is well seated in the socket. Replace the board's retainer screw.

Figure 26.6 Unscrew the retaining screw and remove the slot cover.

Figure 26.7 Push the board in with a rocking motion to seat it in its socket.

Tip

Always hold expansion cards by their edges and try not to touch the metal connectors that fit into the PC's slots. Your body can build up enough static electricity to fry an entire card or one of its components, rendering it useless. When inserting new cards, it makes sense to keep some room between them when you can, to allow more air to circulate between them and keep them cooler.

Caution

Be sure that the internal modem is not touching any other expansion board.

3. At this point, your modem is installed. You can put the cover back on your PC, reconnect power, and go to the next section, which addresses configuring an internal modem. Connect the modem to the telephone line by plugging one end of a phone cord into one of the telephone ports on your modem (usually labeled "line"), then plug the other end into the telephone wall jack. If you would also like to use a telephone with this jack, you can connect the telephone's cord to the other port on your modem (usually labeled "phone").

Configuring An Internal Modem

The next step is to install the modem's software driver. Look for the disks that usually come with a modem and turn on your computer.

If You Have Installed A Plug And Play Modem

Windows 95/98 should boot up and immediately recognize that your new modem is installed in your system. At this point, the program will ask for the disk that contains your modem driver, and you can follow the on-screen instructions to load your driver. With Plug and Play, Windows will perform most of the modem configuration for you.

If Windows 95 or 98 doesn't detect your new modem, click on Start|Settings|Control Panel and double-click on Add New Hardware. When the dialog box appears, have Windows 95/98 search your system for your new modem and then follow the on-screen instructions to install the driver. If this doesn't work, you can also manually install the driver by selecting the appropriate option (see the following section); however, you should probably check your installation first to make sure that your modem is correctly installed.

If You Have Installed A Non–Plug And Play Modem

You can configure a non–Plug and Play modem using Explorer or My Computer.

Configuring A Non–Plug And Play Modem Using Explorer

To configure your non–Plug And Play Modem Using Explorer:

1. Right-click your mouse on the Start button of the Taskbar.
2. Select Explore to open Explorer.
3. Select the A: drive by double-clicking on it (assuming A: is the floppy drive holding the disk). Note that your setup may be different; thus, your drive may be different.
4. Look for a setup file (or whatever file the modem's manual tells you to execute to install the driver). Double-click on this file and then follow the on-screen directions.

Configuring A Non–Plug And Play Modem Using My Computer

To configure your non–Plug and Play modem using My Computer:

1. Double-click on the My Computer icon on the desktop.
2. Double-click on the A: folder (assuming A: is the floppy drive holding the disk). Note that your setup may be different; thus, your drive may be different.
3. Look for a setup file (or whatever file the manual tells you to execute to install the modem driver). Double-click on this file, then follow the on-screen directions.

Setting Up The Communications Software

After installing your modem's driver, you'll want to set up your communications software (e.g., America Online) so that it can run your modem. (This also refers to fax, voice, and any software that supports a modem.) For simplicity, we'll refer to any such software as *communications software*. The basic steps in using the setup feature in your communications software are as follows:

1. Usually, the software will ask you to choose a modem from a list. Try to find your modem's brand and model number, then select it. If your exact model number isn't on the list, you can try another model by the same manufacturer and usually get good results. If your modem's brand isn't listed, check with your modem documentation to see what type

of modem it emulates. More than likely, it will be a Hayes-compatible modem. The best programs on the market will actually search for your modem and suggest one to choose—a major convenience.

2. The software will also ask where your modem resides and will want information such as the port (COM1, COM2, etc.) and the modem's speed. Enter this information, and you're usually ready to go.

Troubleshooting

If you use your software to dial a number and you don't hear a dial tone and then the number dialing, something is probably wrong with your configuration (you can also check your modem's volume control). Examine your system to determine if two devices on your computer are trying to use the same port or system resources.

Windows 95 or Windows 98 can help you troubleshoot the problem. To access Help in Windows 95, follow these steps:

1. Choose Start|Help.
2. Select Troubleshooting.
3. In the list of troubleshooting topics, select If You Have A Hardware Conflict (or similar option). Follow the on-screen suggestions.

Access Help in Windows 98 for fixing a hardware conflict by performing the following steps:

1. Choose Start|Help.
2. Select Troubleshooting.
3. In the list of troubleshooting topics, select Windows 98 Troubleshooters, and then select Hardware Conflict. Follow the on-screen suggestions.

Unfortunately, troubleshooting your modem and getting it to work can be a lengthy trial-and-error process. Hang in there—it will eventually work. If you're having lots of trouble, you can call the modem manufacturer's representative, who is quite accustomed to dealing with these problems.

Moving On

We have gone through the steps necessary to install a new external or internal modem. In the next chapter, I'll talk about how to configure a notebook computer so it can work on your network.

27

Mobile Networking

Throughout this book, I've talked about how you can link your desktop computers together into a network. But what if you want to add a notebook computer to your network? This chapter addresses how to configure a notebook computer that's running Windows 95 or Windows 98, and how to connect it to your network. You'll also find troubleshooting steps that you can use to fix almost any problem that you may encounter when you connect a notebook to your network.

Making Network Connections With Your Notebook

To connect a notebook to your office or home network, you'll need to either install a network Ethernet card that works with your notebook's PC card (PCMCIA) port, or, if you're using your notebook with a docking station, you will need to install a conventional network card into the docking station, and install its drivers. (A *driver* is a file that tells Windows how to use the Ethernet card.)

Definition, Please

PC card—A slot in your notebook that accepts PC card devices (see Figure 27.1). You can purchase various PC card devices, including modems, network cards, and more. PC cards were once known as *PCMCIA devices*. Figure 27.2 shows a PC card Ethernet device.

docking station—A device that connects to a notebook computer and that accepts conventional expansion cards, including network interface cards. With these devices, you can conveniently use your notebook at the office by plugging it into the docking station, which is already connected to a network and which also offers connections to other hard drives, keyboards, and peripherals. Installing a network interface card into a docking station is similar to the process outlined in the "Installing A Network Card" section of Chapter 7.

Figure 27.1 A PC card port.

Figure 27.2 A PC card Ethernet card.

Installing A PC Card Network Device

To install a PC card network device, you can do the following:

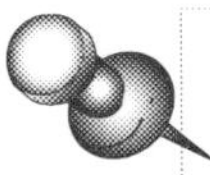

If the instructions that come with your PC Card network device differ from the following steps, use the instructions that come with your device.

1. Turn off your notebook.
2. Open your notebook's PC card port and install the network card by sliding it in until it seats into the slot, as shown in Figure 27.3.
3. Connect your network card to your network, which will typically accept a 10BaseT connector.
4. Turn on your notebook. When it boots, it should automatically recognize the network card in its PC card port. At this point, you can simply tell Windows where your drivers are (they usually come on a floppy disk from the card manufacturer), and then Windows will install the drivers and automatically configure your network card.

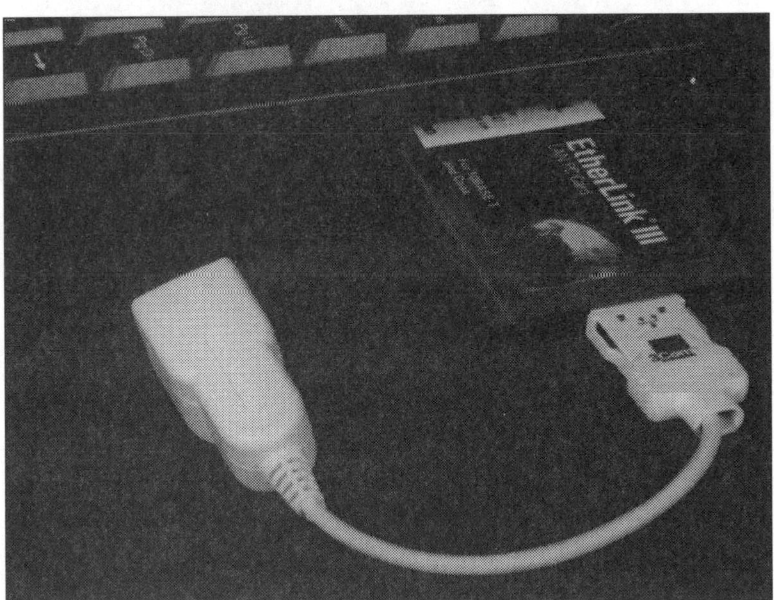

Figure 27.3 Installing a network card into the PC card port.

If Windows Doesn't Recognize Your Network Card

If Windows fails to recognize your network card, you can do the following:

1. Select Start|Settings|Control Panel.
2. Double-click on the Add New Hardware icon. Windows will ask whether you want to have the system try to locate the new hardware or if you want to add it yourself. It's usually best to have Windows look for it first, but only if the network device is Plug and Play compatible. Select Yes (Recommended) and click on OK. Windows will search your system and try to detect your network device. When it's successful, it will ask you where it can find the driver disk. If Windows can't find your network device, go to the next step.
3. If Windows can't locate and recognize your Ethernet card, you will need to tell it what type of card you are installing and then provide it with the driver. By default, Windows selects Driver From Disk Provided By Hardware Manufacturer so that you can install the driver from a floppy. Then click on OK on the bottom of the New Hardware Found screen. In the resulting Install From Disk dialog box, Windows then asks you to insert the manufacturer's disk. If the file is somewhere on your hard drive, you'll need to click on the Browse button to show Windows where to find it. Windows loads the driver and then configures your system.

Checking That Windows Installed Your Network Card

To check that Windows has installed your network card, you can do the following:

1. Select Start|Settings|Control Panel.
2. Double-click on the System icon and select the Device Manager tab. A list of devices attached to the system appears.
3. Scroll through the devices on your screen until you see the PC Card controller icon. Look for a listing of your network device by double-clicking on the icon. If you see your network device there, you should be ready to use your notebook with your network. From here, all of the instructions for sharing files, printers, and other peripherals from the other chapters in this book apply.

Enabling File And Print Sharing

Before you can connect and work with the network, you have to configure the networking features to enable file and print sharing. Here are the steps to enable file and print sharing in Windows 95 and Windows 98. For more on these topics, refer to Chapters 10, 11, and 13:

1. Select Start|Settings|Control Panel.
2. Double-click on the Network icon and click on the Configuration tab.
3. Click on the File And Print Sharing button.
4. If you want others on the network to be able to access your files, place a checkmark next to the I Want To Be Able To Give Others Access To My files box. Do the same with the I Want To Allow Others To Print To My Printers option if you want that option.
5. Click on OK. You'll have to restart your computer for these changes to take effect.
6. After rebooting, click on My Computer, which will show you all of the available disk drives.
7. Right-click on the drive that you wish to share with other users, click on Sharing, and then click on the Sharing tab. Click on Share As and name your drive in the Share Name box. Select one of the following:
    - *Read-Only Access*—Lets others view files on your PC.
    - *Full Access*—Lets users create, change, or delete files on your system.
    - *Depends On Password*—Lets users have Read-Only or Full access, depending on the password that you decide to share with them.

If You Can't Connect With The Network

Try the following if you're not able to connect with the network:

- Check the connection between your Ethernet card and the network itself. Be sure that the connectors are firmly and positively seated. In particular, if the network cable is coiled or kinked, you should straighten it.
- If you can, try swapping the network cable to ensure that there is nothing wrong with the cable itself.

- If you're using coaxial, be sure to check that all terminators are in place.
- Be sure that the Ethernet PC card device is fully seated in its PC card slot.

Checking That Your Card Is Installed Properly

To check that your card is properly installed, you can do the following:

1. Select Start|Settings|Control Panel.
2. Double-click on the PC card (PCMCIA) icon and view the devices installed in its slots, as shown in Figure 27.4. If the resulting dialog box indicates that both sockets are empty, the Ethernet card is not properly installed (or there's something wrong with the card—not likely, but we'll check for this in the next section). Recheck your installation and make sure that the card is seated securely in its slot.

Troubleshooting Your Ethernet Card

You can check to see if there is a problem with the PC card port itself:

1. Select Start|Settings|Control Panel.
2. Double-click on the System icon and select the Device Manager tab. A list of devices attached to the system appears, as shown in Figure 27.5.

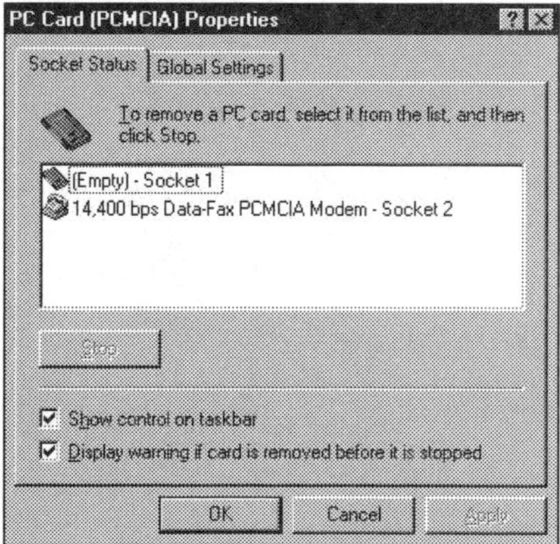

Figure 27.4 View the devices installed in the PC card slot.

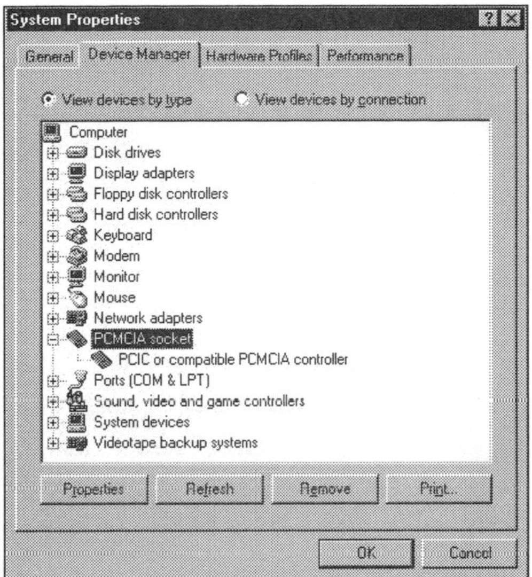

Figure 27.5 The Device Manager tab shows a list of devices, including the PC card.

3. Scroll through the devices on your screen until you see the PC Card controller icon. If you see a yellow oval with an exclamation point in it, this means that your PC card interface is not properly configured, and Windows can't use it. There may be a system conflict. In this case, follow the steps in the "Troubleshooting A System Conflict" section later in this chapter.
4. If you can't find a listing or icon for your PC card, it means that it hasn't been installed or is no longer installed. In this case, you will have to install the driver for that device. Please note that most PC card interfaces work with standard Windows 95 or Windows 98 drivers for these devices. You can usually locate the drivers you need on your Windows 95 CD or installation disks.

If your PC card appears to be working correctly, Windows may be having trouble recognizing your Ethernet card because the card's drivers aren't installed correctly.

To check if Windows can recognize your Ethernet card:

1. Select Start|Settings|Control Panel.
2. Double-click on the System icon and select the Device Manager tab. A list of devices attached to the system appears.

3. Scroll through the devices on your screen until you see the Network Adapters controller icon and double-click on it. If you see a yellow oval with an exclamation point next to your network driver, this means that your Ethernet card is not properly configured, and Windows can't use it. In this case, refer to the "Troubleshooting A System Conflict" later in this chapter. If you can't find a listing or icon for your Ethernet card, it means that it hasn't been installed or is no longer installed. In this case, you will have to install the driver for that device. If your network card appears to be installed correctly, follow the steps in the "Network-Specific Troubleshooting" section later in this chapter.

Installing An Ethernet Device Driver

When you bought your Ethernet card, it should have come with its own set of drivers on a disk or CD-ROM. If you don't have these drivers, you can try accessing the manufacturer's Web site to see if a driver might be available for downloading. If you can't locate the manufacturer's site, try using one of the Web search engines, such as Yahoo! (**www.yahoo.com**) or Alta Vista (**www.altavista.com**). You can also look in Appendixes A and B at the end of this book for help in finding a site or other means to contact the manufacturer.

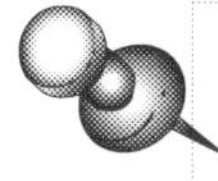

Some downloaded drivers will have setup procedures that differ from the following instructions. Be sure to review the README.TXT files that come with the driver (double-click on the file from Explorer or open it in Windows NotePad) to see if it contains any special instructions.

To add the driver, follow these steps:

1. Select Start|Settings|Control Panel.
2. In the Control Panel, double-click on the Add New Hardware icon. Windows will ask whether you want to have the system try to locate the new hardware, or if you want to add it yourself. It's usually best to have Windows look for it first, but only if the network device is Plug and Play compatible. Select Yes (Recommended) and click on OK. Windows will search your system and try to detect your network

device. When it's successful, it will ask you where it can find the driver disk. If Windows can't find your network device, go to the next step.

3. At times, for whatever reason, Windows won't be able to locate and recognize your Ethernet card. In this case, you will need to tell Windows what type of card you are installing, and then provide it with the driver. By default, Windows selects Driver From Disk Provided By Hardware Manufacturer so that you can install the driver from a floppy. Then, click on OK on the bottom of the New Hardware Found screen. In the resulting Install From Disk dialog box, Windows asks you to insert the manufacturer's disk. If the file is somewhere on your hard drive, you'll need to click on the Browse button to show Windows where to find it. Windows loads the driver and then configures your system.

Troubleshooting A System Conflict

If your Ethernet card is not working correctly, there may be a conflict in your notebook's system (two or more devices are trying to use the same system resources). Windows 95 or 98 can help you troubleshoot the problem. Access Help in Windows 95 by performing the following steps:

1. Select Start|Help|Troubleshooting.
2. In the list of troubleshooting topics, select If You Have A Hardware Conflict or similar option. Follow the on-screen suggestions.

Access Help in Windows 98 for fixing a hardware conflict by performing the following steps:

1. Select Start|Help|Troubleshooting.
2. In the list of troubleshooting topics, select Windows 98 Troubleshooters, and then select Hardware Conflict. Follow the on-screen suggestions.

If you recently added a new piece of hardware and its drivers, this may be causing problems with your network device. If this is the case, try removing the hardware by performing the following:

1. Select Start|Settings|Control Panel.
2. Double-click on Device Manager.

3. Select the Device tab.
4. Find the device that you recently added, highlight it, and then click on the Remove button. Click on OK to continue to remove the hardware's drivers, and then click on Yes to tell Windows to reboot.
5. Turn off your notebook and remove the hardware device from your system.
6. Test your system to see whether your system and network card are now running normally.
7. If the suspect device (the one that you recently added and just removed) is causing the problem, you should consult the manufacturer of that device to see if there are any known problems with it and any suggestions on how to get it running.

Network-Specific Troubleshooting

If your hardware appears to be working correctly, the problem may lie with the network configuration in your notebook, or the configuration of the network itself. Here are several things to consider. You should consult with the administrator of your network for additional guidance and information.

When connecting to a network, be sure that your Ethernet card is configured for the type of cabling that you're using and that your notebook has the correct network drivers. You should normally have all of your network drivers installed before you physically connect your cabling.

To see if you have the correct drivers installed, try the following:

1. Select Start|Settings|Control Panel.
2. Double-click on the Network icon and select the Configuration tab. You should see a list of installed network clients and protocols, such as Client for Microsoft Networks, Client for Netware Networks, IPX/SPX Compatible Protocols, or NetBEUI. If you need to add another client or protocol, make sure that you have the driver, then click on the Add button. Most Ethernet cards will come with their own disk of drivers. For instructions on how to install the network driver, please refer to the "Installing An Ethernet Device Driver" section earlier in this chapter.

You can also double-check that your notebook has a unique computer name.

If you've performed all of the previous diagnostics and you still have a problem, there may be something wrong with your Ethernet card. In this case, you'll need to contact the manufacturer for any further suggestions.

Moving On

In this chapter, I discussed how to connect your notebook computer to your network and offered troubleshooting tips. At this point, I've concluded the discussion of how to build and upgrade a network of your own. I hope this book has helped you with the process. May your network serve you well.

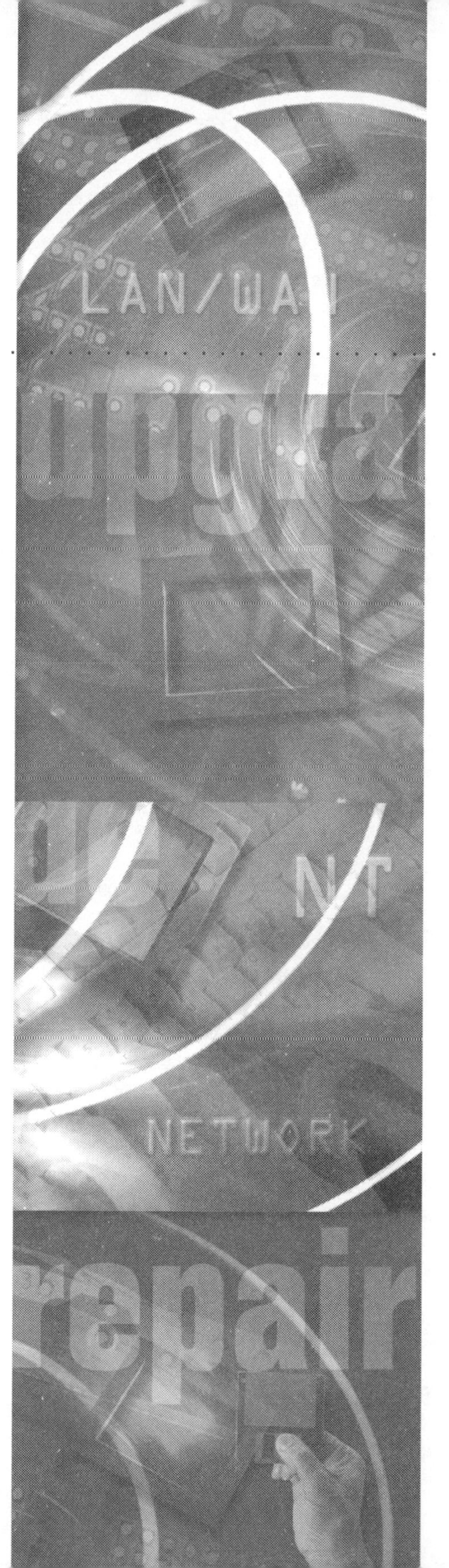

Part 5

Appendixes

Appendix A
Upgrade And Network-Related Vendors

Associations

The Association of Shareware Professionals
545 Grover Rd.
Muskegon, MI 49442-9427
616-788-2765

Hardware: Manufacturers

3COM Corp.
www.3com.com
Hardware: Modems, networking

Acer America Corp.
2641 Orchard Pkwy.
San Jose, CA 95134
800-733-2237, 408-432-6200
www.acer.com
Hardware: Systems

ACS Computer Group
100 San Lucar Ct.
Sunnyvale, CA 94086
408-481-9988
Hardware: Multimedia

Adaptec
691 S. Milpitas Blvd.
Milpitas, CA 95035
408-945-8600
Hardware: Peripherals

Advance Integration Research, Inc.
2188 Del Franco St.
San Jose, CA 95131
800-866-1945, 408-428-0800
Hardware: Motherboards

Advance Micro Research, Inc.
245 Corporate Ct.
San Jose, CA 95131
408-456-9430
Hardware: Systems

Advanced Digital Systems
13909 Bettencourt St.
Cerritos, CA 90703
800-888-5244
Hardware: Multimedia

Advanced Gravis Computer
101-3750 N. Fraser Way
Burnaby, BC V5J 5E9 Canada
604-431-5020
www.gravis.com
Hardware: Entertainment

Advanced Micro Devices
25A Technology Dr., Bldg. 2
Irvine, CA 92718
800-266-0488
www.amd.com
Hardware: CPUs

Aiwa America, Inc.
800 Corporate Dr.
Mahwah, NJ 07430
800-920-2673
Hardware: Backup

Allsop Computer Accessories
4201 Meridian
Bellingham, WA 98226
800-426-4303
Hardware: Mouse pads, glare filters, peripherals

Alps America
3553 N. First St.
San Jose, CA 95134
800-950-2577, 408-432-6000
Hardware: Printers, pointing devices, CD-ROM drives

Altec Lansing Multimedia
Rts. 6 and 209
Milford, PA 18337-0277
717-296-2818
Hardware: Multimedia

American Megatrends, Inc.
6145-F Northbelt Pkwy.
Norcross, GA 30071
800-828-9264, 404-263-8181
www.megatrends.com
Hardware: Motherboards

Apple Computer
1 Infinite Loop
Cupertino, CA 95014
800-776-2333
www.apple.com
Hardware: Systems

AST Research
16215 Alton Pkwy.
Irvine, CA 92718
800-876-4278, 714-727-4141
www.ast.com
Hardware: Systems

ATI Technologies
33 Commerce Valley Dr. E
Thornhill, ON L3T 7N6 Canada
905-882-2600
www.atitech.com
Hardware: Video cards

Aztech Labs, Inc.
47811 Warm Springs Blvd.
Fremont, CA 94539
510-623-8988
Hardware: Multimedia, CD-ROM drives

Bose Corp.
The Mountain
Framingham, MA 01701
508-879-7330
Hardware: Speakers

Brother International Corp.
200 Cottontail La.
Somerset, NJ 08875
909-356-8880
www.brother.com.
Hardware: Printers

C. Itoh Electronics
2701 Dow Ave.
Tustin, CA 92680
800-877-1421
Hardware: Printers

Calcomp, Inc.
14555 N. 82nd St.
Scottsdale, AZ 85260
800-451-7568
www.calcomp.com
Hardware: Printers, pointing devices

Canon USA, Inc.
1 Canon Plaza
Lake Success, NY 11042
516-488-6700
www.usa.canon.com
Hardware: Printers

Cardinal Technologies
1827 Freedom Rd.
Lancaster, PA 17601
717-293-3000
Hardware: Modems

Casio
570 Mt. Pleasant Avenue
Dover, NJ 07801
201-361-5400
Hardware: Digital cameras, image capture devices

Centerpoint Technologies, Inc.
1410 Blair Place, Suite 300
Ottawa, Ontario, K1J 9B9
888-332-9322
Hardware: Telephony

CH Products
970 Park Center Dr.
Vista, CA 92083
619-598-2518
Hardware: Entertainment

Chinon America, Inc.
660 Maple Ave.
Torrance, CA 90503
800-441-0222, 310-441-0222
Hardware: Storage

Cisco Systems, Inc.
255 Tasman
San Jose, CA
408-526-4000
Hardware: Networking

Citizen America Corp.
2450 Broadway, #600
Santa Monica, CA 90411-4003
800-556-1234, 310-453-0614
Hardware: Printers

Cobalt Microserver, Inc.
440 Clyde Avenue
Building B
Mountain View, California 94043
www.cobaltmicro.com
888-702-6225
Hardware: Networking

Colorado Memory Systems, Inc.
800 Taft Ave.
Loveland, CO 80537
303-669-8000
Hardware: Storage

Compaq Computer Corp.
20555 State Hwy. 249
Houston, TX 77070
800-231-0900
www.compaq.com
Hardware: Systems

Computer Peripherals, Inc.
667 Rancho Conejo Blvd.
Newbury Park, CA 91320
800-854-7600
Hardware: Modems

Connectix
2655 Campus Dr.
San Mateo, CA 94403
415-571-5100
Hardware: Digital cameras, image capture devices

Conner Peripherals
3081 Zanker Rd.
San Jose, CA 95134
800-421-1879, 408-456-4500
www.conner.com
Hardware: Storage

Creative Labs
1901 McCarthy Blvd.
Milpitas, CA 95035
408-428-6600
www.creativelabs.com
Hardware: Multimedia upgrade kits, multimedia, sound cards

Curtis by Rolodex
225 Secaucus Rd.
Secaucus, NJ 07094
201-422-0240
Hardware: Peripherals

Cyrix Corp.
P.O. Box 850118
Richardson, TX 75085-0118
800-848-2979
www.cyrix.com
Hardware: CPUs

Dazzle Multimedia
510-360-2300
Hardware: Multimedia

Dell Computer Corp.
9505 Arboretum Blvd.
Austin, TX 78759
800-426-5150, 512-338-4400
www.dell.com
Hardware: Systems

Diamond Multimedia Systems
2880 Junction Ave.
San Jose, CA 95134-1922
408-325-7000
www.diamondmm.com
Hardware: Video cards, multimedia upgrade kits

Digital Equipment Corp.
Digital Dr.
Merrimack, NH 03054
800-722-9332
Hardware: Systems

Eizo Corp.
23535 Telo Ave.
Torrance, CA 90505
310-325-5202
www.eizo.com
Hardware: Monitors

Epson America
20770 Madrona Avenue
800-BUY-EPSON, 310-782-4100
Hardware: Printers, scanners

Fujitsu America, Inc.
3545 North First St.
San Jose, CA 95134
800-642-7617, 408-432-1300
www.fujitsu.com
Hardware: Printers

Future Domain Corp.
2801 McGaw Ave.
Irvine, CA 92714-5835
714-253-0400
Hardware: Peripherals

Gateway 2000
610 Gateway Dr., N.
Sioux City, SD 57049
605-232-2000
www.gw2k.com
Hardware: Systems

Global Village Communication
11144 East Arques Avenue
Sunnyvale, CA 94086
408-523-2458
Hardware: Modems

Goldstar Technology, Inc.
1000 Sylvan Ave.
Englewood Cliff, NJ 07632
201-816-2000
www.lge.co.kr
Hardware: Monitors

GST/Micro City
17707 Valley View Blvd.
Cerritos, CA 90703
714-739-0106
www.aapogee.com

Hard Drives International
1912 W. Fourth St.
Tempe, AZ 85281
800-766-3475
Hardware: Storage

Hauppauge Computer Works, Inc.
91 Cabot Ct.
Happauge, NY 11788-3706
800-443-6284, 516-434-1600
Hardware: Motherboards

Hayes Microcomputer Products, Inc.
5835 Peachtree Corners, E
Norcross, GA 30092
800-377-4377
www.hayes.com
Hardware: Modems, communications software

Hercules Computer Technology, Inc.
3839 Spinnaker Ct.
Fremont, CA 94538
510-623-6030
www.hercules.com
Hardware: Video cards

Hewlett Packard Co.
16399 W. Bernardo Dr.
San Diego, CA 92127
800-752-0990
www.hp.com
Hardware: Printers

Hitachi NSA
1000 Lowder Brook Dr., Suite 2400
Westwood, MA 020914
617-461-8300
www.hitachipc.com
Hardware: Monitors

IBM Corp.
Rt. 100, Box 100
Somers, NY 10589
800-IBM-3333
www.ibm. com
Hardware: Systems

Imation
1 Imation Place
Oakdale, MN 55128
612-704-3200
Hardware: Storage

Intel Corp.
2200 Mission College Blvd.
Santa Clara, CA 95052
408-765-1703
Hardware: CPUs

Iomega Corp.
1821 W. Iomega Way
Roy, UT 84067
801-778-1000
www.iomega.com
Hardware: Storage

Irwin Magnetic Systems, Inc.
2101 Commonwealth Blvd.
Ann Arbor, MI 48105
800-421-1879
Hardware: Storage

Kensington Microware, Ltd.
2855 Campus Dr.
San Mateo, CA 94403
800-535-4242, 415-572-2700
Hardware: Peripherals

Key Tronic Corp.
P.O. Box 14687
Spokane, WA 99214
509-928-8000
Hardware: Keyboards

Kingston Technology
17600 Newhope St.
Fountain Valley, CA 92708
714-435-2600
www.kingston.com
Hardware: Memory

Kyocera Electronics
100 Randolph Rd.
Somerset, NJ 08875-6727
908-563-3400
Hardware: Printers

Lexmark International
740 New Circle Rd. N.W.
Lexington, KY 40511
606-232-5500
Hardware: Printers

Linksys
800-546-5797
Hardware: Networking

Logitech, Inc.
6505 Kaiser Dr.
Fremont, CA 94555
510-795-8500
Hardware: Peripherals, pointing devices, scanners

Matrox Graphics, Inc.
1025 St. Regis
Dorval, PQ H9P 2T4 Canada
514-685-2630
www.matrox.com
Hardware: Video cards

Maxell Corp. of America
22-08 Rt. 208
Fair Lawn, NJ 07410
800-533-2836
Hardware: Storage

Maxtech Corp.
13915 Cerritos Corporate Dr.
Cerritos, CA 90703
310-483-5000
Hardware: Modems

Maxtor
211 River Oaks Pkwy.
San Jose, CA 95134
408-432-1700
www.maxtor.com
Hardware: Storage

MetroBook
888-829-5300
www.metrobook.com
Hardware: Notebooks

MicroClean, Inc.
2050 S. Tenth St.
San Jose, CA 95112
408-995-5062
Hardware: Peripherals

MicroSolutions
800-890-7227, 815-756-3411
Hardware: Notebook peripherals

Microtest, Inc.
4747 N. 22nd St.
Phoenix, AZ 85016-4708
800-526-9675
www.microtest.com
Hardware: Networking

Minden Group
236 N. Santa Cruz Blvd., Suite 237A
Los Gatos, CA 95030
408-399-6645
Hardware: Memory

Minolta Corp.
11150 Hope St.
Cypress, CA 90630
800-808-4888
Hardware: Digital cameras, image capture devices

Mitsuba Corp.
1925 Wright Ave.
La Verne, CA 91750
800-648-7822
Hardware: Systems

Mitsubishi Electronics America
5665 Plaza Dr.
Cypress, CA 90630
800-843-2515, 714-220-2500
www.mela-itg.com
Hardware: Monitors

Mitsumi Electronics Corp.
6210 N. Beltline Rd., Suite 170
Irving, TX 75063
214-550-7300
Hardware: Peripherals, storage

Mustek, Inc.
1702 McGaw Ave.
Irvine, CA 92714
800-468-7835
www.mustek.com
Hardware: Scanners

NEC
475 Ellis St.
Mountain View, CA 94039
800-366-9782
www.nec.com
Hardware: Monitors

Nokia Display Products
3000 Bridgeway Blvd.
Sausalito, CA 94965
415-331-6622
Hardware: Monitors

Number Nine Visual Technology Corp.
18 H Graphicswell Ave.
Lexington, MA 02173
800-GET-NINE
www.nine.com
Hardware: Video cards

Okidata
532 Fellowship Rd.
Mt. Laurel, NJ 08054
800-654-3282, 609-273-0300
www.okidata.com
Hardware: Printers

Orchid Technology, Inc.
45365 North Port Loop W.
Fremont, CA 94538
800-767-2443, 510-683-0300
www.orchid.com
Hardware: Video cards

Panasonic
2 Panasonic Way
Secaucus, NJ 07094
201-348-9090
Hardware: Printers, scanners

Panasonic Computer Peripheral Co.
6550 Katella Avenue
Cypress, CA 90630
714-373-7500
Hardware: Storage

Pinnacle Micro, Inc.
19 Technology
Irvine, CA 92718
800-553-7070
www.pinnaclemicro.com
Hardware: Storage

Pioneer New Media Technologies, Inc.
2265 E. 220th St.
Long Beach, CA 90810
800-444-6784
Hardware: Storage

Play, Inc. (maker of Snappy, a popular video capture device)
2890 Kilgore Rd.
Rancho Cordova, CA 95670
916-851-0800
Hardware: Digital cameras, image capture devices

Plextor
4255 Burton Dr.
Santa Clara, CA 95054
408-980-1838
Hardware: Storage

Plustek USA, Inc.
1362 Bordeaux Dr.
Sunnyvale, CA 94089
408-745-7111
Hardware: Scanners

Practical Peripherals, Inc.
31245 La Baya Dr.
Westlake Village, CA 91362
800-442-4774
www.practinet.com
Hardware: Modems

Princeton Technology, Inc.
2552 White Rd.
Irvine, CA 92714
714-851-7776
Hardware: Memory

Prometheus Products, Inc.
9524 S.W. Tualatin-Sherwood Rd.
Tualatin, OR 97062
503-452-0948
Hardware: Modems

Proxim
295 North Bernardo Avenue
Mountain View, CA 94043
650-960-1630
www.proxim.com
Hardware: Networks

Quickshot Technology, Inc.
950 Yosemite Dr.
Milpitas, CA 95035
408-263-4163
Hardware: Entertainment

R-Tech, Inc.
22129 Sherman Way
Canoga Park, CA 91303
818-347-1100
Hardware: Systems

Ricoh Corp.
475 Lillard Dr.
Sparks, NV 89434
702-352-1600
Hardware: Digital cameras, image capture devices

Samsung Electronics America
105 Challenger Rd.
Ridgefield Park, NJ 07660
201-229-4000
Hardware: Monitors, printers

Samtron
18600 Broadwick St.
Rancho Dominguez, CA 90220
310-537-7000
Hardware: Monitors

Sceptre Technologies, Inc.
16800 E. Gale Ave.
City of Industry, CA 91745
818-369-3698
Hardware: Monitors

Seagate Technology
920 Disc Dr.
Scotts Valley, CA 95066
408-438-6550
www.seagate.com
Hardware: Storage

Sharp Electronics Corp.
Sharp Plaza
Mahwah, NJ 07430
201-529-8200
Hardware: Printers

SimmSaver Technology, Inc.
228 North Pennsylvania
Wichita, KS 69083
316-264-2244
Hardware: Memory

Sony Corp.
1 Sony Dr.
Park Ridge, NJ 07645
201-930-1000
www.sony.com
Hardware: Monitors, systems

Star Micronics America
70 Ethel Rd., W
Piscataway, NJ 08854
908-572-5550
www.smc.com
Hardware: Printers

Storm Technologies
1395 Charleston Rd.
Mountain View, CA 94043
650-691-6600
Hardware: Scanners

Summagraphics Corp.
60 Silvermine Rd.
Seymour, CT 06483
800-729-7866
www.calcomp.com
Hardware: Pointing devices

Teac America
7733 Telegraph Rd.
Montebello, CA 90640
213-726-0303
Hardware: Storage

Techworks
4030 West Braker Lane
Austin, TX 78759
Hardware: Memory

Tektronix, Inc.
26600 S.W. Parkway Ave.
Wilsonville, OR 97070
800-835-6100
Hardware: Printers

Thrustmaster
7175 N.W. Evergreen Parkway #400
Hillsboro, OR 97124
503-615-3200
Hardware: Gaming peripherals

Toshiba
9740 Irvine Blvd.
Irvine, CA 92718
714-583-3000
Hardware: Printers

Umax
3353 Gateway Blvd.
Fremont, CA 94538
510-651-4000
Hardware: Scanners

US Robotics/3Com
7770 N. Frontage Rd.
Skokie, IL 60777
847-676-7000
www.3com.com
Hardware: Modems

Verbatim Corp.
1200 W.T. Harris Blvd.
Charlotte, NC 28262
704-547-6500
Hardware: Storage

ViewSonic Corp.
20480 Business Pkwy.
Walnut, CA 91789
909-869-7976
www.viewsonic.com
Hardware: Monitors

Viking Components
11 Columbia
Laguna Hills, CA 92656
714-643-7255
Hardware: Memory

Visioneer
34800 Campus Dr.
Fremont, CA 94555
510-608-6400
Hardware: Scanners

Wacom Technology Corp.
501 S.E. Columbia Shores Blvd., Suite 300
Vancouver, WA 98661
360-750-8882
Hardware: Pointing devices

Western Digital
8105 Irvine Center Dr.
Costa Mesa, CA 92718
714-932-5000
www.wdc.com
Hardware: Storage

Whistle Communications Corp.
110 Marsh Dr.
Foster City, CA 94404
888-494-4785
www.whistle.com
Hardware: Networking

Wyse Technology
3471 N. First St.
San Jose, CA 95134
408-473-1200
Hardware: Monitors

Yamaha Systems Technology, Inc.
100 Century Center Court
San Jose, CA 95112
408-467-2300
Hardware: Speakers

Zoom Telephonics
207 South St.
Boston, MA 02111
617-423-1072
www.zoomtel.com
Hardware: Modems

Mail-Order Companies

ABC Computer Technologies, Inc.
1295 Johnson Dr.
City of Industry, CA 91745
800-876-8088
www.abscomputers.com
Hardware: Systems

APZ Computers
800-983-8889
Hardware: Systems, peripherals

CDW Computer Centers, Inc.
1020 E. Lake Cook Rd.
Buffalo Grove, IL 60089
800-726-4239
www.cdw.com
Hardware: Peripherals, software, memory

CTX
20470 Walnut Dr.
Walnut, CA 91789
909-595-6293
www.ctxintl.com
Hardware: Systems

Complete Systems -N- More
1740 N. Greenville Ave.
Richardson, TX 75081
800-705-9596, 972-705-9668
Hardware: Peripherals, systems

Computability
P.O. Box 17882
Milwaukee, WI 53217
800-741-7752
www.computability.com
Hardware: Peripherals, software

Computer Discount Warehouse
1020 E. Lake Cook Rd.
Buffalo Grove, IL 60089
708-465-6000
Hardware: Systems, peripherals, software

Computer Gate International
408-730-0673
www.computergate.com
Hardware: Peripherals

CyberMax Computer, Inc.
133 N. 5th St.
Allentown, PA 18102
899-443-9868
www.cybmax.com
Hardware: Systems

Global Computer Supplies
11 Harbor Park Dr.
Port Washington, NY 11050
800-829-0785
Hardware: Systems, peripherals

Hi-Tech USA
1562 Centre Pointe Dr.
Milpitas, CA 95035
800-831-2888
Hardware: Peripherals

Insight
800-INSIGHT
www.insight.com
Hardware: Peripherals

Kenosha Computer Center
2133 91st St.
Kenosha, WI 53143
800-255-2989
www.kcc-online.com
Hardware: Peripherals

Memory 4 Less
2622 W. Lincoln, Suite 104
Anaheim, CA 92801
888-821-3354
Hardware: Memory

Memory Express
800-877-8188
Hardware: Memory

Micro Mall Direct
16812 Hale Ave.
Irvine, CA 92606
800-347-1273
Hardware: Peripherals

Micro X-Press
800-875-9737
www.microxpress.com
Hardware: Systems, peripherals

Micron Electronics
900 Karcher Rd.
Nampa, ID 83687
800-214-6674
http://store.micronpc.com
Hardware: Systems

MicroWareHouse
1720 Oak St.
Lakewood, NJ 08701-3014
800-243-5622
Hardware: Peripherals

Midwest Computer Works
600 Bunker Ct.
Vernon Hills, IL 60061
800-869-6757
Hardware: Systems, peripherals

Midwest Memory Works
600 Bunker Ct.
Vernon Hills, IL 60061
800-770-4341
www.mcworks.com
Hardware: Memory

Midwest Micro
800-728-8590
www.mwmicro.com
Hardware: Peripherals

NECX Direct
800-961-9208
www.necx.com
Hardware: Peripherals

O.S. Computers
58 Second St., 5th Floor
San Francisco, CA 94105
800-938-6722
Hardware: Peripherals

PC Mall
800-681-3282
Hardware: Peripherals

PCs Compleat
PC Mall
800-598-5601
www.pcscompleat.com
Hardware: Systems, peripherals

The PC Zone
800-252-0286
www.pczone.com
Hardware: Systems, peripherals

Programmer's Paradise, Inc.
1163 Shrewsbury Ave.
Shrewsbury, NJ 07702
908-389-8950

Software Developers' Tools
Publishing Perfection
800-716-5000
Hardware: peripherals

Quantex
800-836-0566
www.quantex.com
Hardware: Systems

Royal Computer
1208 John Reed Ct.
Industry, CA 91745
800-486-0008
Hardware: Systems

Storage USA
101 Reighard Ave.
Williamsport, PA 17701
800-538-DISK, 717-327-9200
Hardware: Storage

TC Computers
5005 Bloomfield St.
Jefferson, LA 70121
800-723-8282
www.tccomputers.com
Hardware: Systems

Treasure Chest Peripherals
800-677-9781, 504-733-2527
Hardware: Motherboards, peripherals

Tri State Computer
650 6th Ave.
New York, NY 10011
800-433-5199, 212-633-2530
Hardware: Peripherals

USA Flex, Inc.
444 Scott Dr.
Bloomingdale, IL 60108
800-678-4394, 630-582-6206
Hardware: Systems, peripherals

Vivitar Corp.
1280 Rancho Conejo Blvd.
Newbury Park, CA 91320
805-498-7008
Hardware: Digital cameras, image capture devices

Retail

CompUSA
14951 N. Dallas Pkwy.
Dallas, TX 75240
214-982-4451
Hardware: Systems, peripherals, software

MegaHaus Hard Drives
2201 Pine Dr.
Dickinson, TX 77539
800-786-1185, 713-534-3919
Hardware: Storage

Software Publishers

Activision, Inc.
11601 Wilshire Blvd., Suite 1000
Los Angeles, CA 90025
516-431-0589
www.activision.com
Software: Entertainment

Adobe Systems, Inc.
1585 Charleston Rd.
Mountain View, CA 94043
415-961-4400
www.adobe.com
Software: Graphics/desktop publishing

Alpha Software Corp.
1 North Avenue
Burlington, MA 01803
800-451-1018, 617-272-3680
Software: Database

Asymetrix Corp.
110 110th Ave. N.E. Suite 700
Bellevue, WA 98004
206-637-1673
www.asymetrix.com
Software: Multimedia

Autodesk, Inc.
111 McInnis Pkwy.
San Rafael, CA 94903
800-445-5415, 415-517-5000
www.autodesk.com
Software: Technical

Inprise Corp.
100 Borland Way
Scotts Valley, CA 95066
408-431-1000
www.inprise.com
Software: Developers'

Caere Corp.
100 Cooper Ct.
Los Gatos, CA 95030
408-395-7000
www.caere.com
Software: Business

Computer Associates International, Inc.
1 Computer Associates Plaza
Islandia, NY 11788-7000
800-225-5224
www.cai.com
Software: Business

Connectix
2655 Campus Dr.
San Mateo, CA 94403
415-571-5100
Software: Graphics

Corel Corp.
1600 Carling Ave.
Ottawa, ON K1Z 8R7 Canada
613-728-8200
www.corel.com
Software: Graphics/desktop publishing, educational, entertainment, business

Cybermedia
3000 Ocean Park Blvd.
Suite 2001
Santa Monica, CA 90405
310-581-4700
Software: Utilities

DataViz
55 Corporate Dr.
Trumbull, CT 06611
800-733-0030
www.dataviz.com
Software: Utilities

DeLorme Mapping
P.O. Box 298, Lower Main St.
Freeport, ME 04032
207-865-4171
Software: Mapping

Disney Interactive
500 South Buena Vista St.
Burbank, CA 91521-8404
800-441-1243
www.disney.com
Software: Entertainment, educational

Dr. Solomon
1 New England Executive Park
Burlington, MA 01803
617-273-7400
Software: Utilities

Dragon Systems, Inc.
320 Nevada St.
Newton, MA 02160
617-965-5200
Software: Voice recognition

Executive Software
800-829-6468, 818-547-2050
www.execsoft.com
Software: Network utilities

FileMaker Pro Corp.
5201 Patrick Henry Dr.
Box 58168, Santa Clara, CA 95052
800-544-8554
www.claris.com
Software: Business

Franklin Quest Co.
2550 S. Decker Lake Blvd.
Salt Lake City, UT 84119
801-975-9992
Software: Business

Global Village Communication
1144 E. Arques Ave.
Sunnyvale, CA 94086
408-523-1000
www.globalcenter.net
Software: Communications

GoldMine Software
17383 Sunset Blvd.
Pacific Palisades, CA 90272
310-454-6800
Software: Business

Great Plains Software
1701 S.W. 38th St.
Fargo, ND 58103
800-456-0025
www.gps.com
Software: Accounting

GT Interactive
255 Shorline Dr., Suite 520
Redwood City, CA 94065
415-596-3944
Software: Entertainment

HotOffice Technologies, Inc.
5201 Congress Avenue, Suite 232
Boca Raton, FL
888-446-8633
www.hotoffice.com
Software: Teamware

Individual Software
5870 Stoneridge Dr. #1
Pleasonton, CA 94560
510-734-6767
Software: Business

Interactive Magic
P.O. Box 13491
Research Triangle Park
North Carolina, 27709
919-461-0722
Software: Entertainment

Interplay Productions
17922 Fitch Ave.
Irvine, CA 92714
714-553-6655
www.interplay.com
Software: Entertainment

IntraNetics
18 Commerce Way, Suite 2050
Woburn, MA 01801
888-932-2600
www.intranetics.com
Software: Intranet

Intuit
P.O. Box 3014
Menlo Park, CA 94026
800-624-8742
www.intuit.com
Software: Home, accounting

Janna Systems, Inc.
3080 Yonge St., Suite 6060
Toronto, ON M4N 3N1 Canada
800-268-6107
Software: Business

Jian
1975 W. El Camino Real, Suite 301
Mountain View, CA 94040
415-254-5600
Software: Business

The Learning Company
314 Erin Dr.
Knoxville, TN 37919
615-558-8270
Software: Educational

Lotus Development Corp.
55 Cambridge Pky.
Cambridge, MA 02142
617-577-8500
www.lotus.com
Software: Business

LucasArts Entertainment Co.
P.O. Box 9367
Canoga Park, CA 91309-0367
800-98-LUCAS
www.lucasarts.com
Software: Entertainment

Maxis
2 Theatre Square
Orinda, CA 94563-3346
510-254-9700
Software: Entertainment

Micro Logic Corp.
P.O. Box 70
Hackensack, NJ 07602
800-342-5930
Software: Business

Microsoft Corp.
1 Microsoft Way
Redmond, WA 98052
206-882-8080
Software: Business, entertainment, educational

Software: Business, Operating System, Developers' Tools, Entertainment, Education

Mustang Software, Inc.
6200 Lake Ming Rd.
Bakersfield, CA 93306
805-873-2500
www.mustang.com
Software: Communications

Netopia, Inc.
14285 Midway Rd., Suite 100
Alameda, CA
800-485-5741
www.netopia.com
Software: Teamware

Netscape
501 E. Middlefield Rd.
Mountain View, CA 94043
415-254-1900
Software: Internet

Network Associates
2805 Bowers Ave.
Santa Clair, CA 95051
800-338-8754
www.mcafee.com
Software: Utilities

Palo Alto Software, Inc.
144 E. 14th St., #8
Eugene, OR 97401
503-683-6162
Software: Business

Parsons Technology, Inc.
1 Parsons Dr.
Hiawatha, IA 52233-0100
800-223-6925
www.parsonstech.com
Software: Home

Peachtree Software, Inc.
1505 Pavilion Place
Norcross, GA 30093
404-564-5700
www.peachtree.com
Software: Accounting

PKWare, Inc.
9025 N. Deerwood Dr.
Brown Deer, WI 53226
414-354-8699
Software: Utilities

Pro CD, Inc.
222 Rosewood Dr.
Danvers, MA 01923
508-750-0000
Software: Business

Quark, Inc.
300 S. Jackson, #100
Denver, CO 80209
303-934-2211
www.quark.com
Software: Graphics/DTP

Quarterdeck Corp.
13160 Mindanao Way, Floor 3
Marina Del Rey, CA 90292-9705
310-309-3700
Software: Utilities

Rand McNally
8255 North Central Park
Skokie, IL 60076
847-329-2219
Software: Mapping

Starfish Software
1700 Green Hills Rd.
Scotts Valley, CA 95066
408-461-5899
www.starfish.com
Software: Business

Symantec Corp.
10201 Torre Ave.
Cupertino, CA 95014
408-253-9600
www.symantec.com
Software: Utilities, communications

Ulead Systems, Inc.
970 W. 190th St., Suite 520
Torrance, CA 90502
310-523-9393
www.ulead.com
Software: Graphics/desktop publishing

Visioneer
34800 Campus Dr.
Fremont, CA 94555
510-608-0300
www.visioneer.com
Software: Scanning

Online Services

America Online
8619 Westwood Ctr. Dr.
Vienna, VA 22182
703-448-8700

CompuServe, Inc.
5000 Arlington Centre Blvd.
Columbus, OH 43220
614-457-8600

EarthLink
3100 New York Dr.
Pasadena, CA 91107
800-395-8425
www.earthlink.com

Netcom On-Line Communications Services
3031 Tisch Way
San Jose, CA 95128
800-353-6600

Prodigy Services Co.
445 Hamilton Ave.
White Plains, NY 10601
800-Prodigy

Appendix B
Vendors By Category

This appendix provides a listing of hardware manufacturers, software publishers, and retailers, broken down by category. You can use this list when you're searching for a manufacturer of a particular component, need to find a place to order or buy a certain part or program, or want to see what software is available in a category. When you locate a company in this listing, please refer to Appendix A for the name, address, telephone number, and Web URL for contact information.

CD-ROM Drives

Alps America

Aztech Labs, Inc.

Creative Labs

Mitsumi

NEC

Plextor

Sony

Toshiba

Cleaning

MicroClean, Inc.

CPUs

Advanced Micro Devices

Cyrix Corp.

Intel Corp.

Digital Cameras And Image Capture Devices

Casio

Connectix

Minolta Corp.

Play, Inc.

Ricoh Corp.

Vivitar Corp.

Entertainment Hardware

Advanced Gravis Computer

CH Products

Quickshot Technology, Inc.

Glare Filters

Allsop Computer Accessories

Internet Service Providers

Internet Software

Microsoft Corp.

Netcom On-Line Communications Services

Netscape

Keyboards

Key Tronic Corp.

Memory

Manufacturers

Kingston Technology

Princeton Technology, Inc.

SimmSaver Technology, Inc.

Techworks

Viking Components

Mail Order

Hi-Tech USA

Kenosha Computer Center

Memory Express

Memory 4 Less

Micro Mall Direct

Midwest Memory Works

PCs Compleat

Modems

Manufacturers

Cardinal Technologies

Computer Peripherals, Inc.

Global Village

Hayes Microcomputer Products, Inc.

Maxtech Corp.

Practical Peripherals, Inc.

Prometheus Products, Inc.

Supra Corp.

US Robotics, Inc.

Zoom Telephonics, Inc.

Mail Order

Hi-Tech USA

Kenosha Computer Center

PCs Compleat

Monitors

Manufacturers

Eizo Corp.

Goldstar Technology, Inc.

Hitachi NSA

Mitsubishi Electronics America

NEC

Nokia Display Products

Samsung Electronics America

Samtron

Sceptre Technologies, Inc.

Sony Corp.

ViewSonic Corp.

Wyse Technology

Mail Order

PCs Compleat

Motherboards

Manufacturers

Advance Integration Research, Inc.

American Megatrends, Inc.

Hauppauge Computer Works, Inc.

Mail Order

Hi-Tech USA

Treasure Chest Peripherals

Mouse Pads

Allsop Computer Accessories

Multimedia

Hardware Manufacturers

ACS Computer Group

Advanced Digital Systems

Altec Lansing Multimedia

Aztech Labs, Inc.

Creative Labs

Diamond Multimedia Systems

Media Visio

Thrustmaster

Networking

Hardware Manufacturers

Cisco Systems, Inc.

Cobalt Microserver, Inc.

Linksys Corp.

Microtest, Inc.

Proxim

Whistle Communications Corp.

Online Services

America Online

CompuServe, Inc.

Juno Online Services (email only)

Prodigy Services Co.

Peripherals

Manufacturers

Adaptec

Curtis by Rolodex

Future Domain Corp.

Hewlett Packard

Hitachi America, Ltd.

Iomega Corp.

Kensington Microware, Ltd.

Logitech, Inc.

Mitsumi Electronics Corp.

Mail Order

APZ Computers

CDW Computer Centers, Inc.

Complete Systems-N-More

Computability

Computer Discount Warehouse

Computer Gate

Global Computer Supplies

Insight

Kenosha Computer Center

Micro X-Press

NECX Direct

O.S. Computers

PC Mall

The PC Zone

Publishing Perfection

Treasure Chest Peripherals

Tri State Computer

USA Flex, Inc.

Pointing Devices

Manufacturers

Alps America

Logitech, Inc.

Summagraphics Corp.

Wacom Technology Corp.

Printers

Manufacturers

Alps America

Brother International Corp.

C. Itoh Electronics

Calcomp, Inc.

Canon USA, Inc.

Citizen America Corp.

Epson America, Inc.

Fujitsu America, Inc.

Hewlett Packard Co.

Kyocera Electronics

Lexmark

Minolta

Okidata

Panasonic

Ricoh

Samsung Electronics America

Sharp

Star Micronics America

Tektronics

Toshiba

Scanners

Manufacturers

Epson America, Inc.

Mustek, Inc.

Panasonic

Plustek USA, Inc.

Storm Technologies

Visioneer

Umax

Mail Order

Kenosha Computer Center

Software

Accounting

Great Plains Software

Intuit

Peachtree Software, Inc.

Business

Adobe Systems, Inc.

Alpha Software Corp.

Computer Associates International, Inc.

Corel Corp.

FileMaker Pro Corp.

Franklin Quest Co.

Goldmine Software

Individual Software

Janna Systems, Inc.

Jian

Lotus Development Corp.

Micro Logic Corp.

Microsoft Corp.

Palo Alto Software, Inc.

Pro CD, Inc.

Software Publishing Corp.

Starfish Software

Timeslips Corp.

CAD (Computer Aided Drawing)

Autodesk, Inc.

Communications

Global Village Communication

Mustang Software, Inc.

Symantec Corp.

Mail Order

Programmer's Paradise, Inc.

Educational

Corel Corp.

Cendant Software

Disney Interactive

EdMark Corp.

Learning Company

Microsoft Corp.

Entertainment

Activision, Inc.

Disney Interactive

GT Interactive

Interactive Magic

Interplay Productions

LucasArts Entertainment

Masque Publishing

Maxis

Microsoft Corp.

Graphics/Desktop Publishing

Adobe Systems, Inc.

Corel Corp.

Microsoft Corp.

Quark, Inc.

Ulead Systems, Inc.

Home Finances

Intuit

Parsons Technology, Inc.

Intranet

IntraNetics

Lotus Corp.

Mapping

DeLorme Mapping

Rand McNally

TravRoute

Multimedia Development

Asymetrix Corp.

Teamware

HotOffice Technologies, Inc.

Netopia, Inc.

Utilities

Cybermedia

DataViz

Dr. Solomon

Network Associates

PKWare, Inc.

Quarterdeck Corp.

Seagate

Symantec Corp.

Voice Recognition

Dragon Systems, Inc.

Speakers

Manufacturers

Bose Corp.

Yamaha

Storage

Manufacturers

Chinon America, Inc.

Colorado Memory Systems, Inc.

Conner Peripherals

Imation

Iomega

Irwin Magnetic Systems, Inc.

Maxell Corp. of America

Maxtor

Mitsumi Electronics Corp.

Panasonic Computer Peripheral Co.

Pinnacle Micro, Inc.

Pioneer New Media Technologies, Inc.

Plextor

Seagate Technology

SyQuest Technology

Teac America

Verbatim Corp.

Western Digital

Mail Order

MegaHaus Hard Drives

Storage USA

Systems

Manufacturers

Acer America Corp.

Advance Micro Research, Inc.

Apple Computer

AST Research

Compaq Computer Corp.

Dell Computer Corp.

Digital Equipment Corp.

Gateway 2000

IBM Corp.

Mitsuba Corp.

Sony Corp.

Mail Order

ABC Computer Technologies, Inc.

APZ Computers

CTX

Complete Systems-N-More

Computer Discount Warehouse

CyberMax Computer, Inc.

Global Computer Supplies

Micro X-Press

Micron Electronics

Midwest Computer Works

The PC Zone

PCs Compleat

Quantex

Royal Computer

TC Computers

USA Flex, Inc.

Video Cards

Manufacturers

ATI Technologies

Diamond Multimedia Systems

Hercules Computer Technology, Inc.

Matrox Graphics, Inc.

Number Nine Visual Technology Corp.

Orchid Technology, Inc.

Glossary

10BaseT—A common cable for connecting computers together to form networks. Also known as *unshielded twisted pair (UTP)*.

access rights—Rules that specify whether others have access to your files, and if they can read or change them. Also known as *rights*.

ADSL (Asymmetric Digital Subscriber Line)—A popular flavor of DSL that sends information faster than it receives information (thus, the "asymmetric" in the name).

AGP (Accelerated Graphics Port)—A graphics technology that defines a specific bus standard and uses the main memory on the motherboard.

AT—An IBM computer that features the 80286 processor and supplanted the original IBM PC and XT computers.

attachment—A file that is sent along with an email message. The recipient can download the file and use it.

autoexec.bat—A DOS file that executes a series of commands each time you turn on and boot your PC.

average access time—The average amount of time that it takes for a hard drive's heads (the devices that read and write information to the drive) to move to the different tracks on a disk.

average seek time—The average amount of time it takes for a hard drive's read/write head to move between two adjacent tracks.

backup—A duplicate copy of a file or disk. This may be stored on a different medium, such as tape.

baud—A rate of data transmission that is approximately 1 bit per second.

BIOS (basic input/output system)—Internal built-in software that determines the compatibility of your system.

bits per second (bps)—A measure of the number of information bits that a modem, or any other device, can send and receive in a second. The more bits it can send, the faster you can exchange information.

bus—An internal data highway between key computer components that defines how fast data can travel. The larger or wider the bus, and the faster, the more data can pass.

cable-based Internet access—Fast Internet access that comes through the same cable that provides a home with cable TV.

cache—A memory system that works closely with the processor to read ahead and hold data so that it's immediately available, thus speeding up the performance of your system.

CD-R (compact disc-recordable) drives—Specialized CD drives that let you "burn" or record your own CDs by copying files from a hard drive. You can also copy audio CDs or commercial CD-ROMs. Once you burn a CD, you can read it with just about any computer that's equipped with a CD-ROM drive or play it in your stereo's CD player (if you burn an audio CD). CD-R drives write to a blank CD that accepts data only a single time and may not be erased or reused.

CD-ROM drive—A device much like the one on your stereo that plays music CDs, but reads CDs that hold computer data. In many ways, a CD-ROM drive has the same basic function as a floppy drive, but runs CD-ROMs instead and can't write data.

CD-RW (compact disc-rewriteable) drives—Specialized CD drives that let you reuse and rewrite information to a special CD, almost as you would to a floppy disk. According to the manufacturers, you can overwrite a rewriteable CD some 1,000 times.

CGA (Color Graphics Adapter)—An older industry standard for computer graphics that could show only four colors in a resolution of 320×200 pixels.

client—A computer that is connected to a network and uses the resources of the server; it doesn't share its resources with the other computers on the network.

clone—A computer that works and responds just like any IBM computer, but is not manufactured by IBM. See **IBM compatible**.

clusters—Units that a computer uses to store information on a hard drive.

CMOS (complementary metal-oxide semiconductor)—A medium that stores data. As it relates to a PC, CMOS stores system information that defines some of the hardware.

coax—See **thinnet**.

config.sys—A DOS file that configures the PC each time it's booted.

CPU (central processing unit)—The main processor or chip in your PC. Sometimes, people use CPU to refer to your main PC case.

data transfer rate—A parameter that tells you how fast data can move from the hard drive to the system's memory.

defragger—A software program that rearranges and organizes the data in a hard drive's clusters so a drive can read them as quickly as possible.

Depends On Password access rights—Access rights that let users open and read files, or open, read, and modify files, depending on the passwords that they have.

Digital Subscriber Line—See **DSL (Digital Subscriber Line)**.

DIMM (dual inline memory module)—A small circuit card that contains a standard arrangement of memory that may be plugged into motherboards.

DMA (direct memory access)—A circuit that transfers data between a device and memory.

docking station—A device that connects to a notebook computer and that accepts conventional expansion cards, including network interface cards. With these devices, you can conveniently use your notebook at the office by plugging it into the docking station that is already connected to a network. A docking station also offers connections to hard drives, keyboards, and other peripherals.

DOS (disk operating system)—An operating system of the IBM PC and compatibles. This is a text-based operating system that makes users type in commands to perform basic system functions.

DOS boot disk—A floppy disk that contains the necessary information to boot, or start, a computer.

dot pitch—The size of the pixel or dot that a monitor displays. The lower the number, the better.

DRAM—A memory chip that must have power applied to it periodically to store data.

driver—A specialized program that tells the operating system how to work with an external device, such as a printer.

DSL (Digital Subscriber Line)—Technology that uses existing phone lines to carry voice and digital data.

DVD (digital video disk or **digital versatile disk)**—A CD standard that can hold 4.7GB of data.

DLL (dynamic link library)—Files that serve a function in Windows that can be shared among applications. For example, many CD-ROM programs that show video will install a runtime DLL for Apple's QuickTime for Windows.

EGA (Enhanced Graphics Adapter)—An older industry standard for computer graphics that could display up to 16 colors in a resolution of 640×350 pixels.

EIDE (Enhanced Integrated Drive Electronics)—A hard drive standard that supports large drives, and nondisk devices such as tape drives and CD-ROM drives, and transfers data at a higher rate than IDE.

EISA (Extended Industry-Standard Architecture)—An expansion bus standard that is now obsolete. EISA was developed by a consortium of manufacturers to compete against IBM in the late 1980s.

email—A means to communicate through computers that's similar to writing a letter or fax, but you don't send any paper. The message appears electronically on the recipient's computer screen.

email system—Software for handling email that consists of mail client software that lets users access and read their email, as well as mail server software that runs on the server, sends email, and retrieves it from the Internet.

Ethernet—A standard for connecting computers together into a network. It defines the type of cables that you can use, the way computers send and receive data, and more. For now, Ethernet is the most popular network standard.

expanded memory—Additional memory beyond 640K RAM that can be used by applications that specifically support it.

expansion cards—Specialized computer boards that let you add new functions to your computer. Some expansion cards are essential to a computer's operation—like the board to control your hard and floppy drives, or a video card that sends video to your monitor. Other expansion cards include internal modems and sound cards.

expansion slot—A slot in your PC that accepts an expansion board, allowing the board to connect to the motherboard.

extended memory—Memory beyond 1MB that a 386 or higher processor can access and use.

extranet—A type of intranet that lets authorized users on the outside access limited data.

Fast Ethernet—A standard for connecting computers together into a network that is 10 times faster than Standard Ethernet.

FAT (file allocation table)—Part of a DOS disk that stores information on the location of files and available space.

file—The unit in which data is stored on a PC. Data files can contain any type of information, including graphics, text, or programs.

file allocation table—See **FAT (file allocation table)**.

firewall—Specialized hardware or software (or both) that checks all the data that enters your network. Some firewalls use a technique called *packet filtering* that closely examines data to ensure that it comes from a known or trusted location, as defined by the administrator. These firewalls are typically less expensive. Another type of firewall, known as a *proxy server,* creates a barrier called a *bastion host.* This approach is generally more effective because it creates a physical barrier that places the firewall server between your network and the outside world.

format—A process by which a PC prepares a disk to receive and store data.

fragmentation—A process that occurs during normal computer operation and describes the phenomenon in which files are broken into segments and distributed across a hard drive, which slows the drive's performance.

Full Access rights—Access rights that give users full access to the files in a folder so they can open, read, and modify the files.

hard drive—An internal disk medium that acts as your computer's file cabinet to store application (software) and data.

host—A computer that answers incoming calls and lets a remote computer (the *remote* or *client*) connect to it.

hub—A device that accepts 10BaseT cables from all of the computers on the network and joins them together.

IBM compatible—A type of computer that acts like IBM computers. These computers are also known as *clones*.

IDE (Integrated Drive Electronics)—A popular hard drive standard for systems and drives that defines how they connect together.

interlace monitor—A monitor that draws each screen in a way that results in a slight flicker.

Internet—A huge network that connects thousands of commercial, academic, private, and government computers and networks in almost 100 countries. Originally developed by the military, the Internet has grown to be used by millions of users to exchange and share information.

Internet Service Provider—See **ISP (Internet Service Provider)**.

intranet—A specialized network that looks and works like a company version of the Web. To use an intranet, workers use the same browsers that they would use to surf the Web in order to look at company documents, work on databases, and refer to other business information.

IRQ (interrupt request)—A parameter that connects hardware devices and a system's interrupt controller.

ISA (Industry Standard Architecture)—A type of bus with a 16-bit data path. It is found on most computers, from the old 80286-based ATs to many of today's Pentiums.

ISDN (Integrated Services Digital Network)—A digital telephone line that can communicate at speeds up to 128Kbps—approximately twice that of a 56Kbps modem.

ISO.90—A standard for transmitting data across telephone lines at 56Kbps. This modem standard largely replaces K56flex and X2.

ISP (Internet Service Provider)—A company that provides Internet access services. When you open an account with one of these companies, you typically obtain an email address and can use your modem to dial a modem at the ISP to access the Internet.

jumpers—Board switches that let you apply settings and configure boards.

K56flex—A standard for transmitting information across a telephone line at 56Kbps.

Kbps (kilobits per second)—The amount of information bits that a modem can send and receive in a second. The more bits it can send or receive, the faster the modem.

kilobyte—1,024 bytes. Abbreviated as KB or K.

LAN (local area network)—A network in a home or office.

local drive—A drive that is part of the computer that you're working on.

local printer—A printer that is connected to the computer that you're working on.

mail client—The software that runs on a PC and lets users retrieve their email. This is the software that you use to compose messages, add attachments, and tell the computer where to send them.

mail server—The software that runs on a server and sends and retrieves email. This software sends email to others on the network or routes it across the Internet.

mapping—Making a drive that's on another PC look like one that is on your own system.

math (or numeric) coprocessor—A special chip that crunches numbers. If you're working with lots of mathematical functions—spreadsheets, for example—a numeric coprocessor will speed up your performance.

MCA (Micro Channel Architecture)—A bus standard created by IBM.

MDA (Monochrome Display Adapter)—An older display standard that displays text in only a single color.

megabyte—1,024 kilobytes. Abbreviated as MB.

megahertz—One million cycles per second. Abbreviated as MHz.

memory—Your computer's workspace, where it loads applications and processes data.

MMX (multimedia extensions)—Additional processor instructions designed by Intel to process the multimedia instructions used in common audio, video, and 2D and 3D graphics. This enhancement was added to Intel's Pentium line.

modem (modulator/demodulator)—A device that lets a PC talk with another computer over telephone lines. A modem converts signals from your PC into a form that can be sent across a telephone line. At the other end of the phone line, a modem converts the signal back to its original form so that a computer can read and use the information.

motherboard—A PC's main printed circuitboard, which holds the CPU, expansion cards, and memory.

mounting components—The adapter rails, nuts, bolts, and other hardware that you use to mount a drive in your PC.

MPEG—A compression standard for displaying video on a PC.

multimedia—The convergence of sound, text, video, and graphics in a computer application.

multimedia upgrade kits—Kits that include everything you need to upgrade your computer to handle multimedia. These kits typically include a CD-ROM drive, sound board, speakers, and some software.

nanosecond—One-billionth of a second. Abbreviated as *ns*.

network—A system that consists of two or more computers that are connected together, either with cables or a wireless system, so that they can share resources (printers, drives, modems, and so on) and information, usually in the form of files.

network interface card—See **NIC (network interface card)**.

Network Neighborhood—Windows' designation for the network resources that you can work with.

network operating system—See **NOS (network operating system)**.

network printer—A printer that is physically connected to another computer that's on the same network. Also known as a *shared printer*.

NIC (network interface card)—A special kind of expansion card that installs in your computer and connects with network cables so a computer can become part of a network.

noninterlaced monitor—A monitor that draws data to the screen in such a way as to reduce flicker.

NOS (network operating system)—An operating system that is designed to support a network. Popular network operating systems include Linux, Novell NetWare, Unix, and Windows NT Server.

numeric coprocessor—See **math (or numeric) coprocessor**.

operating system—See **OS (operating system)**.

OS (operating system)—A specialized program that lets a computer perform file, disk, and memory tasks, and accepts input from a mouse and keyboard.

OS/2—An operating system originally developed by Microsoft and IBM that was introduced after DOS.

OS/2 warp—A graphical operating system introduced by IBM.

parallel ports—Known also as *LPT1* and *LPT2*, parallel ports are used mostly for connecting with a printer.

PC card—A slot in your notebook that accepts PC card devices, such as modems, network cards, and more. PC cards were once known as *PCMCIA devices*.

PCI (peripheral component interconnect)—A type of bus with a 64-bit data path that is found on most computers, from late 486s to today's Pentium II systems.

PCMCIA device—See **PC card**.

peer-to-peer—A type of network that links computers together, and for all practical purposes, the computers have equal status within the network. Each computer shares its resources, which can include files, printers, and more, and uses the resources found on other computers.

pixel—The smallest unit or dot of color that a computer monitor displays.

port—A connection on your computer that provides the physical link between a computer and another device.

power supply—An electrical device in a PC that takes household current and prepares it for use by the computer.

print queue—A line of documents waiting to be output to a printer.

processor—The chip at the center of your computer's operations that controls everything the system does. The processor is what you're referring to when you call a computer a 386, 486, or Pentium. Also referred to as the *CPU.*

RAM (random access memory)—The memory in your computer where applications and data are loaded so the computer may work with them.

Read-Only access rights—Access rights that let users open and "read" the files within the folder. However, they can't make changes to them.

refresh rate—Indicates how often a video card redraws the picture on your screen. The slower the rate, the more chance that you'll see in-between flicker.

remote—A computer that connects to the host and uses its resources.

resolution—The number of physical dots on a computer screen. The more dots that appear, the higher the resolution, and the better the image looks.

rights—See **access rights**.

RLL (Run-Length Limited) encoding—An obsolete hard drive standard.

ROM (Read-Only memory)—Permanent memory that stores information.

RS-232—The PC's serial interface that connects with a mouse and external modem, and transfers data.

sampling rate—Refers to how often your sound card samples or records sounds. The more times a sound card samples a sound, the higher the quality of the recording.

SCSI (Small Computer System Interface)—A popular standard for connecting peripherals, such as hard drives and CD-ROM drives.

sector—A portion of a disk where the computer can store data.

server—The central system on a computer network that houses the drives and other resources. A server typically shares its resources, but doesn't use the resources of other computers on the network.

Share-Level access—Access control that lets you assign passwords to shared folders so only the users who know the passwords will be able to access the files in those folders.

SIMM (single inline memory module)—A small circuit card that contains a standard arrangement of memory that may be plugged into motherboards.

slot 1—The motherboard socket that accepts Pentium II and Celeron chips.

slot 2—The socket that accepts Pentium Xeon chips.

sneakernet—A humorous term that describes the low-tech method of transferring files from one computer to another by copying them to floppy disks, carrying them to another machine, and then copying them from the floppy to the hard drive.

socket 5—The motherboard socket that accepts Pentium chips.

socket 7—The motherboard socket that accepts a Pentium with MMX, AMD K-6, and Cyrix M-2 chips.

software—Computer programs or applications that run on a computer.

sound card—An expansion board that makes it possible for your PC to play sounds and music.

swap file—A part of your hard drive that's set aside to accept overflow of programs and data from RAM or memory. When Windows uses your hard drive in this way, it's called *virtual memory*.

switch box—A simple device that accepts the printer cables from two or more PCs and provides a connection to a single printer. When you want to print from a certain PC, you set the switch box to accept information from that PC, so the device can route it to the printer.

T1—A type of connection to the Internet that can transfer data at speeds up to 1.544Mbps and support up to 24 simultaneous users.

T3—A type of connection to the Internet that can transfer data at 44.184 Mbps and handle up to 672 users.

thinnet—A common cable for connecting computers together to form a network. Also known as *coax cable*.

USB (Universal Serial Bus)—A universal port that is designed to replace a PC's serial and parallel ports.

User-Level access—Access control that lets you assign access rights to users or groups, and is more sophisticated than share-level access. However, this is a feature that can be used only when the Windows 95 or Windows 98 system is part of a network that is running Windows NT.

utilities—Programs that assist you in diagnosing or fixing your system's problems.

UTP (unshielded twisted pair)—A common cable for connecting computers together to form networks. Also known as *10BaseT*.

VGA (Video Graphics Array)—An industry standard for displaying computer graphics.

video card—A card in your computer that translates (outputs) video from your computer onto your computer's screen or monitor.

virtual private network—A means to connect to the office network via an Internet connection.

voice modem—A special modem that supports voice capabilities.

Web—See **World Wide Web**.

World Wide Web—A part of the Internet that emphasizes graphics and is the most popular aspect of the Internet. Today, the Web is what most people have in mind when they say "cruising" or "surfing" the Internet. You view Web pages with software called a Web browser. The most popular Web browsers are Netscape Communicator and Microsoft Internet Explorer.

X2—A standard for transmitting data across telephone lines at 56 KBPS. X2 is a standard from US Robotics.

XT—A variation of the original 8088-based IBM PC that could work with a hard drive.

Index

D

E

H

I

J

K

L

M

N

O

P

Q

R

S

T

U

V

W

Z

What's On The CD-ROM

To help you build your network and perform your system upgrades, this book's CD-ROM includes multimedia videos that show you how to perform the key steps. You can refer to these to see how to perform a particular task and familiarize yourself with the techniques.

To help you with your system diagnostics, the companion CD-ROM is full of software utilities and other helpful programs. You'll find that these utilities will be invaluable as you evaluate your network and individual systems, upgrade systems by installing new components, and troubleshoot problems. I've also included a few programs you might enjoy in your regular computing.

- *CuteFTP*—Lets you easily work with FTP by providing an intuitive and easy-to-use browsing system. (30-day trial version)
- *Dr. Hardware*—A PC testing program that recognizes and describes PC components and configuration.
- *eSafe Protect*—Protects against vandals and viruses you might encounter on the Internet as you browse, download, or communicate.
- *Lockup95*—A system tray applet to start the default screensaver immediately.
- *PC-Doctor*—Performs more than 250 hardware diagnostic tests.
- *SiSoft Sandra 98*—Provides detailed information about your hardware and software, and includes powerful benchmarking, diagnostic, and troubleshooting utilities.
- *SYSCHK*—Gives you details about your system and devices, and prints a complete configuration report.